D1714716

Palgrave Studies in International Relations Series

General Editors:

Knud Erik Jørgensen, Department of Political Science, University of Aarhus, Denmark

Audie Klotz, Department of Political Science, Maxwell School of Citizenship and Public Affairs Syracuse University, USA

Palgrave Studies in International Relations, produced in association with the ECPR Standing Group for International Relations, will provide students and scholars with the best theoretically-informed scholarship on the global issues of our time. Edited by Knud Erik Jørgensen and Audie Klotz, this new book series will comprise cutting-edge monographs and edited collections which bridge schools of thought and cross the boundaries of conventional fields of study.

Titles include:

Mathias Albert, Lars-Erik Cederman and Alexander Wendt (*editors*)
NEW SYSTEMS THEORIES OF WORLD POLITICS

Barry Buzan and Ana Gonzalez-Pelaez (*editors*)
INTERNATIONAL SOCIETY AND THE MIDDLE EAST
English School Theory at the Regional Level

Geir Hønneland
BORDERLAND RUSSIANS
Identity, Narrative and International Relations

Oliver Kessler, Rodney Bruce Hall, Cecelia Lynch and Nicholas G. Onuf (*editors*)
ON RULES, POLITICS AND KNOWLEDGE
Friedrich Kratochwil, International Relations, and Domestic Affairs

Pierre P. Lizée
A WHOLE NEW WORLD
Reinventing International Studies for the Post-Western World

Cornelia Navari (*editor*)
THEORISING INTERNATIONAL SOCIETY
English School Methods

Dirk Peters
CONSTRAINED BALANCING: THE EU'S SECURITY POLICY

Simon F. Reich
GLOBAL NORMS, AMERICAN SPONSORSHIP AND THE EMERGING PATTERNS
OF WORLD POLITICS

Robbie Shilliam
GERMAN THOUGHT AND INTERNATIONAL RELATIONS
The Rise and Fall of a Liberal Project

Daniel C. Thomas (*editor*)
MAKING EU FOREIGN POLICY
National Preferences, European Norms and Common Policies

Rens van Munster
SECURITIZING IMMIGRATION
The Politics of Risk in the EU

Palgrave Studies In International Relations Series
Series Standing Order ISBN 978–0–230–20063–0 (hardback)
978–0–230–24115–2 (paperback)
(*outside North America only*)

You can receive future titles in this series as they are published by placing a standing order. Please contact your bookseller or, in case of difficulty, write to us at the address below with your name and address, the title of the series and the ISBNs quoted above.

Customer Services Department, Macmillan Distribution Ltd, Houndmills, Basingstoke, Hampshire RG21 6XS, England

A Whole New World

Reinventing International Studies for the Post-Western World

Pierre P. Lizée

Chancellor's Research Chair in Global Studies, Department of Political Science, Brock University, Canada

First published 2011 by
PALGRAVE MACMILLAN

Palgrave Macmillan in the UK is an imprint of Macmillan Publishers Limited, registered in England, company number 785998, of Houndmills, Basingstoke, Hampshire RG21 6XS.

Palgrave Macmillan in the US is a division of St Martin's Press LLC, 175 Fifth Avenue, New York, NY 10010.

Palgrave Macmillan is the global academic imprint of the above companies and has companies and representatives throughout the world.

Palgrave® and Macmillan® are registered trademarks in the United States, the United Kingdom, Europe and other countries.

ISBN 978–0–230–28039–7 hardback

This book is printed on paper suitable for recycling and made from fully managed and sustained forest sources. Logging, pulping and manufacturing processes are expected to conform to the environmental regulations of the country of origin.

A catalogue record for this book is available from the British Library.

Library of Congress Cataloging-in-Publication Data
Lizée, Pierre P.
   A whole new world : reinventing international studies for the post-Western world / Pierre P. Lizée.
       p.   cm.
   Includes bibliographical references and index.
   ISBN 978–0–230–28039–7 (alk. paper)
   1. International relations—Study and teaching—Developing countries.   2. International relations—Study and teaching—Western countries.   3. International relations—Philosophy.
   4. World politics—21st century.   I. Title.
   JZ1238.D44L59 2011
   327.1071—dc22   2011012064

10   9   8   7   6   5   4   3   2   1
20   19   18   17   16   15   14   13   12   11

Transferred to Digital Printing in 2012

Contents

Acknowledgments

I started the research involved in some components of this book a few years ago, when I was a post-doctoral fellow at the University of California at Berkeley. I was at Berkeley at the invitation of Joyce Kallgren, and I should thank Joyce for the kindness and interest with which she supported my work there.

I was then invited to join Brock University, near Toronto, as Chancellor's Research Chair in Global Studies. In this way, Brock gave me the most precious gift one can give an academic: time. While at Brock, I had the time to travel, live, and do research across the world, and the time also to reflect and move my work forward. Without that support I could never have written this book.

I should thank as well three colleagues who have been extremely helpful to me as I was writing this text: Amitav Acharya, from the American University, in Washington, D.C.; Paul Evans, from the University of British Columbia, in Vancouver; and Brian Job, also from the University of British Columbia. It is often said that your enemies critique you behind your back, while your friends critique you to your face. By that measure, I can say, with a half-smile, that Amitav, Paul, and Brian; have been the very best of friends. They have critiqued me endlessly; they have forced me to revise every argument, and they have made me doubt what I assumed was certain: for all of this I am extremely grateful.

As I was writing this book, I spent different lengths of time living and teaching in Asia. Many colleagues with whom I interacted in this context have also been very supportive of my work. In particular, I should thank Jusuf Wanandi, the leading force at the Center for Strategic and International Studies, in Jakarta; Mely Caballero Anthony, from the S. Rajaratnam School of International Studies, in Singapore; Carolina Hernandez, from the University of the Philippines, in Manila; and Sorpong Peou, from Sophia University, in Tokyo.

I should express my gratitude to Knud Erik Jørgensen and Audie Klotz, the Series Editors for the Palgrave Studies in International Relations, for their assistance and support. Alexandra Webster, at Palgrave Macmillan, believed in this book from the start, and for this I thank her. Christina Brian and Liz Blackmore, also at Palgrave Macmillan, were as efficient as they were helpful throughout the entire publication process. Two anonymous reviewers suggested important revisions to the text. I should also thank Melissa Mucci, my research assistant at Brock University, who helped me organize the final version of this book.

I should say a word, lastly, about my two children: Megan and Ethan. One of life's melancholy truths is that children grow up too quickly and academics write books far too slowly, thus losing some of the time they should have spent with their children. Megan and Ethan have dealt with this situation, though, with the utmost understanding and grace, and for this I thank them. As is the case with everything I do, it is to the two of them that I dedicate this book, with all my heart.

Introduction: Understanding the Post-Western World

International studies is beset by an important problem: it is inherently Western-centric. Stanley Hoffmann, surely one of the key figures in the development of the field over the past few decades, once famously went so far as to describe it as being, in essence, "an American social science." The images, concepts, and theories which underlie international studies, Hoffmann argued, must be recognized for what they are: products of the post-1945 era, when "to study United States foreign policy was to study the international system and to study the international system could not fail to bring one back to the role of the United States."[1] This is, of course, something of an exaggeration. Other intellectual traditions, most notably those coming from the United Kingdom and France, have also influenced the evolution of international studies. It is still the case, though, that the field has remained a profoundly Western affair. It is American and European authors that have given it its basic vocabulary. This vocabulary – the understandings of the state, the market, and similar concepts, which have framed the central claims and debates in the field – was drawn from the European and North American experience of all these realities. Finally, the problems that have constituted the main focus of international studies are, more than anything else, the problems of the Western world. How to prevent war between the superpowers, how to spur forward economic development and security in the West in the post–Cold War era, or how to deal with the rest of the world through all of this – these have been key questions in the development of the field.[2]

The situation described above has placed the entire discipline with unavoidable and crucially important questions. What exactly does it mean to say that international studies is Western-centric? What has been overlooked or misunderstood, when it comes to the international politics of the non-Western world? Furthermore, what would a discipline which is no longer Western-centric, one which pays greater heed to the realities of the non-Western world and integrates them in its logic and its claims, actually look like? These are vexing questions for all of us who work in

1

international studies, not least because the field does not yet appear to have the intellectual tools and insights that would allow us to answer them in full.

More to the point, these questions are troublesome because they leave us with a great deal of uncertainty and ambiguity in everything we do in the field. When we discuss or critique the notion of balance of power, for instance, are we describing a fundamentally Western-centric concept, which requires Western understandings of the state, power, and rationality, in order for it to make sense? If we use that notion in a non-Western context, for example to probe how power balancing is likely to operate between China and India, do we know what we are overlooking or misinterpreting because of that ambiguity? Is it possible for us to formulate, then, a more inclusive understanding of the balance of power, one which is also sensitive to the realities of that part of the world and gives us a greater degree of assurance when we discuss how the notion operates there?

How far should we go, finally, in this reinvention of the field? What is claimed and debated in international studies always follows from a series of key premises. We go to Machiavelli or Morgenthau to comprehend power and violence; we read Kant to learn about peace; and, more recently, we have started studying Foucault or Wendt to understand the forms of rationality and knowledge at play in the work of these other authors. It is these debates that we engage in, these notions that we use as we advise policy makers and as we teach our students the rudiments of the discipline in undergraduate courses. Is all of this, though, eminently Western-centric? When Hobbes talks about the state, is he overlooking significant aspects of what makes the state unique in the non-Western world? Conversely, how, then, should we read him to garner from his writings insights which will also apply to the non-Western world? How would that principle apply to all the other authors that form the canon of international studies – should we study and teach Machiavelli, Morgenthau, and now Wendt differently, in order to address all such issues? These are all important questions, and yet we still lack answers to them.

The issue today, though, is that global politics is such that finding answers to all these questions can no longer wait. We live in a world which is less and less Western-centric. The key transformation at play in global politics is the "rise of the rest," as Fareed Zakaria puts it,[3] and the way in which it challenges the configurations of international power, which in the past were based on the continued pre-eminence of the West. The issue is not, as Zakaria makes clear, that the West is losing its power, or that ours is a world "defined by the decline of America": the point is instead that the world is now swayed by "the rise of everyone else."[4] Non-Western powers – China, India, and the like – constitute some of the world's dominant economies. Their capacity to influence or shape geostrategic realities and to challenge, for instance, the supremacy of the American military in many parts of the globe is growing accordingly, and will continue to do so in the medium and long term.

This is a first component of the changes now unfolding in global politics. A second component in these changes is perhaps even more important. At the moment the new power allows those "in the rest" to start "dissecting the assumptions and narratives of the West, and providing alternative views."[5] Americans and other Westerners are bound to feel, in response, that they live in a world that is "being shaped in distant lands and by foreign people."[6] To what extent, for example, will China's growing role in global economic institutions allow it to redefine the models of economic and political development which have underlain the work of these institutions since they were established? The understandings of politics, economics, and international affairs that have defined the post–World War II global architecture were dominated by the United States and its allies. They radiated outward, toward the "rest." Now there is much more of a dialogue on these issues: China and other rising powers bring the "rest" within the very core of any meaningful debate on the concepts and approaches which should guide the evolution of global economics and politics.

In that sense, we now inhabit a planet, Parag Khanna tells us, where the "second world" of China and of other non-Western states is increasing its global clout to such a degree that a "new geography of power" must be developed in order to understand international politics.[7] This is the "Post-American World" described by Zakaria.[8] It is a world where shifts in global politics are such that America is "decentered," as Jessica Gienow-Hecht puts it.[9] More than anything else, it is a world which, in the words of David Rothkopf, pushes the US and other dominant Western powers toward an "age of ambiguity,"[10] where exercising power, let alone defining it, remains subject to uncertain and complex developments unfolding in the non-Western world.

Some may disagree with the scope and extent of these changes. Others might want to frame the problem somewhat differently. It is certainly possible to suggest, for example, that we live in a world which is becoming "post-Western" more than "post-American," since Western values *per se* are what is being reassessed through these global changes, just as much as American power and culture is.[11] The key point, though, is that international studies cannot proceed further without at least considering all these issues. The question, then, is forced on the entire discipline: does international studies have within itself the concepts and theories that allow it to look at all these problems? Can a field of study which is deeply Western-centric in its language and worldview explain a world which is now less and less Western-centric? To put it even more bluntly, can the "American social science" of Hoffmann as much as comprehend the "Post-American World" of Zakaria?

This is the challenge of our times for international studies. The discipline needs to develop the models which will allow it to explain how the "rise of the rest" is likely to transform the very nature of global politics. Just as much, though, the discipline must also lay out precisely how it is required to change itself, its very makeup, in order to do that. It must determine, essentially, how its concepts and its theories must be altered or amended so that it may come to understand the "rest," the non-Western world, and the way in which forces emanating from that part of the world will shape global politics. This is what is so striking about the new global politics emerging around us. It demands of all of us in the field that we find answers to the questions about the Western-centric aspects of our discipline, which we have left pending for so long. If we fail to do it, we will remain unsure of ourselves as we ponder some of the most important developments in contemporary global politics.

Most obviously, the issue is not that the non-Western world should start to matter just now. It has always been present in global politics. No understanding of the global political economy, for instance, can proceed without reference to the patterns of trade and production which have linked non-Western economies to the rest of the world for the past centuries. The non-Western world has also been always present, evidently, in international studies itself. There have always been certain conceptions of it, implicit or perhaps at times more explicit, in everything we have said in the field about global politics. The problem was, however, that our discussion of the non-Western world in international studies was framed by concepts and theories which, we knew, were geared much more toward Western problems and worldviews. This is what can no longer stand and must be addressed now. More and more, discussions about global politics will be discussions about the non-Western world, its nature and its changing place in international affairs. This means that the questions left pending in the past will become too flagrant, too pressing for everyone in the field to be ignored. We will need to be much clearer and detailed about the biases which block our understanding of the non-Western world, and we will also have to be much more decisive about moving beyond these biases. This is what is now placing the non-Western world at the top of our agenda in international studies.

Also, the point should not be that we need to return through this exercise to overwrought clichés about what separates the West from the "rest." There are plenty of those. Huntington's thesis about the "clash of civilizations,"[12] for instance, is well known and has regained widespread currency in the post-9/11 world. Nevertheless, these clichés do not help us: they tell us about the often strained assumptions and unexamined conjectures of their proponents, but much less about the issues which these people aim to explore. What international studies requires now is something rather more measured and detailed. We know, in our field, that we work on the basis of a certain vocabulary about the state, civil society, rationality, and so on. We also know that there are aspects of these realities which necessitate some further distinctions when it comes to certain parts of the non-Western world. The relationship between civil society and the state, for example, and the one between violence and rationality are often very specific in those instances where the state-building process is still fragile and ongoing. We also know, then, that we need to recalibrate some of our key terms if we are to look more closely at the non-Western world and its role in the rise of the post-Western world. But this is all. Such an exercise should not take us back to hackneyed clichés. It should, on the contrary, allow us to move away from them, by forcing a detailed reexamination of their logic and claims.

This book addresses these questions and these challenges. It is divided into three parts, which correspond to three main steps in the case it puts forward. The first part examines the current state of play in international studies. What are the main issues on which the discipline is focused, and what debates divide it today? The sections of this first part serve to present a key argument: international studies speaks at all times a language of universals, in the sense of assuming that its insights pertain to all of the international politics throughout the world. This is true of realism and liberalism, the two main poles of the discipline. The proponents of both kinds of approach assume that their insights on matters ranging from the nature of human rationality to that of state behavior encapsulate universal human and political traits, and thus that the explanations of international politics which they put forward on the basis of these insights also have universal value. The most significant texts and authors which have allowed this assumption of universality to permeate international studies are examined. The writings of Machiavelli on violence and those of Waltz on the state, for instance, or those of Kant and his contemporary followers on the nature of peace, are brought into analysis at this point. This is an essential element of the case presented in this book. It is these key authors and texts that have instilled in international studies the habit of using unexamined postulates and a mode of thought which underlies the assumption that this discipline could address international politics throughout the world. By using these authors and their texts as constant points of reference while we do our research or teach the rudiments of our discipline, it is suggested, we have sustained this assumption of universality in all the aspects of our work.

This state of affairs explains why so many in the field have not felt that they should confront head-on the question of what is specific to the international politics of the non-Western world and of how these issues should be incorporated into the workings of international studies. The assumption of universality which underlies the entire discipline quite immediately leads one to think that such a line of inquiry is unnecessary, if not completely illogical. If we know for sure that the nature of power, the nature of the state, or the nature of rationality are the same always and everywhere, why should we imagine that we need to study the specific nature of these elements in the non-Western world?

This part of the book also argues, somewhat more controversially, that even those approaches in international studies which claim to challenge the presumption of universality inherent to the discipline end up returning to it themselves. The post-modern literature, for instance, which is currently giving impetus to the continued development of constructivism in international studies, aims to show that the discipline rests on forms of knowledge and on constellations of ideas which are socially and historically constructed. The notions of power and state sovereignty, which animate, for example, the realist approach, should not be seen as expressions of universal realities so much as one particular formulation of these realities – one embedded in specific historical and social circumstances. The universals which constitute much of the language of international studies, in a word, should give way to particulars: they are mere conventions emerging out of a given context of intellectual *a priori* positions and specific circumstances, and they should be recognized as such.

The problem with this sort of critique of more mainstream approaches, however, is that it duplicates the oversights of these approaches when it comes to the non-Western world. The understanding of the state within realism, for instance, misses much of what makes up the state in that part of the world. When post-modern or constructivist writers take this realist understanding of the state as the point of departure of their own work, they also miss what realism itself misses, and they carry these oversights throughout their entire line of reasoning. They fail, however, to acknowledge these oversights. As is shown in the same part of the book, these writers, on the contrary, still come to assume that what they say will pertain to the whole of international politics. This is how they return to the assumption of universality, which they condemn at the beginning of their analysis: they believe that their critique of mainstream international studies allows them to make claims which speak to international affairs *per se*, throughout the entire world.

Next, the second part of the book examines what is overlooked or misinterpreted in all these different approaches and theories when the international life of the non-Western world is at stake. What is specific to the international politics of these parts of the world? To what extent are such elements ignored or misunderstood in the main approaches which comprise international studies at the moment? What might the discipline overlook or misread, then, as it attempts to understand the rising impact of non-Western countries on the global politics of the post-Western world as a whole?

This entire second part of the book certainly acknowledges the degree to which the rubric that drives such arguments – the notion of a "non-Western world" – is an ambiguous one. As is explained in the sections of this part, the borders of the non-Western world are uncertain, its nature is multifaceted, and any attempt to define it rests, in any case, on categories which refer as much to the ideological premises one brings to this exercise as to the reality of the non-Western world itself. There is a vast literature, however, which attempts to work through these problems and the dilemmas they pose and endeavors to bring to light the specificity of non-Western international politics. This part of the book draws on that literature and underlines some of its main conclusions. The core elements that mark the specificity of international life in the non-Western world are thus outlined in these sections. The nature of the state, for instance, the nature of violence, and how these realities influence the character of international affairs in the non-Western world are topics presented one by one. The character of the interactions between the state, the market, and civil society is examined, together with how these interactions influence the conduct of international politics in the relevant parts of the world. The second part also discusses how these elements play within issues of economic interdependence and democratization, how they fit with changing notions of self-identity, and how all these questions, in turn, influence the forms of international politics that emanate at the present from the non-Western world.

Concrete examples are given throughout these sections of the book. They are all drawn from the Asian context, and they help give a more tangible tone to the discussion. Talking about the recent evolution of Chinese economy, for instance, still involves a fair degree of generalization, but it does also bring to mind more defined images and dilemmas. Asia was chosen as the source of these examples because it remains, more often than not, the key point of reference when one speaks of the "rise of the rest" and the way it should entail a reorientation of basic understandings of global politics: the growing influence of China, India, or Japan as a case in point is, most definitely, always part of this sort of debate.[13]

A crucial issue that this part of the book brings to light is the difficulty of addressing the problems studied here within international studies as the discipline stands at the moment. International studies is a language of universals. What is argued in the literature surveyed in these sections, in contrast, is that the nature of international politics in the non-Western world has never been fully captured by the language of universals. This is where the problem arises. How can a discipline whose driving logic assumes that it speaks to the whole of international politics throughout the world recognize at the same time that it does not really do that? To put it another way, do all the claims to universality which structure international studies make it impossible for the discipline as much as to comprehend that some aspects of international politics in the non-Western world lie, quite literally, outside of its scope? This is a major problem if one is trying to make international studies more sensitive to the realities of the non-Western world. There is a resistance to these questions which is ingrained in the very logic of the discipline. In that perspective, introducing a more nuanced and comprehensive account of non-Western international politics into international studies requires much more than a simple enumeration of elements such as the specific nature of the state in the non-Western world, which might be overlooked in the discipline at the moment.

This point leads to another of the more controversial aspects of the argument advanced in this book. The literature exploring the nature of international politics in the non-Western world is extremely useful because it points out elements which are often overlooked in international studies. Indeed, this literature is used in the present text precisely for that reason. What also becomes apparent here, however, is that the key project underlying this literature is not without its problems. The goal of this literature is to make international studies less Western-centric. We should understand, for instance, how international studies looks from the perspective of Asian or African countries – the argument goes in these writings; or we should study how definitions of self-identity in the non-Western world have been shaped and constrained by the colonial experience. We should then bring these new perspectives and these additional insights within international studies. This would make for a discipline which is less self-enclosed, and thus more sensitive to a number of realities it has ignored in the past. This sort of process, in the end, will compel international studies to correct its past oversights and to become less Western-centric.

The argument advanced here demonstrates that this cannot be done; the assumption of universality which drives international studies completely blocks the entire project. How can something lie beyond explanations which cover everything? How can non-Western international politics exist beyond theories which already explain all international politics? Evidently, the response of those who attempt to bring to light the specificity of international life in the non-Western world is that international studies has to change and to abandon its assumption of universality. The point made here, though, is that this argument cannot be heard, or even recognized as valid, within international studies. The logic of universals which structures the discipline precludes this. And repeating the argument time and again, as is done in the literature focused on the non-Western world, will not change the situation. This is a literature which wants to introduce a language of particulars in international studies, a language which underscores the specific nature of the different forms of international politics found in various regions of the world. It addresses this language of particulars, though, to a discipline which speaks a language of universals. This does not make for a new dialogue, one that may push international studies outside of its usual concepts and vocabulary. It simply means, on the contrary, that people talk past one another, using languages and logics which simply cannot be understood by the other side.

What is specific about international politics in the non-Western world has not become an intrinsic part of international studies; in fact the exact reverse has happened. The literature focused on the non-Western world has not been integrated into international studies in order to produce a more global discipline. On the contrary, it has lingered on the margins of the discipline, while the more mainstream approaches in international studies, even though they are recognized as Western-centric, have remained the key point of reference for scholars and practitioners alike in international affairs. This situation has led many to lament in recent publications that we still have to learn how to "world" international studies,[14] as others have noted how "non-Western international relations theory" has yet to be brought into the discipline.[15]

There is also a second unresolved problem in this literature devoted to the international politics of the non-Western world. Just like the more mainstream approaches in international studies, it still needs to address more directly the new global conditions created by the "rise of the rest." This is a literature which, by its very nature, is turned inward, toward the specific elements of international affairs in the non-Western world and toward the set of global and local forces which have shaped the development of these realities. However, the fundamental point emerging at the moment about the post-Western world as a result of the "rise of the rest" is that the non-Western world is redefining in crucial ways what happens outside of it. In this sense, then, the literature focused on the non-Western world must also reorient itself: it must turn itself outward, toward the growing impact of the realities it studies on the evolution of all of global politics.

This means that the core objective of this literature must be readjusted accordingly. It is impossible to talk of global politics in universal terms, which aim to capture the essence of international life throughout the entire world – this literature claims. Those who do so merely use a set of Western-centric criteria, which they superimpose on changing and dissimilar international contexts throughout the world. On the contrary, we should emphasize all that is particular, all that is different in the international politics of the non-Western world, in order to force those who speak of international politics in universal terms to recognize how they have often overlooked most of these realties. The issue at the moment, though, is that, as it were, the particular resembles more and more the universal. The forces, actors, and approaches to international affairs which could once be seen as specific to the non-Western world are now in fact becoming global. This is the key point that the arguments surrounding the "rise of the rest" invite us to integrate in our thinking: what was different about the non-Western world, outside the established ways of global politics, will inform the norms and practices of all of global international politics from this point on. Or, at least, any debate about what is universal in international politics, what traverses all areas of the world and shapes the core elements of global politics, will not be able to proceed in the future without reference to the non-Western world and its increasing role in the definition of those images and worldviews. The literature devoted to the international politics of the non-Western world can make a formidable contribution to these discussions if it engages them fully. But here this literature must also reexamine some of its logic. This is a literature which has always seen the search for a language of universals in international affairs, a language that could speak to all global politics, in an intrinsically suspect process, driven, in its very essence, by self-referential Western norms and agendas. Now this literature must itself speak to some extent a language of universals. This is the challenge that the "rise of the rest" makes to these writings: they must address what is specific about the non-Western world, but they must also help develop the concepts and images which will extend beyond the non-Western world and help explain the character of the whole post-Western world emerging at the moment around us. How that might be done, how that would change the tension between this literature and the language of universals of the more mainstream literature, and how, ultimately, this whole process could add to our understanding of the post-Western world – all remain, however, open questions in this literature.

The third and last part of the book then brings all these elements together. How is it possible to ensure that international studies explains well the global politics of the post-Western world? What should be kept or changed in the major approaches which have defined the evolution of international studies? How can approaches more specifically devoted to the international politics of the non-Western world help? What about all the difficulties just outlined?

The argument presented here suggests that developing an understanding of international affairs which is less Western-centric, and thus better able to capture the impact of the non-Western world on the construction of the post-Western global order, should not at all involve abandoning the main approaches that have framed the development of international studies up to this point. Quite the reverse, in fact, should be the goal. Machiavelli, Hobbes, and Kant, or, today, Waltz and Wendt – all these crucial signposts surveyed in the first part of this book – still raise fundamentally important questions regarding, for instance, the spread of democratic values through-out the world, or the conduct of foreign policy during periods of acute global change. The simple point, though, is that this canon should now be read in a way which is more sensitive to the realities of the non-Western world. In that sense, the elements presented in the second part of this book do need to become part of the vernacular of international studies as a discipline.

What is presented here, then, is a middle road between two approaches which, up to this point, have evolved largely in opposition to each other. International studies has developed as a discipline in a way which has led it to ignore many of the realities of the non-Western world. In contrast, the literature focused on the non-Western world has sought to challenge the very legitimacy of these more mainstream approaches and to substitute for them quite different outlooks on international affairs. What is suggested here is that each approach can, in fact, enrich the other. Alexander Wendt has suggested that the attempt to find a middle way, a *via media*,[16] can help to reconcile positions which might have appeared to oppose each to other at the outset; this is exactly what is proposed in this last part of the book.

Indeed the argument is that the new global politics of the post-Western world, with its attendant need for an engagement of both Western and non-Western approaches to international affairs, requires now nothing more than just this sort of dialogue between previously distinct perspectives.

The problem, though, is that things are never that simple. There is a reason why such a dialogue has not taken place. Those are approaches which proceed on the basis of diametrically opposed logics. International studies has developed on the assumption that it could capture in its explanations the core forces and issues which define international politics throughout the world. The literature focused on the non-Western world has evolved in direct opposition to this way of thinking. And this tension, in turn, has prevented the two approaches from connecting to each other. This is also what is shown in the first two parts of the book. Bringing these two approaches together entails much more than the amalgamation of the insights on international affairs which each body of literature has put forward. The process requires, in effect, nothing less than some form of resolution of the debate which has opposed them.

The way out of the problem that is proposed in the last part of the book represents an attempt, here again, to find a middle road. Or perhaps, to put things in a better way, the argument proposed in these pages revolves around the idea that it is time for international studies to move *beyond* this problem.[17] International studies has been locked in a debate which, by its very nature, could not be resolved. One had to speak a language of universals or a language of the particular and, once that choice was made, a meaningful dialogue with the other side was impossible. The changes developing at the moment in global politics, however, invite a reevaluation of the terms of this debate. The self-enclosed language of universals, which has been a crucial component in the evolution of international studies, is being forced open by the "rise of the rest." Our sense of global politics must be more sensitive to aspects of non-Western international politics that we have ignored in the past. In counterpoint, though, the "rise of the rest" also compels the literature focused on the non-Western world to help devise a language on international affairs which can speak to the nature of global politics throughout the world, and to the way it is evolving at the moment. Our sense of the specificity of international politics in the non-Western world requires, in this sense, some connection with the language of universals at the core of international studies. In this, it is argued here, lies the chance to connect the logic animating each of these approaches and to move beyond the tensions that have divided them in the past.

Indeed, as is suggested here as well, this type of project is crucially important for the future of international studies. Debates about the nature of international politics have always been, in some way, debates about the question of universals – what is global, so to say, in global politics, what is not, and how do we know it? It is suggested here, in essence, that such debates have often proceeded on the basis of categories which led to quite unproductive divisions and arguments within international studies. Shifts in the nature of global politics, however, are forcing us to reexamine these issues and the divisions they have created in the discipline. It is by entering in this discussion that we will be able to bring together the insights on world politics put forward by approaches that have remained isolated from each other up to this point.

The last part of the book also gives concrete examples in order to illustrate how all these questions relate to some of the most important concerns in global politics at the moment. For instance, the questionable success of the broad operations of state-building and post-conflict reconstruction launched in many parts of the non-Western world in recent years is considered. China's rise in power and its impact on global geopolitics is also examined. Debates about the nature of human rights, self-identity, and democratization in the non-Western world are discussed. So is the rise of the so-called emerging markets. By any measure, these are issues which are fundamentally important for the global community. Crucially, though, all these issues underscore the importance of the argument advanced in this book. They require students and practitioners in international studies to draw on many of the insights provided by the discipline in order to study and explain them. But, in equal measure, they demand of everyone working in international studies a great sensitivity to the political and international realities of the non-Western world and to the extent to which these realities will shape the evolution of global affairs in the future. Showing in some way how this type of analysis can be achieved on the basis of the arguments presented here is the goal of these examples.

Finally, the last part of the book also returns to some of the key texts and authors which have influenced the evolution of international studies. It is these key texts and authors that provide the constituent logic of the discipline and divide it along the series of debates that shape its development at this moment. If international studies is to move in the direction proposed here, if it is to develop a better sense of international life in the non-Western world and of its impact on the character of global politics, this canon has to be brought in the process. How can we read Machiavelli, Hobbes, or Kant, for instance, in a way which is not Western-centric? How do more contemporary authors figure in these questions? How can such an exercise add to the manner in which we study the international politics of the post-Western world? These are very significant issues for international studies today, when the discipline considers the "rise of the rest," and the sections of the book dealing with them offer some reflections concerning the way in which the discipline should approach them.

It may be that this gives the truest measure of the challenge facing international studies at this point. Like any other discipline, international studies has always been concerned with the question of the next step.[18] Where do current debates lead us? What is the next big argument, and what sorts of debates will it set in motion? What is shown in this book, more than anything else, is that any movement forward in international studies, any step toward the next big argument, will be assessed in light of the new global politics created by the "rise of the rest." This is the world that will need to be explained, and this is where the discipline will be required to turn its attention.

This means that international studies as a whole must be concerned in some way with the questions raised by the "rise of the rest." To what extent is the discipline Western-centric, how can it go beyond these problems to understand the growing influence of the non-Western world in global politics – these are not questions which can remain on the fringe of international studies. On the contrary, they go to the very nature of the discipline. And this means, in turn, that the key authors and texts which have shaped the nature and evolution of international studies as a discipline must be brought in when we consider these issues. To do otherwise would leave unresolved the one issue which must be addressed by international studies at the moment: the core canon of the discipline would remain unchanged, the "rise of the rest" would proceed apace, and the gap between the discipline and the world it now has to explain would grow, without ever being bridged. This is where, in the end, the most crucial challenge for international studies could lie at this time. Hopefully, this book will add in some way to the reflections that this challenge is bound to bring about in international studies in the immediate future.

Part I

How Do We Think about Global Politics? Universals in International Studies

1
Competing Universals: Realism

The first part of this book puts forward one simple argument: international studies as a discipline assumes that it speaks to the nature of international politics throughout the entire world.[1] The logic which underlies the discipline, the series of postulates and claims it calls upon to explain global affairs all support this idea that international studies captures in its explanations universal forces and problems that go to the core of international affairs in all parts of the globe. To make this case, this part of the book examines the main authors, claims, and debates that have marked the evolution of international studies. Some authors, for instance, serve as constant points of reference in the study of international affairs. Students and policy makers alike refer to Machiavelli to situate their understanding of power; they reference Hobbes to describe the nature of the international realm; or they invoke Kant to find a rationale for their search for peace and rationality in global politics. More recent authors – Foucault, for example – serve as the anchoring point of a critique of this more traditional canon. In all of this, basic images of the world are set, and lines of debate are established.

What is shown here is that this entire series of worldviews and debates goes to the same claim: what is said by specialists of international studies applies to international politics throughout the whole world. Hobbes, for instance, develops his understanding of the state through a logic that, he claims, applies to all states. When contemporary thinkers draw on that same logic, they arrive at the same conclusion: what is said about the state, its character, and its impact on the nature of international politics speaks to all states throughout the world. The same is true of those who offer critiques of that conception of the state. They implicitly acknowledge that contemporary understandings of the state drawn from the writings of Hobbes and others speak to universal realities. They then assume that their own critique of that notion of state will itself also capture universal realities.

What will then be shown in the second part of the book is how this situation affects international studies at the moment, as the field considers the "rise of the rest." To understand the international politics of the non-Western world and to gauge the rising impact of non-Western actors on global politics, one must study what is inherently specific about international life in those countries. It is here, though, that a crucial problem emerges. How is it possible to situate in a logic that assumes that it speaks to universal problems and realities the idea that some forms of international politics stand beyond its purview, and indeed completely escape this logic? From this problem follow many difficulties for international studies – some conceptual and some much more practical. It is these difficulties that must be resolved, as will be shown later on, if the discipline is to understand better the consequences of the "rise of the rest."

First, though, the argument defended in this part of the book must be introduced. The presentation of this argument, in turn, must start with realism. As all students of international politics learn from their very first classes, and as all those who teach these classes also know, the realist approach to international affairs is in fact always the starting point in the study of the field. Those who position themselves as critics of the approach also, in truth, always start with realism and then try to push the literature in directions that are different from those followed by the realists. There is, however, much more. Realism, as will be shown in a moment, is essentially a discourse on what is universal in international affairs. The force of realism has been its ability to carry this sense of a universal scope through its different interpretations and critiques. This is why the story told here must start with realism: it sets up the assumption that international studies speaks to all of international politics, and this assumption then locks the field in the belief that what it says, either in support of realism or in opposition to it, will apply to the entire realm of international affairs.

How does realism do that? One must start here with Machiavelli. Or, more exactly – as Rob Walker aptly puts it in *Inside/Outside: International Relations as Political Theory*, his best-known examination of the realist tradition – one must start with "what is has come to mean to claim that one should begin with Machiavelli."[2] What there is for the realists in Machiavelli is, in essence, the impression that egotism and self-interest, ambitions and desires, and, just as much, the fear caused by the knowledge that others, also motivated by the same traits, will do anything to further their own aims all constitute the fundamental building blocks of political life. These elements remain, in that light, constant points of reference, which ultimately define both political analysis and political prescription. This is what students learn while sitting in university classrooms, and this is what decision-makers in international circles feel they should keep in mind as they gauge the circumstances of the day.

The issue of what Machiavelli "has come to mean" to the realists acquires a new significance, though, when considered in the context of the problems studied here. What emerges then is the strong universalism which follows from Machiavelli's construction of politics and violence. What also becomes apparent, in turn, is how this universalism then permeates the work of those who use Machiavelli in their analysis, whether to support their adoption of realist tenets or to offer an alternative vision of the realist tradition. There is here a language learned and a whole storyline, which make it so that all those who use that language and repeat that story always come to the same conclusion: they are speaking to realities which are the same all the time and everywhere.

How is universalism a corollary of Machiavelli's writing? Before anything else, Machiavelli wants to teach us how politics comes into existence and what its nature is bound to be. As he notes in one of his best known aphorisms,

> You should know, then, that there are two ways of contending: one by using laws, the other, force. The first is appropriate for men, the second for animals: but because the former is often ineffective, one must recourse to the latter. Therefore, a ruler must know well how to imitate beasts as well as employing properly human means.[3]

Violence exists, in others words, in a beast-like world, which is "as yet uninstitutionalized and unpurposed" – to use the phrase employed by Michael Doyle to describe the nascent Italian principalities, still riven by violence, which form the backdrop of Machiavelli's reflections.[4] This is a world where the lack of institutions and "laws" creates a perpetual violence, which blocks any attempt at rational behavior. Indeed the very notion of agency is absent here. The world is "unpurposed." This is because there is no space where individuals can transform the world or act in it on the basis of self-defined objectives and in rational pursuit of these objectives. Violence, on the contrary, cuts them short at every turn. The fundamental point is that agency, rationality, and the judicious use of brutality – the world of politics, according to Machiavelli – emerge only once violence comes under the control of the ruler. It is only then that is it possible to think that non-violent politics can exist. It is only then, in consequence, that it is possible even to think that violence represents one currency of power among many. And it is only then, finally, that it is possible to conceptualize notions like agency and rationality, which are able to formulate political objectives and approach violence as one of the means through which these objectives can be pursued.

The "economy of violence," which Sheldon Wolin describes in order to show how the Prince counseled by Machiavelli must modulate violence and politics, rationality and cruelty so as to survive and prosper,[5] also involves, in that perspective, the very creation of the world where this choice is possible. Violence must be constrained and controlled by the Prince before he can even think of it as means at his disposal, capable of being shaped and made efficient by his will. Machiavelli thus establishes a distinction between what could be termed contextual violence, the unpurposed violence of the beasts, and a much more instrumental understanding of violence, linked to the idea that violence remains a means at the service of humanly determined objectives. As he insists, seeing violence as such an instrument, and even conceiving of the elements of rationality, purpose, and choice, which that notion entails, requires a prior success in the control of contextual violence and an endless effort to maintain that control. Politics will thus be possible once the sheer and constant violence of the beasts is evacuated from social relations, so that rational and purposive behavior, possibly violent and possibly not, becomes possible. Politics will always have to be concerned, before anything else, with making sure that this movement cannot be reversed.

It is this understanding of the source and nature of politics that sets up a universalist bent to the study of the political. This happens in two ways. First, there is an essentialism here which leads to universalism. Politics can only emerge if and when the movement away from this sheer and constant violence is successful. The absence of this process does not lead to the possibility of other forms of politics, but rather to the utter absence of politics. In turn, the success of that process fixes the nature of the politics that will follow and forecloses all other possibilities. Politics will thus be the same all the time and everywhere, or it will not be. Politics cannot be different, it can only be present or absent. This logic also sets up a second path to universalism, this time linked to the impossibility of pluralism. There is no other principle of political organization, no force exterior to the world painted by Machiavelli, which can come from the outside, now or ever, to challenge the principles he puts forward, since there cannot be different types of politics, but only one. Machiavelli does note that Princes learn over time and behavior differs from republic to republic, for instance between young and mature ones, but they can only be different within the parameters set by the unavoidable need to control violence and by the sort of politics that this need puts in place. Moving away from these parameters would bring back the beast-like world where violence is everything, and politics impossible. Differences that could bring about, and then sustain, any form of political pluralism are thus themselves impossible.

The epistemological stance adopted by Machiavelli also lends a deeply universalist streak to his work. He draws his teachings from historical events which have value of lessons because, as he explains in a well-known passage,

> Prudent men are wont to say – and this is not rashly or without good ground – that he who would foresee what has to be, should reflect on what has been, for everything that happens in the world at any time has a genuine resemblance to what happened in ancient times. This is due to the fact that the agents who bring such things about are men, and that men have, and always have had, the same passions, whence it necessarily comes about that the same effects are produced.[6]

The way Machiavelli presents his lessons is central. Most often, they are articulated around binary oppositions whereby the Prince has to learn to act in a certain way if he is to avoid violence and defeat at the hand of his enemies, or has to think along the lines of a particular subterfuge or political stratagem if he is to ward off their own ambitions and cruelty. What Machiavelli aims to introduce in this fashion, nonetheless, is not a series of laws of political survival. Rather, and at a much more basic level, he is trying to account for the tension between rationality and knowledge, on one side, and, on the other side, violence and chaos. For him, in accordance with his understanding of the nature of politics, rationality and knowledge emerge only once endemic violence has been evacuated from social relations. The movement toward a more restrained violence, a *useful* violence, is a crucial prerequisite to the idea that rational individuals, rather than weapons and blind violence, can constitute means of political agency. Instrumental violence brings about, in this sense, instrumental rationality. As the individual comes to control violence, instead of invariably remaining its passive victim, he can then plausibly be seen as a self-determined and self-thinking actor, able to shape and change the nature of the social order through his capacity for reflection and purposeful behavior. In turn, Machiavelli insists, instrumental rationality is necessary if politics is to exist at all. A detached look at the world, a belief that it can be bent and fashioned according to one's will, leads to the world of politics, where violence can be a means among others to attain one's ends, and where other means and preoccupations can create space for the pursuit of one's objectives or that of a more common good. The absence of this type of rationality, conversely, leads back to a world of unending and purposeless violence, which negates the very possibility of politics, reflection, and meaningful behavior.

It is here that Machiavelli's epistemology makes him a universalist thinker. Rational thought, he argues, can only emerge through the control of violence in society. The absence of that process of control of violence signals not the possibility of other forms of thought, but the impossibility of thought itself: only violence will dominate and shape the social order, and there will be no space where the rational individual, able to shape society, can appear. Rationality, therefore, can only be the same everywhere and all the time. Difference here is also an impossibility, because only presence or absence are possible. Everywhere and all the time, there will be this dimension of self-reference and control of nature, because they are the only possible channel toward an instrumental conception of violence without which thought and rationality themselves cannot exist. There can be no pluralism of rationality. Rational thought without the prior control of violence is impossible, and any control of violence will bring rationality back toward the same common form.

Machiavelli's approach to normativity, lastly, also leads him to universalism. His sense of the normative, though, is eminently political rather than religious. Values, he insists, can be defined and safeguarded only if politics has replaced violence as the currency of power in society, indeed only as long as politics remains the sole template of power. Morality, in that context, remains embedded in politics. It only emerges once – and where – politics has been constituted. Nor can it set standards which undermine the conduct of political life, with all its intrigues and treacheries: doing so would destroy the very structures that keep the beast-like world of omnipresent violence at bay and allow the pursuit of morality in the first place. The quest for value-driven political and social behavior must therefore remain circumscribed by the search for security and control of violence. As David Boucher remarks, "morality must be subordinate to politics if statesmen and states are to sustain the necessary flexibility for creating and maintaining a stable political environment both internally and externally."[7] Morality will thus come to be after politics, after rationality, and it will be able to develop in the parameters set by these elements. The rational use of instrumental violence – force at the service of political ends – will be morally defensible because it protects the political community from its internal and external enemies, and that community is essential to morality itself. The values that are generated in the moral sphere remain uncertain. Machiavelli sees around him the beginnings of a new moral order, not the clear characterization of the end-point of that new order. He knows, though, that these new values should not be allowed to impede the exercise of violence as a means of defense of the community.

The universalism linked to this conception of morality follows from Machiavelli's belief that he has uncovered the sole process through which values can be created and defended in society. He posits a sequence that starts with the existence of omnipresent, contextual violence and then extends to the development of politics, the rational use of instrumental violence to sustain and defend that community, and the creation of a moral realm in the space constituted by this community. The logic leading to universalism at the normative level is thus the same one used to bring about a universalist dimension to the ontological and epistemological components of his teachings. There is here also an essentialism at play, which leads to universalism. There can only be morality if violence is controlled and if the rationality necessary to the control of violence is also in place, in counterpoint: the absence of these elements cannot lead to other types of morality, but to the absence of morality itself. And, furthermore, the norms which will be established in that context will be the same, everywhere and all the time, since morality can only come from one process and then lead to the same outcome. Different sorts of morality – religious ones, for instance – cannot sustain themselves, since they do not address adequately the problems of violence and rationality that must be resolved if any morality is to have purchase on social and political life.

"What it has come to mean" for the realists to start with Machiavelli, then, is that, when this most central of realist questions is posed – how are politics, rationality, and morality, possible in a world of violence and sheer brutality? – the answer can only be given in universalist terms. Politics, the realists will say after reading Machiavelli and incorporating in their work his fundamental concern with the omnipresent nature of violence, can emerge only if violence becomes instrumental, only if it is controlled and channeled, instead of remaining an omnipresent and unyielding force escaping all restraint and preventing any other form of power from emerging in society. Politics can only exist as a result of that process, and thus will always reflect its demands: it will be defined at its core by the need to control and channel violence and nothing else, and it will disappear in the sheer chaos of unending bloodshed and brutality if it steers away from that primordial concern. Rationality can only be, and thus will be, always and everywhere, a corollary of this movement, away from constant, sheer violence and toward a more measured, instrumental violence. The control of violence and the logic of ends and means, choice and purpose that it allows must be in place if the notion of purposeful reflection able to have purchase on reality is to have any plausibility. The absence of that process will leave in place the total irrationality of total violence where there is no space for rationality to become a vector of political agency. Rationality will need to be and remain instrumental: a detached calculus of means and ends, causes and effects, is the only way to sustain politics and thus to create an alternative to a world of endless and purposeless violence. Finally, morality will be anchored in politics, always and everywhere, because it is only politics that can provide the space of non-violence, where higher ideals can be asserted and implemented. Morality will at all times follow politics, rather than the reverse, lest it undermine the very structure it needs to develop itself.

These terms – violence, rationality, politics, or morality – can thus mean only one thing, everywhere and all the time. They all serve as so many postulates in the realist paradigm, starting points which can be taken for granted before the explanation moves to something else, and they carry within them the assumption that the view of the world they embody carries universally across space and time. When other writers follow Machiavelli in starting with violence, and when they abide by the logic he himself follows from that starting point or by the meaning he imparts to terms like rationality, violence, or morality, they consequently offer points of relay in the realist tradition for those universalist assumptions. The story they tell is such that it can only lead them to the conclusions, and to the universalist worldview, contained in Machiavelli's writings.

For instance, Morgenthau's *Politics Among Nations*,[8] the cornerstone of post–World War II realism and the obligatory textbook for all students in international politics, is very much a case in point. The beginning of the argument put forth in the book is in parallel with the logic advanced by

Machiavelli. The "struggle for power," Morgenthau tells us, is "universal in time and in space."[9] That struggle encompasses all forms of

> domination of man by man, both when it is disciplined by moral ends and controlled by constitutional safeguards, as in Western democracies, and when it is that untamed and barbaric force which finds its laws in nothing but its own strength, and its sole justification in its aggrandizement.[10]

It is the movement from the "untamed" sway of violence, which "finds its laws in nothing but its own strength," to the "disciplined" use of force that marks the emergence of political power:

> Political power, however, must be distinguished from force in the sense of the actual exercise of physical violence. The threat of physical violence in the form of police action, imprisonment, capital punishment, or war is an intrinsic element of politics. When violence becomes an actuality, it signifies the abdication of political power in favor of military or pseudo-military power. In international politics, in particular, armed strength as a threat or potentiality is the most important material factor making for the political power of a nation. If it becomes an actuality in war, it signifies the substitution of military for political power.[11]

It is this very use of violence, when it becomes "an intrinsic element of politics," that can allow political power to come into existence and then to be exercised through force or not. There is therefore here also a universalism rooted in the logical sequence positing, first, that violence is a universal, and second, that politics arises out of the progress toward an instrumental form of violence and stands in tension with that violence: universally, then, politics will reflect this process and the particular nature it instills in political life. It is on the basis of this universalism, of this unqualified certainty, that Morgenthau can then talk simply of "politics" or of "all politics" when he builds his argument.[12]

The epistemology at the heart of this argument follows from this understanding of the nature of politics and of the assumption of universality attached to it. One cannot assume that rationality can be built out of a conception of the world and of knowledge that "assumes the essential goodness and infinite malleability of human nature."[13] Rationality, on the contrary, can only exist in a world of universal violence, but against violence, as a bulwark against the "untamed and barbaric" force it can bring to bear in politics. Realists will then, according to Morgenthau,

> believe[...] that the world, imperfect as it is from the rational point of view, is the result of forces inherent in human nature. To improve the

world, one must work with those forces, not against them. This being inherently a world of opposing interests and of conflict among them, moral principles can never fully be realized, but must at best be approximated through the ever temporary balancing of interests and the ever precarious settlement of conflict. [...Realism] appeals to historic precedent rather than to abstract principles, and aims at the realization of the lesser evil rather than of the absolute good.[14]

Rationality emerges in the violent world linked to the "forces inherent in human nature." It can only unfold if it offsets violence to "improve the world," but it will always remain tied to these efforts to counter the role of violence in politics: it must "work with those forces" and "aim at the realization of the lesser evil rather than of the absolute good." Rationality, always and all the time, then, will exist as a response to the violence inherent in human nature. It will support deeds and thought only if it can provide a somber assessment of the human potential for improvement, but also for violent and vile behavior, and if it can propose principles of political action that promote the former and guard against the latter. The omnipresent potential for violence in human nature compels rationality to be that way, universally.

Morgenthau, finally, also follows in that path when he considers morality. Politics minimizes the impact of violence in social life, and morality, in turn, should only work within the bounds set by politics so as to not undermine its only defense against the regression and destruction entailed by a return to omnipresent violence. Morgenthau notes in that perspective that

[t]here can be no political morality without consideration of the political consequences of moral action. Realism, then, considers prudence – the weighing of the consequences of alternative political actions – to be the supreme virtue in politics. Ethics in the abstract judges action by its conformity with the moral law; political ethics judges action by its political consequences.[15]

All morality in politics, everywhere, will be of that sort, because "there can be no morality" without this regard for its political consequences. The choice cannot be between different types of morality. We live in a world where there is either the morality described by Morgenthau, or none at all. This is so for all of us, everywhere and all the time.

The other foundational text of modern realism read time and again by generations of scholars, E. H. Carr's *The Twenty Years' Crisis 1919–1939*,[16] follows the same logic and ends up with comparable universalist overtones. Completed in 1939, just as World War II broke out, it thus bookends the war together with Morgenthau's *Politics Among Nations*, which was published in 1948. Both books stem from a similar sense that the events of the time demonstrated beyond doubt that international politics can only be understood if the ever present violence that underlies it is fully acknowledged and met face on. In what he presents as a refutation of the "exuberance of utopianism"[17] in the pre-war period and of the widely held belief that international politics could be based on considerations other than the unvarying need to counter force and brutality in world affairs, Carr insists that progress in international politics can be achieved only if these elements are addressed directly and decisively. The realism he propounds, therefore, will

> [e]mphasize the irresistible strength of existing forces and the inevitable character of existing tendencies, and [...] insist that the highest wisdom lies in accepting, and adapting oneself to these forces and these tendencies.[18]

The "inevitable character" of force and violence, their "irresistible strength," means for Carr that politics will always need to deal with them. The universalist aspect of his argument follows from this belief that politics, and then progress and morality, simply cannot exist otherwise: "power," he tells us, "is a necessary ingredient of every political order."[19] Rationality, in turn, will always need to rely on the "acceptance of [these] facts" and to accept that "the function of thinking is to study a sequence of events which it is powerless to influence or alter."[20] It is only if it is detached and calculating in its approach to the reality of violence and brutality, only if it is *realist* when faced with these facts, that it will be able to have some resonance and impact in the world: it is then, and only then, that "political thought [will become] itself a form of political action" and that "political science [will be] the science not only of what is, but of what could be."[21] A rationality with some purchase on the world will thus, always and all the time, have that realist character. Morality, for its part, will remain at all times embedded in politics and in the space it creates for normative progress beside the chaos of constant violence: "morality can only be relative, not universal," Carr notes, and "ethics must be interpreted in terms of politics [because] the search for an ethical norm outside politics is doomed to frustration."[22] There again, claims about the nature of morality lead to a belief that morality can only be this way, everywhere and all the time.

Machiavelli's role in framing a *problématique* of violence, rationality, and morality, imbued with universal implications, which echoes throughout the entire realist tradition, is in fact explicitly recognized by Carr. Machiavelli is "the first important realist," Carr argues, because the

> three essential tenets in [his] doctrine are the foundation-stones of the realist philosophy. In the first place, history is a sequence of cause and effect, whose course can be analysed and understood by intellectual effort,

but not (as the utopians believe) directed by "imagination". Secondly, theory does not (as the utopians assume) create practice, but practice theory. In Machiavelli's words, "good counsels, whencesoever they come, are born of the wisdom of the prince, and not the wisdom of the prince from good counsels". Thirdly, politics are not (as the utopians pretend) a function of ethics, but ethics of morality. Men "are kept honest by constraints". Machiavelli recognized the importance of morality, but thought that there could be no effective morality where there was no effective authority. Morality is the product of power.[23]

The realists understand, in other words, that the world is shaped by the "causes and effects" of violence which escape the "utopians." Rationality will remain a function of these realities, as will morality. Further nuances of place or context are unnecessary because this will remain so all the time and everywhere: violence is omnipresent and shapes all politics, rationality, and morality in that way.

All of this is fundamental. Machiavelli sets out, as was just seen, a series of oft-reprised categories which have now been inscribed in the deeper recesses of the realist imagination and carry with them this feel of unquestionable universality. It is by drawing on that language and its inherent assumptions of universality that countless realists now speak, for instance, of the permanence and omnipresence of violence. The logic of what is said here holds within its constituent parts this sense of universality.

Another fundamental point is that these categories, and this sense of universalism, then provide the starting points of many of the critiques addressed to the realist tradition. It is these elements, in other words, that set the course of that critique, its nature, scope, and agenda. And the problem, in that context, is that these critiques remain caught within the assumption of universalism contained in realism. They cannot escape that assumption of universality because, so to speak, they have no points of reference *outside* of it: the tradition from which they work does not allow them to see what that outside world, beyond realism, would look like.

An example can be given now for these issues, which will be considered in much more detail later on. Post-modernist writers argue that violence in international politics is the reflection of specific socio-political configurations of rationality and principles of community building, and that these configurations can be reconstructed to bring about a lesser degree of violence in politics, which is not readily envisaged by the realists because of their universalist bent. There nonetheless remains in that literature, as will be demonstrated later here, an assumption that brute violence itself need not be deconstructed, that violence is violence, which follows directly from an unquestioned and direct acceptance of the belief in the universality of instrumental violence at the center of the realist tradition. Some of the universals of realism, to put it differently, are so fixed within the literature that they carry through to the language of those who profess to question or repudiate most of the realist tradition.

The questions asked in this work, though, remain central. To what extent, if we stay with the example of violence, does beginning from a different starting point modify the trajectory followed by the realist approach and its various critiques? Much of the non-Western world has not experienced what has been described here as the movement from contextual to instrumental violence. Violence has not been evacuated from society and politics in the rising number of so-called failed states, for instance, and this movement remains incomplete in many regions of the non-Western world. As will be shown later, this has created in many instances a social environment of constant violence, where there is no zone of autonomy and agency surrounding the individual and where, consequently, the individual has not fully emerged as a site of political and moral power to the extent he has in the West. How, then, does this set up a different relationship between violence, politics, rationality, and morality? How does this affect the very nature of each of these elements and set them on a course quite dissimilar from the one envisaged by realism? How, subsequently, does this contradict the sequences of claims upon which the universalist logic of realism is predicated? How does this also, in turn, destabilize the critiques of realism, and how does this compel a readjustment of the view of the world that they offer in opposition to the realist one? And how, finally, can these sorts of questions bring about a new slant in international studies, one more congruent with the character of international politics in both Western and non-Western areas?

The examination of the assumptions upon which the universalist claims of realism are based must first be completed, though, before all the elements necessary to answer these questions are in place. It is Hobbes who puts in place the second fundamental series of tenets, which imbue realism with the assumption of a universalist scope. Hobbes published his masterpiece *Leviathan* in 1651, in reaction to the English Civil Wars, and indeed the object of this book – as well as that of his entire lifework, as C. B. Macpherson notes in his masterly introduction to one of the key editions of the text – was in essence to "find how to prevent future civil wars."[24] The solution he proposed is well known. Individuals must mutually consent to surrender all their rights, save for the right of self-preservation, to a commonwealth, a state, which will then control all these individuals, but will also preserve them from the violence that each could exercise against the others. This line of reasoning has served over time to introduce three central and interrelated elements in the discourse of international studies. First, Hobbes brings a structural element to the study of international politics. Violence, he contends, is to be controlled not by the individuals who populate society, but rather by the institutions and modes of organization that regulate the interactions between these individuals. It is only an overarching structure, standing above and separately from individual will – the Leviathan that emerges in opposition to the state of nature where life would always stay "brutish and short"[25] – that can resolve the issue of violence. In fact, it is through the very surrender to that structure that individuals can move away from violence. This logic establishes, at a second level, the role of the state as the primordial form of delineation of politics. The Hobbesian line of reasoning sets up a space inside the state where politics is possible, and, conversely, a space outside the state where it is impossible. The area between the Leviathans will then continue to be a place of violence, literally on the exterior of the lone structure able to control the violent impulses of human beings. Third, these arguments lead to a belief in the unity and coherence of international politics: all of international affairs are to remain defined, always, by the constant use or threat of violence. With these three elements, to paraphrase another remark in Macpherson's introduction to *Leviathan*, "there ought not to be any question as to whether Hobbes [put himself] in the main stream [of international studies]; it should rather be acknowledged that he dug the channel in which the main stream subsequently flowed."[26] These three elements, though, also connect realism and universalism ever so closely.

The starting point of Hobbes' argumentation is the tension between rationality and violence. "The condition of Man," he tells us, "is a condition of Warre of every one against everyone; in which case every one is governed by his own Reason; and there is nothing he can make use of, that may not be a help unto him, in preserving his life against his enemyes."[27] This is the "state of nature" of human beings. It never can really exist as such, but it shows to all the latent possibilities inherent in violence and reason, which underlie all human activities. Humans are "governed by Reason," but they have to face others and the danger that these others could use their shrewdness and intelligence to triumph over their peers, even to a degree where violence, the "war of everyone against everyone," will be the most likely prospect. This compels human beings to establish the Leviathan, the sovereign able to protect them and bring peace to social relations.

This is where the structural element central to Hobbes' work comes into play. The state of nature, as Gregory S. Kavka notes, is a "relational concept"[28]. It speaks to the fact that the risk of violence in society does not rest with what one does, but much more with what others choose to do – I may act with reason, but others can still use violence against me. The "war of all against all" is rooted in something that escapes the control of any one individual and is much more closely tied to the sort of context in which they all have to evolve. The route out of the state of nature, then, is to change that context and to create a new social institution, able to have power over all individuals. Therefore the solution, for Hobbes, does not have to do with somehow changing the individual. It has to do, instead, with changing the social structure in which this individual evolves. Reason in human beings, to put it even more starkly, does not compel them to act rationally but structurally, at the level of the milieu that connects them all, rather than through personal attempts to act with reason and through appeals to others to do the same.

The creation of the Leviathan thus follows logically, unavoidably, from the rationality that animates all human beings. Reason can only lead to its creation. The Leviathan, the state, determines in that perspective a radical fissure in politics between the domestic and the international, the inside of the state and its outside. The movement away from the state of nature can only take place within the space covered by the state, where it can force individuals to forego violence in their relations and to act always with reason. Once the state is created, it allows a level of security to its citizens that satisfies them enough to make them let things be, instead of risking the coherence and legitimacy of the state by attempting to build a more global and inclusive Leviathan. The space left outside the state is where violence will continue to exist and where reason, so to speak, will not be able to reach it because it will remain unable to operate the structural transformation it managed to carry out within the state. Therefore, just as the movement toward the state in unavoidable, embedded as it is in human reason, so is its consequence. By creating a space where it can prevail, reason also demarcates one where it cannot and where violence will still reign: international politics will thus be the realm of violence, untouched by the structures that could change it and bring a degree of reason to its evolution. All states, then, will find themselves much as the individuals within society did before the advent of the Leviathan. They will hope for cooperation, perhaps establish some degree of trust amongst themselves, but they will nonetheless always have to prepare for violence, because no structure will be in place to prevent its use and to provide an effective guarantee of security for all.

This is the consensual understanding of international politics, which has been inherited from repeated readings of Hobbes throughout the development of international studies. The series of ontological commitments about the individual, the state, and the nature of international politics contained in these assumptions is also coextensive, though, with a claim to universality that has equally been constitutive of the discipline itself and of the image it has constructed of its object of study. Hobbes' initial postulates about the rationality of all human beings, where "every one is governed by his own Reason," and the confrontation of rationality with the "Warre of every one against everyone," are introduced as matters of universal principle. All human beings are rational, everywhere and all the time, and violence is also a universal, challenging, and limiting reason everywhere and all the time. It is this universality of the human predicament that sets up the universality of the only possible solution to that predicament. The state is structurally unavoidable and inescapable because it provides the single way out of the human desire to do away with violence; everywhere there are humans, the state will need to appear as a result of the very nature of these human beings. The universality of the movement toward the state, in turn, sets up the universal character of the spaces left between states. This will be a realm of violence, undivided and unbroken, universal in its very nature. The universality of human reason, its necessary movement toward the state, will entail, always and everywhere, a zone outside the state where only the irrational rather than the rational can prevail, and where violence remains at all times its possible instrument. The universal nature of international politics thus follows logically, structurally, from the universal nature of human beings.

Hobbes' epistemology also leads him to the assumption that his work has universal applicability. It has been suggested time and again that his attempt to devise what amounted in his mind to a science of politics is best understood against the background of the broad paradigmatic shift toward scientificity and calculable rigor, set in motion by the advances in mathematics, geometry, and applied mechanics of his era. He is often placed, on the basis of that logic, in the historical sweep linked in the natural sciences to the findings of Newton and Galileo and their efforts to anchor scientific discovery in an attempt to uncover the fundamental laws of nature.[29] For Hobbes, the fundamental law of his object of study – politics – is that the threat of violence always compels rational human beings to change the nature of their interaction through the creation of the Leviathan. Science, which is, as Hobbes tells us, "the knowledge of Consequences, and dependance of one fact upon another,"[30] can lay out the logical, the structural chain of "consequences," which will lead from rationality to fear of violence, to the creation of the Leviathan, and, lastly, to the nature of the anarchic realm left beyond the sovereign Leviathan. This is a law of human life that can be established with all the certainty and accuracy of the mathematical formulae used to describe the effects of gravity or the curvature of the Earth.

This gears-like sequence of enmeshed claims where each sets in motion the next – Macpherson calls Hobbes a "mechanical philosopher"[31] – brings to *Leviathan* two of the central components of what would later become the positivist tradition in international studies. First, it circumscribes objects of study and the sets of relationships that define their interrelationship. We know what rationality, the state, or the international realm are in their true nature, because they can only be that way: each is created through structural processes which lead logically and inescapably to that specific nature. The form through which they manifest themselves will vary according to time and place, but there will always be a nature, an identity, to each of these realities, which will remain present irrespective of these elements of context. Second, this approach to knowledge presents the observer of politics as an outsider vis-à-vis the phenomena that are studied: the sequences of cause and effect that create domestic and international politics stand on their own, whether or not they are observed, and indeed their nature is entirely independent from the makeup and disposition of the observer. This view of science then leads to a belief in the universality of the findings put forward as a result of the scientific observation of human affairs. The universality of reason, and, in counterpoint, the universality of violence set about an inescapable series of consequences, which then will itself have a universal scope. The process of scientific inquiry, because it brings to light the unavoidability, the very necessity of this chain of consequences, also shows that it will shape the character of politics always and all the time. What science is able to uncover, in other words, is precisely the universal in politics and society. And these laws of politics and society can only remain the same universally, whatever the diverse nature of the observers attempting to discern them through different contexts of time and place.

Hobbes' moral theory, finally, also possesses strong universalist overtones. The entire second half of *Leviathan* – Part III, devoted to the notion of the "Christian Common-Wealth," and Part IV, to that of the "Kingdom of Darkness" – is intended not only to demonstrate a thorough understanding of the canons of Christian morality but also to show how Christianity can acquire meaning and impact only if the prescriptions laid out in the first half of the text are first fully implemented. The point which Hobbes is trying to get across here is the eminently political character of religion. The aspiration to morality is given by God, but it can only exist in the world of humans if it is endorsed by them in the social and political orders that they build so as to relate to each other and to the moral ideals that they espouse. Morality is built as much as it is revealed. More than that, it is built through the politics that Hobbes has spent the first half of *Leviathan* exploring. Developing the state, in other words, is the only process through which the prerequisites to morality can be set in place. The search for morality thus remains for Hobbes, as is the case with his understanding of politics, profoundly structural: a moral life can only be achieved through the structural transformation of human affairs that the Leviathan can bring about, and that first allows the civil peace necessary to the very pursuit of morality in social affairs to emerge. Hence, morality speaks most of all in Hobbes' mind to a series of structural prerequisites to which human beings must, before anything else, surrender themselves. For its part, the realm outside the state will remain, in that context, an amoral space. It will be so not because the pursuit of morality is absent from that realm, but rather because the structural prerequisites necessary to that pursuit and to its success are themselves absent there. Many might therefore want peace and justice in international affairs, but endeavoring to bring about these goals will be useless if the context allowing them to emerge is not set in place first.

It is this structural component in the formulation of Hobbes' moral theory that gives it its universal reach. Morality can only exist if there is this surrender to what escapes individual behavior and if it is achieved through the structural movement toward civil peace brought about by the establishment of the Leviathan. Morality cannot, therefore, come about outside of this movement, regardless of time and place. Morality will not arise in human affairs, anywhere at any time, if the sovereign state has not first marginalized violence in society. The international realm that emerges in counterpoint to this process will, always and all the time, remain amoral precisely because it is *exterior* to that process of structural marginalization of violence.

The series of conceptual sequences set up by Hobbes, which shape so much of the inherited patterns of reasoning that underlie current understandings of international politics, thus implant an unquestioned, and unquestionable, universalism in these understandings of international affairs. The postulates drawn from Hobbes, the lines of argument they initiate, entail as so many automatic and implicit reflexes the belief that the claims about international politics to which they lead explain the totality, and in fact the very identity, of all international politics. Assuming that there is a structural force to violence – an inescapable need that violence establishes for a structural response to the devastation it can unleash in social relations – leads to an inexorable, and thus universal, need for the creation of states able to pacify social relations. This process, in turn, produces a space outside the state which remains unified at all times and everywhere in its inability to transcend violence. Three fundamental tenets of contemporary realism follow directly from this sort of logic: first, the belief that violence imposes structural constraints on human relations; second, the belief that there is a clear and fundamental difference between domestic and international politics; and, third, the belief that the character of international politics requires that it be considered as a unified and unchanging object of study. Universality is entrenched in all these claims. The realities created by the structural forces identified by Hobbes – the state, the distance between domestic and international politics, the unity of the international realm – have an intrinsic and unchanging nature. They constitute so many objects of study that can be assumed always to remain the same and thus to stand above all matters of context. The forms that international life adopts in different circumstances, the varying agendas and perspectives of those who participate in this life or comment on it, will not change them.

The author who most often invokes these series of assumptions – and the claims to universality they comprise – in order to construct his understanding of the nature of international politics is, of course, Kenneth Waltz. Indeed, his most accomplished reprise of these themes in his classic *Theory of International Politics*[32] has now not only helped assemble a large part of the vocabulary most widely employed today to discuss international affairs, it has also instilled in those students, academics, and policy makers who draw on that vocabulary a belief that it can describe the sheer totality of international politics. He is, without exaggeration, a constant reference in international studies – as such, he represents another point of relay for the notion that the field speaks to universal realities.

Much as Hobbes would have liked, Waltz declares at the outset of *Theory of International Politics* that his work revolves around one basic goal;

> the aim is to try to find the central tendency among a confusion of tendencies, to single out the propelling principle even though other principles operate, to seek the essential factors where innumerable factors are present.[33]

What is, in Waltz's view, the basic "propelling principle," which will give form and substance to international politics? At the outset of his response to this question, Waltz follows Hobbes in underscoring the fact that only a "relational," a structural movement can allow the passage from violence to politics in human affairs. He employs the analogy of the market, where "the individual unit acts for itself," but where also "from the coaction of like units emerges a structure that affects and constrains all of them."[34] Domestic politics represents a realm where violence has been evacuated from social relations because its structure has allowed this movement from violent to non-violent interaction to occur. The "ordering principle" of international politics, though, is "distinctly different, indeed, contrary"[35] to that of domestic politics, since it has not produced a structure able to force violence out of the units which interact within it. Within the state, violence might thus remain one instrument of politics, and can in fact perhaps be used by state authority in one instance or the other. Outside the state, though, violence is politics itself – power does not exist outside of violence, and can only be exercised through its use. No other form of power has any significance or importance in that realm. This is the fundamental "propelling principle" of international politics that Waltz wants to underscore. He claims that

> the difference between national and international politics lies not in the use of force but in the different modes or organization for doing something about it. A government, ruling by some standard of legitimacy, arrogates to itself the right to use force – that is, to apply a variety of sanctions to control the use of force by its subjects. If some use private force, others may appeal to the government. A government has no monopoly on the use of force, as is all too evident. An effective government, however, has a monopoly on the *legitimate* use of force, and legitimate here means that public agents are organized to prevent and to counter the private use of force. Citizens need not prepare to defend themselves. Public agencies do that. A national system is not one of self-help. The international system is.[36]

Therefore one sees, with Waltz, a logic that reproduces step by step the sequence of arguments advanced by Hobbes. The nature of violence, first, requires a structural response to it: non-violent politics is only possible if the state extirpates violence from social interaction. The state thus creates a delineation in human affairs between a space within it, where politics is possible, and one outside of it, where the structural preconditions for the emergence of politics, progress, or rationality are lacking. In that space between states that constitutes the realm of international affairs, politics is consequently not only absent, it is impossible.

If the logic follows that of Hobbes, so does the claim to universalism that underlay *Leviathan*. The international realm, in Waltz's view, can never be divided by differences of identity or behavior. It remains, everywhere and at all times, unified in its inescapable focus on violence beyond all contrasts related to these questions: identity and behavior vary, of course, but only within the boundaries created by the possible use of violence. This sense of universality is what allows Waltz to summarize, in one short sentence, the nature of all international politics – "the international system is [one of self-help]." It is also what leads him to argue that the claims he puts forward speak to "continuities" which transcend history – just like, he tells us, "Hobbes experiencing the contemporaneity of Thucydides."[37]

Waltz's approach to epistemology also draws immediate parallels with the approach found in *Leviathan*, and it involves just as strong a claim to universality. "How," he asks at the outset, "can a theory of international politics be constructed?"[38] He then answers:

> First, one must conceive of international politics as a bounded realm or domain; second, one must discover some law-like regularities within it; and third, one must develop a way of explaining the observed regularities.[39]

International politics is a "bounded realm" because its "ordering principle" differs from that of all other political spaces: it is only there that violence remains unrestrained and uncontrollable. This is what is shown by the "system-level" approach to theory propounded by Waltz.[40] Violence can only be addressed by a change in the structures of human interaction – a change at the level of the system of interaction – and outside of those structures violence remains. It is, then, this violence that establishes "law-like regularities" within the international realm. And it is, then, the working of these laws – different configurations of threat and violence associated, for instance, with variations in the balance of power arrangements – that explains international behavior. In echo to the epistemology found in *Leviathan*, Waltz thus posits, first, that it is possible for students of politics to uncover an immutable law of human behavior: violence requires a structural response, all the time and everywhere. This immutable law will thus entail, again everywhere and all the time, a differentiation between spaces where a structural framework able to contain violence has been set in place and spaces where it has not. From this law, therefore, unchanging objects of study can be delineated. Domestic politics will always be defined by the control of violence, because its very nature is linked precisely to that control over chaos and brutality. The nature of the state will always be the same, as a border between spaces where politics is possible and spaces where it remains unachievable. And the nature of international politics will remain fixed forever in its intrinsic inability to move beyond the rule of violence and mercilessness. This is what leads Waltz to assert, again echoing his reading of Hobbes, that the "enduring anarchic character of international politics accounts for the striking sameness in the quality of international life through the millennia"[41] and that, "since Thucydides in Greece and Kautilya in India, the use of force and the possibility of controlling it have been the preoccupations of international–political studies."[42] It follows from these claims – and this is a further reverberation of the Hobbesian epistemology – that the outlook and behavior of students of international politics will never be of any consequence for its nature. The character of the international realm is a matter of structural necessity, and it thus stands apart, always, from the outlooks and opinions of those observing it.

In terms of his views on morality in international affairs, lastly, Waltz also starts and ends at points very close to those set in place by Hobbes. The state builds a space where an overarching authority can remove violence from social relations and allow political, legal, and moral progress to emerge in its place. The "ordering principle" of international affairs, though, remains steeped in violence. The quest for morality, in that specific space that exists on the exterior of states and thus outside of politics and law, will therefore remain cautious and ever faltering. Some sense of stability and organization, some sense of order provided by a measure of authority in the international realm, constitutes the only possible starting position for that quest. It might well, though, remain elusive. "Whatever elements of authority emerge internationally," Waltz notes, "are barely once removed from the capability that provides the foundation for the appearance of those elements."[43] And these elements, if they are indeed to appear, will be set in place by the strongest states in the international system, states that will, more often than not, define the good of the international community on the basis of their own interests.[44] The movement toward morality is thus uncertain, because it is caught between these contradictory tendencies: the need, if law and morality are to emerge, to rely on those who can control or at least establish a certain management of violence in international affairs; and the impossibility of preventing those with the power to do so to use that power in their own interest. "States, and especially the strong ones," Waltz adds, "do not act only for their own sakes. They also act for the world's common good. But the common good is defined by each of them for all of us, and the definitions conflict."[45] The inescapable constraints established by the very nature of the international space are such, however, that this is the only path to morality which can be opened up in that space. The structural necessities which extend from the presence of violence in human affairs all the way to the constitution of the international space outside a rigid control over violence dictate that this be the case, throughout time and also throughout the entirety of the international realm.

In his structuro-realism, or neo-realism, which provides the second moment in the post–World War II realism inaugurated by Morgenthau and Carr, Waltz thus sets terms of debate about international politics which are just as much universalist as those employed by these two writers. His work embodies an engagement with a series of preoccupations that appear to stretch from Hobbes to contemporary international questions. They aim to demonstrate, furthermore, that a text like *Leviathan* points to perennial themes of international politics, which remain constant over both time and space.

As will be demonstrated later, though, the nature of international politics in much of the non-Western world is such that most of these assumptions are not valid there. The impression of universality that stands at the very core of these assumptions must also, therefore, be questioned and revised. For one thing, the structural composition of domestic and international spaces where the "ordering principles" guiding violence and politics are in their essence dissimilar – the core anchoring point of the neo-realist approach – operates quite differently in the non-Western world. Someone like Mohammed Ayoob, among others, would point to what he describes as the "inadequate stateness"[46] of large parts of the non-Western world in order to underscore the degree to which the state in these regions is too frail to prevent violence within its borders, and also to prevent violence from its neighbors from spilling within its own territory. The control of violence, in that context, thus requires efforts which are regional as much as they are national, in that each state must ensure that its neighbors are successful in their attempts to control violence within their own borders. This mix of continued violence inside and outside the state, with parallel strategies to control it both from within the state and from above it, in regional institutions and regimes, leads to the constitution of political spaces which are far removed from those anticipated by the neo-realists. In these spaces where the inside and the outside of the state are not mutually exclusive, the regulation of violence by the state and the emergence of different "ordering principles" of politics domestically and internationally is not as unambiguous as the neo-realist literature would have it. Where a direct opposition between the nature of domestic and that of international politics is presupposed, first, a much more nuanced gradation between the two types of politics has to be imagined. And where only two "ordering principles" of politics are proposed with reference to the domestic and international realms, a greater range must be envisioned. Neo-realism must engage in this reimagining of political spaces and of the relationship they have with violence if it is to explain the international politics of the non-Western world. Conversely, as long as it does not engage in this exercise, it will not know the limits of its explanatory power, and it will not perceive where it can illuminate the nature of international politics and where it cannot.

The key point that needs to be made at this stage, however, is that realism always remains a language of universals. Its core assumption is that it speaks to the very nature of international politics, all the time and everywhere. This is why, as will be demonstrated later on, the critiques of realism can assume that their response to this literature also speaks to the nature of international relations as such, and thus does not require further nuances of context in dealing with the character of international politics in the non-Western world. This is, in truth, the strength of the realist tradition: it presents itself as bringing to light, for every one of us in the field, the very essence of international politics throughout the entire world. The elements it studies – violence and rationality – are presented as being among the most rudimentary components of all international politics, the lowest common denominators which underlie all form of international affairs. The critiques of realism have thus operated permutations in the relationship between these elements, questioning for instance the relationship between rationality and the state underlying the neo-realist approach, but they have always started their analysis from these basic elements, which they also believe to be some of the smallest irreducible expression of the constituent parts of all international politics. This has been the core effect of realism: to instill this sense, in international studies, that there are such things as violence *per se*, or rationality *per se*, and to then force a sequence of responses and critiques which have followed different trajectories – all starting, however, from these confined set of definitions.

The question raised here, however, still remains: what if the tradition had started elsewhere? How does the difference in the nature of the violence, which underlies the international politics of the non-Western world, lead, for instance, to dissimilar notions of rational and irrational violence? How does this destabilize both realism and the literature that has grown in reaction to realist tenets about violence and rationality? How can the development of international studies, finally, take into account all these problems? The other central source of universalist claims in international studies must be considered as well, however, before these questions are considered in detail. This other source is, of course, the liberal approach.

2
Competing Universals: Liberalism

Liberalism is the great Other vis-à-vis realism – the "historical alternative," as Tim Dunne puts it[1] – set out in counterpart to the traditional pre-eminence of the realist paradigm in international studies. The liberal literature is in fact in precise opposition to realism, so to say, because it reverses the most fundamental premise of realist thought. Realism assumes that violence precedes the emergence of rationality and society, and that the way in which it is handled and managed then determines the nature of both the rational and the social in human affairs. Liberalism, on the contrary, presupposes the existence of an intrinsic sense of rationality and sociability in humans, which exists aside from violence and therefore can limit its sway in the constitution and evolution of society.

However, what is central to the argument pursued here is that liberalism, exactly like realism, is essentially an attempt to identify universals in international politics. In that, it also participates in the intellectual processes which allow international studies to imagine that it speaks to universal realities in world affairs. Moreover, just as is the case with realism, the claims to universality of liberalism lock critiques of the approach within worldviews and categories which lead them to overlook a good part of what constitutes international politics in the non-Western world. Liberalism misses much because of its assumption that it speaks to universal realities, and those who position their work as a critique of the liberal approach fail to see what the approach itself neglects.

The origins of liberalism in international studies are usually traced back to the work of John Locke. When, in the wake of the English Revolution of 1688, Locke put forth his own views on the State of Nature and State of War, he was certainly responding to the line of thought that extends from Machiavelli to Hobbes and is now associated with the realist approach. "Here we have," he tells us,

> the plain *difference between the State of Nature and the State of War*, which however some Men have confounded, are as far distant, as a State of

Peace, Good Will, Mutual Assistance, and Preservation, and a State of Enmity, Malice, Violence, and Mutual Destruction are one from another. Men living together according to reason, without a common Superior on Earth, with Authority to judge between them, is *properly the State of Nature.* But force, or a declared design of force upon the Person of another, where there is no common Superior on Earth to appeal to for relief, *is the State of War.*[2]

Some have been "confounded" into thinking that a State of Nature among human beings corresponds to a State of "Enmity and Violence" – a State of War. In truth, Locke wants us to understand, the point of origin we should have in mind when conceptualizing the development of society, this State of Nature, is one where people "live together according to Reason." The State of War – that is, the recourse to "force" – can intrude upon this State of Nature, but it cannot precede it. The State of War, Locke tells us just before the passage quoted above,

is a State of Enmity and Destruction; And therefore declaring by Word or Action, not a passionate and hasty, but a sedate setled Design, upon another Mans life, *puts him in a State of War* with him against whom he has declared such an Intension [...][3]

Violence is not "passionate and hasty," born outside of rationality; on the contrary, it exists by "design" and is very much a product of rationality. The use of force against oneself allows for self-defense, the "Right of War" against an aggressor, "though he be in Society and a fellow Subject." But rational human beings – and this is the central argument advanced by Locke – can also devise forms of governance which will build on their common rationality and desire for peace in order to obviate the emergence of violence among them.

To avoid this State of War [...] is one great *reason of Mens putting themselves into Society,* and quitting the State of Nature.[4]

The creation of a social architecture where human beings "put themselves in Society" builds between them modes of interaction which stand in counterpoint to their shared rationality and allow them to "avoid the State of War" by instituting non-violent forms of conflict resolution.

What Locke establishes in these passages remains, to this day, the cornerstone of liberal thinking in international studies: the notion of a moral autonomy of the individual, which allows him or her to sidestep the violent conditions by which he or she is often confronted and to build a political order that will minimize the impact of violence upon his or her life. The international realm need not be a place of aggression and fear, as the realists claim – liberals contend, in echo to Locke's argument – because human rationality and morality introduce the possibility that the forms of governance which lead to belligerence at the international level can be changed in ways that make them less conducive to violence. From this, everything else in the liberal worldview follows.

This worldview has generally been divided into two main series of claims. One follows from Kant and his belief that the moral imperatives that animate human beings can lead them to seek a universal moral order, which will force states to behave in a more peaceful manner toward their counterparts. The other is derived from Adam Smith's notion that market dynamics can create frameworks of harmonization and order among human beings that act at cross-cutting purposes from those of the state and constrain its ability to wage war. It is these thinkers, Kant and Smith, who now constitute the two constant points of reference in any class devoted to the liberal approach in international studies – or indeed, for that matter, in any reflection on matters of morality, peace, and economic interdependence in world affairs. What is fundamental for the case advanced in this book, though, is how all the arguments set forth today in echo to the claims of Kant and Smith bring an inherent assumption of universal scope to liberal thinking in international affairs.

But, first, let us turn to Immanuel Kant and the way in which he opens up a sequence of arguments central to the development of an assumption of universality within the liberal literature. Kant's thoughts on international politics are most often gleaned from a very precise series of texts. The *Critique of Pure Reason* and the *Critique of Practical Reason* are normally used when one wants to describe his views on the relation between rationality and reality; *Idea for a Universal History from a Cosmopolitan Point of View* is studied for the political dimensions of these views; and *Perpetual Peace: A Philosophical Sketch* is then called upon to set out the implications of both kinds of reflection for international politics.[5]

What is usually taken from these texts? In the first instance, Kant's approach to rationality is understood to operate what Lewis White Beck, certainly one of his greatest interpreters, has described as two "Copernican revolutions," in echo to Kant's own use of the phrase in the Preface to the second edition of the *Critique of Pure Reason*.[6] Kant initially wants to reverse prevailing understandings of rationality, epistemology, and ontology. This is the first Copernican revolution. It is not "our knowledge [that] must conform to objects," he tells us, it is rather the "objects [that] must conform to our modes of cognition."[7] Assuming that true knowledge can come out of the experience of the object is wrong, because that experience is always limited precisely to the context and conditions in which the object is experienced: it is not the object that is known, but its experience. It is only rationality, then, that can set the categories and concepts through which this true nature of the object can be established.

Kant's second Copernican revolution follows from the first one. If our rationality is what creates our world, he asks, according to what precepts and rules should we develop this world? The revolutionary aspect of this question lies in its refusal to see the normative principles that should guide human beings as something preordained, and then revealed to them through some process of discovery or enlightenment. Rather differently from that, Kant claims, morality is produced by rationality – the normative follows from our understanding of the true nature of the epistemological and of the ontological. The freedom given to human beings by the fact that they possess rationality, and thus the power to shape their world and their destiny, also entails an ability to develop moral standards of conduct and to act according to these standards. Our rationality, in a word, leads to our duty to act morally.

The issue, then, becomes: What is it that should guide this responsibility to act morally? Fundamentally, it is the recognition that all human beings possess that rationality, that potential for morality, and therefore that each of us must respect all others. "Every rational being exists as an end in himself," Kant tells us, "and not merely as a means to be arbitrarily used by this or that will."[8] Our quest for morality requires that we treat others as "ends in themselves, and not merely as means," and we must above all learn to see each other as such equal "ends rather than means" – ends whose individual fulfillment requires that of all others.

The reflections presented in *Idea for a Universal History from a Cosmopolitan Point of View* establish, then, a bridge between these ideas and Kant's views on politics and war. The presence of violence in human affairs, and the realization of its sheer foolishness when set against the ability of human beings to move beyond it, compels a movement toward peace and morality. This movement requires humanity to develop modes of association which will value in the utmost way the rationality, freedom, and aspiration to morality of each and every individual. The goal for humanity is therefore the attainment of a "universal civic society."[9] However, the movement toward this goal demands, first, the instauration of a commonwealth, a state, which will "force [individuals] to obey a will that is universally valid, under which each can be free."[10] A framework must be found, Kant admits, which permits the creation of a just social order, and the state provides at the moment the best means of doing that. The problem that follows, however, is how to ensure that relations between states do not stand in the way of the ideals of freedom and morality each state is supposed to facilitate.

It is to this problem that *Perpetual Peace* – the last and most important among the texts by Kant that are frequently used for reference in international studies – is devoted. The well-known response provided by Kant is described in the three "definitive articles for perpetual peace among states," which deal respectively with principles of law and politics within the state (*ius civitatis*), between states (*ius gentium*), and within humankind as a whole (*ius cosmopoliticum*).[11] The first definitive article on perpetual peace posits that "the civil constitution of every state shall be republican."[12] Kant follows at this point his argumentation in *Idea for a Universal History*: he asserts that the constant possibility of relapse into the absurdity of violence leads humans to create a constitutional framework which preserves order, but also enhances the freedom and equality of all those who participate in the creation of this constitutional framework. This is the republican constitution which, "besides the purity of its origin" linked to its untainted expression of human rationality and morality, also "gives a favorable prospect for the desired consequence – perpetual peace."[13]

It is at this point that Kant's argument takes flight. A republican constitution which puts human beings at the center of the life of the state has, in the first instance, an immediate impact on the ability of state authorities to wage war. There is a harsh human and a social cost to war, which makes it so prohibitive as to render it implausible. But this is only the beginning of a process whereby human rationality, now confronted by the violence which exists outside the state, attempts to address it. This is the second article on perpetual peace. The morality which animates the citizens of a state finds its counterpart, each of them knows, in the morality underlying the actions and thoughts of the citizens of other states where a republican constitution allows that morality to flourish. Peace will be most likely between all these states, because their citizens will recognize that they can relate to each other on the basis of the rationality and morality that is part of all of them. This leads to a complete realignment of inter-state relations, where rationality and morality can be used to regulate, and even to marginalize, the tendency of states to resort to violence. And the peace which emerges between these states with republican constitutions can then serve as a demonstration, to citizens from other types of states, of the benefits, domestic and international, of moving toward a constitution which allows the expression of individual liberty and rationality. All states are then likely to emulate this movement toward republicanism and eventual integration into an ever-larger zone of peace.

The third definitive article on the "law of world citizenship" then adds a final dimension to this process of pacification of inter-state relations by showing the need – as Wade L. Huntley puts it in a seminal essay on this one portion of *Perpetual Peace* – to "reconcile the common rights of humanity to the planet with the rights of states."[14] Kant suggests to us that "the human race can gradually be brought closer and closer to a constitution establishing world citizenship."[15] This world citizenship will be based on the recognition of our common humanity. It will not displace or undermine state sovereignty, but rather reinforce and give a clearer focus to the standards of freedom, rationality, and morality, which are supposed to underlie the exercise of sovereignty at all times.

This understanding of international politics – of its nature and of its potential for change – is, most obviously, deeply intertwined with Kant's conception of epistemology, ontology, and morality. To put it differently, it is because he starts from his Copernican revolutions on the nature of knowledge, reality, and morality that Kant can subsequently elaborate a system of thought concerning the role of the rational and of the moral in international affairs. His conception of knowledge first initiates a movement away from the physical determinism of violence and, in counterpoint, an arrogation of rationality and freedom on behalf of all individuals. It is this movement that allows notions of self-determination, rationality, and change to anchor Kant's views on international affairs. It is also this movement that makes his position the main counterpart to realism. To the determinism of violence advocated by Machiavelli and Hobbes, Kant substitutes an inner rationality, which liberates human beings from it and establishes the cornerstone of the liberal tradition in international studies. And Kant's belief that the pursuit of morality can come to determine international behavior, and that the violence which is part of the international realm should in fact push that process forward, underlies his entire way of thinking on these matters. Through this analysis, he also inquires into questions which dominate the liberal tradition and set it up as a commanding alternative to realist thinking.

The interweaving of ontological, epistemological, and normative considerations in Kant's thought is profoundly influenced by the universalism that underlies each of these elements. This is where his universalist scope becomes apparent. And Kant's universalist dimension also courses its way through the work of those inspired by his views. This is why his influence matters so much in the context of the argument examined here: his discourse is one of universals, and those who draw from it always come back to all these universals as much as he does.

The point of departure of Kant's universalism is his understanding of human rationality. Knowledge, in his view, does not come from experience, but from reason. Regarded in this light, humans are never defined by the surroundings in which they find themselves, but rather by the principles and categories with which they understand that world and give it shape and meaning. It is out of that autonomous character of human rationality that universalism then emerges: if human rationality is always independent of circumstances, it remains the same everywhere and all the time. Every human being, everywhere and all the time, will share this ability to know and judge, to impose her reason on the particularities of time and place in which she finds herself. This is part of the very fabric of humanity; there cannot be, then, zones of space or time where human beings are different and depart from this ability ascribed to them by Kant.

The moral universalism of Kant is a corollary of this universality of rationality. In the first instance, it is the case that all individuals have the capacity to participate in the construction of a moral social order, since they all possess the rationality that is to set in motion and guide this project. At a second level, the nature of this moral order – the fact that every individual should be recognized as "an end in itself, and not as a means for others" – will also have a universal scope. It must remain the same, all the time and everywhere, in order always to respect the rational nature of every human being, which is itself universal. Kant tells us, in this regard, that our rational duty to act morally, which is enshrined in the categorical imperative, will always be tested by whether or not it "hold[s] for all rational beings (to which alone an imperative can apply), and only for that reason can it be a law for all human wills."[16] This is an expression of the moral formalism associated with Kant's work, which also provides the universalist overtone of all his writings.[17] He describes to us a form of moral judgment, a general principle of action, which he knows to be of universal value because it flows directly from the universality of human rationality.

This universality of rationality and morality then gives a universal quality to the problem of politics and, even more, to the problem of international politics. There is a "universal violence," Kant tells us.[18] But, if violence is universal, so is rationality. The "distress [violence] produces," Kant adds, "must eventually make a people decide to submit to the coercion which reason itself prescribes (i.e. the coercion of public law), and to enter into a civil constitution."[19] Politics always entails, in that optic, a movement away from social relations predicated on the use (or threat) of violence and on the creation – first in the domestic realm, then at the inter-state and global levels – of new configurations, which are moral and legitimate because they respect the autonomy and rationality of all those who live in them. The recourse to violence on the part of any individual, will then be most unlikely in these new configurations, because it would threaten the rule of law and the general morality, both of which allow him to thrive personally and socially. This is the moral order that Kant wants us to pursue. It is the movement toward this order beyond the state that he traces in the three definitive articles of *Perpetual Peace* as he maps out the pursuit of rationality and morality in politics through the development of civil law, then of international law, and finally of global cosmopolitan law.

The vital point for the argument defended here, though, is that politics is universally the same. It is always about the pursuit of rationality and morality over the propensity for violence, and about the creation of the social forms which will protect and give further impetus to that project. To say things differently, politics does not change as one moves from the domestic to the inter-state or to the global levels. As David Boucher notes in this regard, "both domestic and international morality [and law and politics] have the same basis, that is, what reason demands a priori."[20] International politics, then, is always the same: it is either rational and moral, or it is bound to remain a realm of violence. The "universal violence" possible in all human affairs offers only this alternative throughout all international contexts, irrespective of place and circumstances. But the fundamental element which Kant wants us to understand is that this alternative is always present.

Our rationality and our freedom offer us at all times the possibility of moving toward peace in the international realm. International politics is never a separate space, out of our reach as individuals or societies. International affairs can always evolve in ways which reflect our pursuit of rationality and morality. Furthermore, the route to peace is clear, because it is always the same throughout all international politics. Peace will at all times and everywhere be determined, Kant tells us, by the presence or absence of a commitment – embodied both within habits of inter-state relations and within global norms and institutions – to the development and respect of human freedoms and human rights.

The numerous contemporary international relations theorists inspired by Kant adopt the same logic, and then arrive at the same conclusions regarding the universality of their findings. They assume a rationality and a sense of ethical purpose in human beings that can at all times transcend the violent circumstances of international politics. They then attempt to show that the forms of international behavior and the institutions that flow from this rationality and from this sense of ethical purpose can always serve to change international politics in order to make it less violent and more rational and peaceful.

The literature produced by all these contemporary thinkers is divided into two main strands. One strand is inspired by the second definitive article of *Perpetual Peace*, which is devoted to the laws of inter-state behavior and revolves around the so-called democratic peace theory. Another strand follows, for its part, from the third definitive article, where Kant describes his views on global cosmopolitan law, and it revolves around notions of global civil society and global governance.

The literature on the democratic peace theory – "which attributes the dearth of militarized disputes between democracies to the pacific predilections of liberal polities"[21] – builds on Kant's account of the ability of democracies to build non-violent forms of interaction among themselves. This is a literature which is enormously popular now in international studies and is seen, here again, as speaking to unquestionable, and thus universal, truths. For instance Jack Levy (among others) has famously argued in this regard that "the absence of war between democracies comes as close as anything to an empirical law in international relations."[22]

This sort of assertion rests on a vast array of quantitative studies linking democracy and peace. The question of the degree to which the historical record demonstrates the presence of an "empirical law" of causation between the two factors first generated widespread interest in the late 1970s because of the debate generated by scholars like Small and Singer, who questioned the link between democracy and peace,[23] and Rummel, who argued in its favor.[24] An ever-growing list of studies ensued, though the work of Oneal and Russet is now considered in a great majority of circles to offer the most central and detailed statistical demonstration of the democratic peace theory.[25]

The question of why exactly this link between democracy and peace exists has itself been the object of a considerable number of studies. Michael Doyle, who became one of the leading lights of the democratic peace research program with the publication of two celebrated articles in *Philosophy and Public Affairs*,[26] ascribes the relationship between democracy and peace to the factors brought forward in what he terms the "Kantian road to peace."[27] Kant's "account of why Liberal states do maintain peace among themselves" highlights, in his view, how the "habit of respect for individual rights," which is at the core of democracy, leads democratic regimes to acknowledge, in their relations with one another, that each one is "consensual, just, and therefore deserving of accommodation."[28] At a second level, there is also a "material incentive [added] to moral commitment." Accommodation permits cooperation on a range of issues (commerce chiefly among them) which make democracy "mutually beneficial."[29] The twin sets of factors identified by Kant as pushing democracies toward peaceful relations with one another are thus, according to Doyle, those which explain mutual non-aggression between democracies to this day. Democratic regimes recognize that every one of them should be engaged through accommodation and negotiation instead of violence, because each regime embodies principles of rationality and legitimacy which have to be respected. Moreover, these regimes also understand that the peaceful relations which then become possible between them are much more beneficial than violence and should thus be preserved. Bruce Russett also echoes this appeal to a Kantian logic when he opens one of his studies of the democratic peace theory by stating that "democracies rarely fight each other" because they know they can find non-violent and more mutually beneficial ways of resolving their conflicts – and also, more bluntly, because "they believe that democracies should not fight each other."[30]

It is on this basis that the proponents of the democratic peace theory claim that the theory has universal relevance. Michael Doyle, for instance, is among those who put forward some of the most accomplished work on the possible use of the democratic peace theory to understand, and to change, the nature of international politics outside the Western world. He suggests, essentially, a two-track approach. The first track involves continually strengthening the series of political and economic links that underlie the liberal democratic community centered on the West. The second track, subsequently, entails extending this "zone of liberal peace" through three strategies. First, "inspiration" – that is, a sustained and vocal appeal to all people living in non-democratic regimes in the non-Western world to make them demand that universal human rights and freedoms be recognized in their country. Second, "instigation" – a determined and long-term program of support given to the politico-economic reforms that can facilitate the democratization process in these regimes. And there is, possibly, a third strategy: "intervention." If a great majority of people in these regimes is asserting the need for democratization, and if a government in place responds through widespread violence and repression, the international community might have to intervene through force, to compel that government to abide by international standards of rights and freedoms and to allow greater democratization to develop within the borders of its jurisdiction. Once such strategies have brought about democratization in these regimes, the logic of the liberal peace will prevail and the Western zone of peace will then incorporate them as well.[31]

There is here, therefore, the assumption that all individuals throughout the non-Western world share in a common sphere of human rights, freedoms, and identity, which subsists in spite of the context of violence and authoritarian repression in which these individuals might find themselves, no matter what that might be. Following the "inspiration" that the liberal democratic West can give to those individuals by underscoring this common global heritage of rights and freedoms, they will set in motion, in concert with the policies of "instigation" or even "intervention" pursued by Western democracies, a series of reforms within their political and foreign policy doctrines which will reflect these values. These reforms, in turn – and in line with Kantian logic – will then allow them to join the liberal zone of peace. This is also why the proponents of the democratic peace theory can claim that this theory represents "an empirical law in international relations" *per se*. There is, within this language, the claim that human identity and human rights remain identical whatsoever the contexts of place and time, and then the assumption that they are able to initiate a cascading series of domestic and international changes – again, without regard to circumstances and surroundings. It is thus possible to talk of the resonance of the theory in international relations as such, without qualifications related to geography or time. Built within the democratic peace theory is – in a word – the assumption of its universality. This assumption rests on the notion that the factors it underscores in international politics escape the particularities of various contexts; the assumption can thus be seen as having sway over all international politics. This is what Kant gives, to all the proponents of this approach: a detailed and convincing assessment of the irreducibility of human rationality and morality, which then allows them to believe that the international politics of change and legitimacy built upon that understanding of the human spirit will always prevail, irrespective of context and location.

The other strand in this type of literature draws from the logic proposed in the third definitive article of *Perpetual Peace*, which is on global cosmopolitan law. It examines how the peace-inducing effects of democracy can prevail not only within, and then between, states, but also above them, in the changes that democratic life establishes within the entire milieu in which inter-state relations are conducted. Though not yet as developed as the body of work revolving around the democratic peace theory, this literature is now pushing its study of notions of global governance and global civil society to the forefront of current liberal thinking on emerging forms of global politics. The logic that allows the main representatives of this literature to assume that their views on global politics do indeed speak to universal elements in international affairs is also deeply anchored in Kantian postulates about the universality of human reason and its global reach in international politics.

David Held is currently the theorist most closely associated with such attempts to explore the implications of the work of Kant, whom he calls the "foremost interpreter of the idea of a cosmopolitan law," for the study of global governance.[32] Held argues that a "cosmopolitan model of democracy"[33] should underlie efforts to reconstruct models of governance above the state in the wake of the withering away of national sovereignty caused by phenomena of economic and cultural globalization. Rather than being circumscribed by the state, democratic institutional configurations should be redeployed, he suggests, in a series of interlocking regional and global institutions which will provide countervailing points of pressure, ultimately forcing all individuals and states to respect basic human rights and freedoms. Held tells us that

> it could be said, adapting Kant, that the individuals who composed the states and societies whose constitutions were formed in accordance with cosmopolitan law might be regarded as citizens, not just of their national communities or regions, but of a universal system of [...] governance. Such a system connotes nothing more or less than the entrenchment and enforcement of democratic public law across all peoples.[34]

This "universal system of governance" predicated on the "entrenchment and enforcement of democratic public law across all peoples," through a multi-level approach to governance linking domestic, national, and global norms and institutions, could emerge when

> people would come [...] to enjoy multiple citizenships – political membership in the diverse political communities which significantly [affect] them. They would be citizens of their immediate political communities, and of the wider regional and global networks which [impact] their lives.[35]

The central assumption which then lets Held build his argument about the fact that this focus on the "entrenchment and enforcement of democratic public law across all peoples" would allow each individual, throughout the world, imagine himself "citizen of its [*sic*] immediate political community,

and of a regional and global one," is what he terms the "principle of autonomy," which is evidently drawn from Kant's emphasis on the autonomous
nature of human rationality.

"Democracy entails a commitment to what I call the 'principle of autonomy,' " Held says,

> and a set of "empowering rights and obligations" – rights and obligations
> which must cut across all [...] sites of power, whether rooted in poli-
> tics, economics, or culture, which can erode or undercut autonomy, for
> individuals and groups. Such a principle and set of rights and obligations
> create the possibility of what [I refer] to as a "common structure of politi-
> cal action". Such a structure [...] needs to be entrenched and enforced in
> a "democratic public law" if it is to be effective as the basis of a fair and
> circumscribed system of power.[36]

It is thus by assuming an autonomy of human beings derived from "rights
and obligations which cut across all sites of political, economic, or cultural
power" that Held can then move on to his arguments about the development of "common structures of political action" which, to his mind, will in
due course attain global dimensions.

By starting where Kant himself starts, from a fundamental belief in the
autonomy of human rationality, Held therefore also ends where the Kantian
logic itself reaches its conclusion. Human rationality is present at all times
and everywhere – it "cuts across all sites of power" – and it always ultimately
entails the creation of democratic political arrangements that respect and
celebrate this sense of the rational in people. Democracy is thus both possible and necessary in all political contexts, whether one speaks of national or
of global circumstances. And this logic has universal validity because it flows
from human rationality, which itself is universal.

The notion, championed by someone like Richard Falk,[37] that an incipient
global civil society can gain strength in parallel with this process follows the
same logical sequence. Falk argues that a "people-oriented" model of global
politics supportive of "global public goods"[38] should guide and give impetus
to the more institutional developments surveyed by Held. The "unifying ideology" which, to Falk's mind, can permit this "[mobilization and unification]
of the disparate social forces that constitute global civil society" is what he
labels "normative democracy": the attempt to "reconnect politics with moral
purpose and values"[39] in international politics in ways inspired by Kantian
logic. There is also in this type of argument, therefore, the assumption of
a singular nature of human rationality and morality, an unvarying sense of
"purpose and values" that should be found in every human being and can
then serve as a global "unifying ideology," able to transform the nature of
international politics. The leap from a belief in the universality of human

nature to a corresponding assumption about the universality of the international politics rooted in this human nature – the core of Kant's discourse on the issue – is thus also present along this line of thinking.

It is these approaches to Kant that now prevail in the field and determine much of the current liberal thinking about issues of change – and change in global politics. To echo Doyle's phrase, Kant's epistemological, ontological, and normative postulates have opened up a road in international affairs that has remained well traveled. Those who follow Kant today on that road believe that he points them toward universal principles in international politics. These principles emphasize how human rationality creates a distance between individuals and the violence and chaos of international life, and how such a zone of autonomy can be used to develop approaches to foreign policy, global civil society, and global governance that reflect the potential for morality and legitimacy contained in the human spirit.

But what if this zone of self-governing rationality, which surrounds the individual and gives her control over violence, were nonetheless absent, or different? As was briefly mentioned earlier and as will be argued in detail in the second part of this book, the movement away from violence has not always occurred in the non-Western world in a fashion that corresponds to the postulates underlying the Kantian heritage in liberal thinking. Unceasing and probing violence has often remained a constant impediment for the individual, preventing him from constituting himself as a site of self-governing power and rationality. The idea that rationality precedes violence and is able to control it, the engine which propels the entire Kantian logic, might thus not apply here. Political life also often unfolds in the non-Western world in fractured social spaces within and between states, where violence often coexists with non-violent forms of politics in a manner that is quite different from the domestic, inter-state, and global levels of politics delineated by Kant and his followers. The series of strategies that are derived from these spaces – the focus, for instance, on particular foreign policies that should be adopted by the state, or the idea that all national civil societies can somehow connect through a global civil society – might well not be appropriate here. To what extent, then, does this undermine the universalist overtones of the postulates, explanations, and prescriptions upon which the liberal literature of Kantian inspiration has been based? As will be shown later, it is only by engaging in a reconstruction of the liberal tenets that has its starting point in the particular relationship between rationality and violence prevalent in the non-Western world that the liberal approach can convey the international realities which exist there. And only when this has been done can it hope truly to have global resonance.

Just as was the case with the realist tradition, however, there is in liberalism an added structural element, which also participates in the creation of a worldview presumed to be of universal scope. This is, as was noted before, the social rationalism of Adam Smith, most often studied in the liberal literature in counterpoint to the individual rationalism of Kant. This second, more structural, element of liberalism must be considered here before the argumentation proceeds further.

The usual point of entry into Adam Smith's views on human rationality, society, and international politics is the tension which he established between his two main works: *The Theory of Moral Sentiments*, published in 1759, and *Inquiry into the Nature and Causes of the Wealth of Nations*, published for its part in 1776 (a mere few months, as has been noted so often,[40] before the American Revolution would come to embody for many the spirit of capitalism and freedom that Adam Smith is said to have defined so well in that text). Smith bases the argumentation he puts forward in *The Theory of Moral Sentiments* on the notion of sympathy, which in his mind entails a "general fellow-feeling we have with every other man, merely because he is our fellow creature."[41] Moral progress, according to Smith, will be derived from sympathy, and it will require of individuals that they extend the understanding they have of themselves to the situation of others, and to how all their counterparts in society would like to be treated. Morality thus revolves, before anything else, around what Glenn Morrow once termed the "participation in the feelings of others" and, even more starkly, "the ability of passing beyond the limits of individuality"[42] in conceptions of the self and society. Morality, in this perspective, will above all be social: it will arise only when and where there is a mutual recognition, among the members of a society, of the freedom and rights which animate all human beings. The pursuit of the moral life will thus demand that institutions and norms be created with reference to this concern for the respect of the other – Smith talks about using the idea of an "impartial spectator"[43] as a compass in that project – which will harness and guide interpersonal relationships in ways that promote moral behavior in social interactions.

The crucial point, then, is that the movement toward morality and progress in social affairs remains external to human rationality. Morality is fervently pursued by rational human beings, but it is not through rationality that it can be attained. Morality will rather be the effect of the construction of a social order which will allow it to manifest itself through the sort of interactions it will force amongst these rational human beings. It comes from the outside, from the concrete connections society is able to institute amongst human beings, rather than from a more diffuse and internal search initiated from within the human mind.

The logic introduced here is therefore in counterpoint to the one underlying Kant's writings. Where Kant sees rationality as a constant impulse pushing forward the development of morality within the world of society and politics, Smith feels that this world of the social and political can cut short any aspirations to rationality and morality, and must thus be reconfigured in ways that will allow them to manifest themselves. In this sense, Smith personifies within the liberal literature the need to enter into an analysis of the extent to which the concrete social forms human beings build around themselves impede or give greater impetus to the project of human emancipation and freedom at the core of the entire liberal agenda.

It is within the *Inquiry into the Nature and Causes of the Wealth of Nations* that Smith reveals his own views on the subject and puts forward insights which resonate to this day in liberal thinking on international politics. The book has often been presented as an apology of the self-interest and greediness inherent in human beings on account of its determined defense of the free market as the best means of organizing economic forces in society – a stance seemingly at odds with the reverse emphasis, on "fellow-feeling" and regard for others, found in the *Theory of Moral Sentiments*. However, the general impression in the literature of today is that, as C.R. Fay put it, "Adam Smith [...] was philosopher first and economist second; the author of the *Theory of Moral Sentiments* in 1759 and of the *Wealth of Nations* in 1776."[44] Or, as someone like Billet would put it, Smith's embrace of the market is part of his search for a "just economy," which is "not about acquisition, but betterment."[45] The *Wealth of Nations*, in other words, should not be seen as a contradiction to the *Theory of Moral Sentiments*, but instead as an analysis of the means through which the market can come to change society and provide for its advancement along the lines suggested by the more philosophical observations of Smith's first work.

For Smith, the development of wealth in society, at a first level, at least provides ever greater numbers of people with the means of subsistence and with the possibility of moving from constant concerns with survival and hunger to a more sustained engagement with issues of personal development, public life, and morality. At a second level, moreover, the market provides the most natural way of recognizing the freedom of all individuals, as expressed through their labor. The market is thus the most moral of social forms, because it is the most respectful of the freedom and rationality of all individuals. Indeed the market requires that every individual recognize and abide by this freedom and rationality of all the others; and it does so through the constant confrontation it forces between one's labor and that of everybody else in society. It is here, most crucially, that the *Theory of Moral Sentiments* links up with the *Wealth of Nations*. The structural aspect at the core of the pursuit of morality in the first book – the idea that social frameworks must be put in place that will compel human beings to recognize each other's freedoms and rights – connects in the second book with the idea that the market will impose precisely that type of framework on social interactions.

Smith then draws on these insights as he moves on, in the following sections of *Wealth of Nations*, to a discussion of the relationship between the state and the market. It is this discussion that brings him to an examination of the nature of international politics. The underpinnings of his remarks at this level are the virulent attacks he launches against the mercantilist policies that dominated the international politics of his day. This is still, obviously, the *credo* of those who embrace free trade policies. More than being simply a plea for economic freedom, though, Smith's remarks also amount to a severe denunciation of the state itself.

> What is the species of domestic industry which his capital can employ, and of which the produce is likely to be of the greatest value, every individual, it is evident, can, in his local situation, judge much better than any statesman or lawgiver can do for him. The statesman, who should attempt to direct private people in what manner they ought to employ their capitals, would not only load himself with a most unnecessary attention, but assume an authority which could safely be trusted, not only to no single person, but no council or senate whatever, and which would no-where be so dangerous as in the hands of a man who had folly and presumption enough to fancy himself fit to exercise it.[46]

The state is not only unable to maximize wealth for all the members of society; the mere idea that it could attempt to control human beings as it pursues economic growth is in fact "folly and presumption." The market is the most natural structure that can be imposed on human relations; and the state, or any other structural arrangements that aim to regulate human behavior in ways that detract from market dynamics, Smith tells us, must thus be unnatural and inimical to the expression of individual freedom and rationality.

If the state is an unnatural structure, so are the interests and policies generated by it. This is where Smith attacks the understandings of international politics prevailing in his time. The discourse about national interest and balance of power, which gives legitimacy to the mercantilist policies of his day, are for him artificial constructions developed by a small minority of "statesmen and lawgivers" with a view to entrenching their power and to giving it greater legitimacy. Market forces provide a critique of this sort of international politics by showing the possibility of a movement toward a much more participatory international system, where individuals rather than the states define the agenda, and where that agenda is geared toward the twin development of freedom and wealth rather than toward protecting the state and its power.

The key point to be made here, though, is that Smith also instills into his views a universalism – which, as will be seen later, carries to this day among his contemporary followers. This universalism is rooted in the ontological, normative, and epistemological premises that underlie his writings. The central ontological claim of Smith's entire work is that there is a natural order to human affairs, which can only be attained when both the welfare of the individual and that of society have been reconciled. The two elements, in Smith's mind, are thus mutually constitutive: the freedom and rationality of the individual can emerge only if these values are enshrined in concrete social institutions and structures, which will force every individual in society to respect the freedom and rationality of any other. This is also where the source of the universalist bent of Smith's work lies. There can only be *one* natural order. It cannot be constructed other than through this dualism between the individual pursuit of freedom and rationality and the social structures which make the two possible. Nor can it diverge from the principles and forms envisaged by Smith: the social order that is natural will be, always and everywhere, the one that builds upon, and respects, the freedom and rationality of all individuals.

This is why the market is, according to Smith, so important. Its central role is precisely to assert the freedom and rationality of the individual, and also to force the acknowledgment of this individual freedom and rationality upon all members of society, through the unmediated and natural interaction it maintains between them. The power of the market to accomplish these goals will be universal as well, since it so closely embodies this natural social order that, Smith believes, has a universal scope. Conversely, the state cannot be, anywhere or at any time, an acceptable basis for the constitution of proper social interactions and for the delineation of the social space in which these interactions should unfold. Its purpose is to establish control where there should be freedom and to accentuate the distance between citizens and noncitizens where there should be instead a recognition of the mutual interests of all individuals, be they citizens of the same state or not. The state's very nature, therefore, is always contrary to the natural social order, which should prevail among human beings.

The normative element that arises in counterpoint to these insights will also, according to Smith, necessarily be universal. The natural social order is, in his view, the most moral one. If this natural order has a universal dimension, the morality it entails will also be universal: it will always be the case that establishing social frameworks which defer to human rationality and freedom, irrespective of state or other boundaries, is the most moral way of devising social relations. The epistemological basis of Smith's views reflects these insights, and also incorporates the universalism which underlies them. For him, the laws of society can only become known, like everything else, through a profoundly social process. "Our continual observations upon the conduct of others," Smith notes, "insensibly leads us to form to ourselves certain general rules concerning what is fit and proper either to be done or to be avoided."[47] That is to say, individual conscience develops as it encounters the rationality of others and as it endlessly adjusts itself to the opinions and behaviors that generate approval from them. What is bound to emerge in that context is laws of human behavior emphasizing, for instance, the pre-eminence of the market over all other institutions as a framework through which human freedom can be expressed. These laws, in turn, will be universal because they will correspond to the universality of the natural social order founded on rationality and freedom, which is depicted by Smith.

Much of contemporary liberal thinking follows the logic articulated by Smith. This is an approach to international politics which, to the notion of a democratic peace anchored in Kant's work, opposes the notion of a commercial peace, rooted this time in the idea that international trade imposes on states structural constraints that force them to act more peacefully and openly toward each other. In the same way in which Smith's logic leads him to believe in the universality of his insights, this approach proceeds from the assumption that its conclusions speak to the whole of international politics.

The sources of this literature are most often traced to the study of European integration, inaugurated by David Mitrany's renowned *A Working Peace System*.[48] Mitrany's "functionalist" approach holds that the different functions of social and economic life are bound to become closely coordinated throughout the international sphere, regardless of national boundaries. These aspects of social life are then able, as Mitrany puts it, to "determine themselves."[49] They bring to light a commonality of interests among people and underscore how barriers to their further development are in fact unnatural and contrary to human progress itself. This poses a direct challenge to the power of the state. The functionalist approach, Mitrany argues, points to

> the expansion of [...] positive and constructive common work, of common habits and interests, making frontier lines meaningless by overlaying them with a natural growth of common activities and common administrative agencies. Insofar as [this could be achieved], it would also impress a different complexion upon the problem of security. That way alone lies the prospect of turning "defense" into "police," as in the national state, and especially of giving "security" the sense of an undisturbed social life, to be preserved by common government, in lieu of the outdated sense of the security of a physical territory, to be protected by tanks and planes.[50]

Ernst B. Haas' *Beyond the Nation-State* provides the other best-known formulation of this argument.[51] Drawing from the work of Mitrany, Haas posits the same progression, which extends from the need of human beings to establish structures that reflect and promote their basic interests to the unavoidable growth of these structures first to supranational dimensions, and then to becoming a challenge to the power of the state. Haas tells us that those who believe in this logic

> are interested in identifying those aspects of human needs and desires that exist and clamor for attention outside the realm of the political. They believe in the possibility of specifying technical and "non-controversial" aspects of governmental conduct, and of weaving an ever-spreading web of international institutional relationships on the basis of meeting such

needs. They would concentrate on commonly experienced needs initially, expecting the circle of the non-controversial to expand at the expense of the political, as practical cooperation became coterminous with the totality of interstate relations. At that point, a true world community will have arisen.[52]

The purest expression of this line of reasoning, however, and the basis of what is now the core point of reference of this component of liberal thought is undoubtedly the work of Robert O. Keohane. In particular, his now classic *Power and Interdependence*, written in collaboration with Joseph S. Nye,[53] stands out. The book traces the "major features of world politics when interdependence, particularly economic interdependence, is extensive."[54] In opposition to the realist worldview, which rests on the belief that "international politics, like all other politics, is a struggle for power but, unlike domestic politics, a struggle dominated by organized violence,"[55] economic interdependence entails in fact a situation where the character of international politics is quite different. First, the "interstate relations [which are] assumed by the realists to be the normal channels" of international politics are constrained by "multiple channels [which] connect societies" in a variety of informal, transnational, and institutional forms.[56] Second, this changes the "agenda of interstate relationships" and ushers in a new "hierarchy of issues" and priorities, where "military security does not consistently dominate the agenda – many issues arise from what used to be considered domestic policy, and the distinction between domestic and foreign issues becomes blurred."[57] Third, "military force is thus not used by governments towards other governments" where these sorts of transnational economic and social ties exist, because force is "irrelevant to resolving disagreements on economic issues" and because social ties create an harmonization of interests and identity which makes violence unthinkable. If violence remains likely, it is only between states whose interests and actions are not constrained by economic and social interdependence.[58]

Keohane has developed these arguments in a series of works dealing with the cooperative arrangements which can emerge between market economies, the most noteworthy of which certainly remains *After Hegemony*.[59] Others have also defended this notion of a so-called commercial peace through writings which borrow from the same logic. As a well-known example, Richard Rosecrance, in his *The Rise of the Trading State*,[60] defends the thesis that

a new "trading world" of international relations [is emerging and] offers the possibility of escaping the vicious cycle [of conflict and warfare] and finding new patterns of cooperation among nation-states. Indeed, [this] suggests that the benefit of trade and cooperation today greatly exceeds that of military competition and territorial aggrandizement.[61]

Today a sizeable literature attempts to develop, in the wake of the research agenda launched by these writings, the one linked to the logic of the commercial peace. Works by Mansfield and Pevehouse,[62] for instance, or by Russett and Oneal,[63] particularly stand out.

Not all of these texts acknowledge a direct debt to Adam Smith – for instance to the extent that Rosecrance does when he notes that his work on the "trading world" challenges the "military-political world" in a manner that echoes the claims made by Smith in the eighteenth century.[64] All develop their logic, however, from the way in which, as Erik Gartzke and Quang Li put it in their "War, Peace, and the Invisible Hand," "Adam Smith identified in markets autonomous forces with serendipitous effects."[65] Smith establishes, in other words, a core logic, an interlocking series of assumptions about commerce, society, and international politics, from which these authors draw sequences of arguments which provide the opening line of reasoning of their own analysis.

Smith's writings contain, however, much more than these assumptions about the commercial peace thesis. They also comprise, as was shown above, claims above the universality of this thesis. When all these authors adopt Smith's premises, they in fact import in their work the universalist stance these premises entail. In the first instance, to argue that commerce establishes – to use Mitrany's phase – "common work and common habits," which in turn leads to the "natural growth" of common interests across borders and then to constraints being imposed on the state by these transnational common interests that reduce inter-state conflict, these authors must assume an account of the state, of the market, and of the individual which parallels the one established by Smith. They must assume that the market enhances freedom and equality, and that it does so for all individuals whom it connects, either within the social space delimited by the state or transnationally, across different states. They must also believe that the market exposes a freedom and a rationality in the individual which will serve as the best potential basis for the construction of a community of interests across all individuals, either nationally or transnationally, because it will be recognized by all of them as the closest possible approximation of their true personal freedom and rationality. Lastly, these authors must think that the state cannot encompass or represent this true freedom and rationality of the individual, and that its interests and as well as its propensity for war will be marginalized as communities of interest that are much closer to the real nature of all individuals emerge at cross-purposes from those that are state-based.

Thus this approach to international affairs is brought in line with Adam Smith's most important ontological, normative, and epistemological premises. Market relations, it is assumed here, in echo to Smith, entail changes in the nature of social relations, and these changes facilitate the expression of what is natural in human beings. The state, in contrast, remains unnatural. In its attempts to control the freedom of individuals, it runs counter to what is natural in each of them. This is why inter-state conflict, and the state interests from which it stems, will always be delegitimized by the emergence of the more legitimate, the more natural community of interests between all individuals, which is made possible by the market.

This sense of the realities which underlie international politics is complemented by normative and epistemological assumptions which also parallel those put forward by Smith. It follows from these assumptions that there is something intrinsically moral in the search for market-based communities, if these communities bring out the natural freedom and rationality of individuals. Underlying all of this, just as Smith thinks, there will be a learning process, which will be innately social and shared among all individuals who live in these market-based communities of interests, but which will lead all of them to these same conclusions. The adjustments of life within the communities created by the market and within those set in place by the state will show over time that the former are much more conducive to the protection of individual free will and to the search for peace than the latter. This will lead to a wider and wider recognition that, as a rule, the commercial peace thesis is correct and stands as an appropriate point of entry in efforts to move international politics away from the constant threat or use of violence.

Just as, for Smith, these assumptions contained, in their very logic, a universal scope, so do they contain it here. To assume that the market installs a natural social order, which corresponds to the most direct expression of the intrinsic free will and rationality of human beings, confers the market an unchanging and universal character: human nature will not change, wherever and whenever one might be, and the market will thus always provide the best manifestation of its core qualities. The state will never be able to do that, and the communities built around market relations and the ambit of personal freedom they provide will always trump the artificial and restrictive state-based communities. Thus the pursuit of morality in international affairs will always necessitate this search for natural and peaceful modes of community-building above the more violent and artificial boundaries created by the state. And what is natural and moral, what favors in the end the freedom and rationality of all individuals will always gain more adherents and will thus impose itself all the time and everywhere. The dynamics which underlie the commercial peace thesis will thus be present and effective wherever and whenever one looks at the nature of international politics.

What Michael Mousseau describes in one of his studies of the commercial peace as the sense of a "universal extension of trust," inherent in the nature of market relations,[66] speaks to this universalist bent. The market builds trust, and then peace, among all individuals because it draws out what unites each and every one of them. This is also what Mitrany indicates when he says, in the preface to *A Working Peace System*, that his approach to economic integration allows "the opportunity and the promise [to build] a peaceful *world* community."[67] Economic interdependence, he adds, can help usher in "new nationalisms," new communities, which will be "essentially social" and have the "central characteristic that they are *universal*"[68] and underscore what can unite in peace all human beings. This is also, as a last example, part of the assumptions which allow Keohane and Nye, in the opening arguments of *Power and Interdependence*, to assert that the book will show the "major features of *world politics* when economic interdependence is extensive."[69] The idea in all this literature is not that the totality of international politics can be described by the commercial peace approach. As Keohane and Nye themselves note in the first chapter of *Power and Interdependence*, "world politics varies, over time and from place to place, [and] there is no reason to believe that a single set of conditions will always and everywhere apply, or that any one model is likely to be universally applicable."[70] Not all the world, in other words, has attained the sort of economic interdependence portrayed in this literature, or has witnessed the emergence of conditions where the peace it engenders is not threatened by other factors. What remains universal, though, is that economic interdependence, where it exists, will transform international politics in the way described more than two centuries ago by Adam Smith.

Just as in the case of other approaches to international studies surveyed so far, however, the idea that these arguments speak to the whole of international politics throughout the world must be questioned. As will be demonstrated in the next section of this book, such arguments rest on understandings of individual free will, state and market interaction, and the place of violence in society that do not fit easily with the non-Western world. It is not, as Keohane and Nye would have it, that the logic conveyed by these arguments has to be tempered by the different contexts in which it unfolds: it is rather that this very logic does not correspond to what is happening in this one context. Before this point is examined in detail, though, one last series of approaches to international studies must be introduced.

3
Situating the Particular: After Constructivism

If the tension between realism and liberalism provides the main axis of debate within international studies, there is also a series of critiques that have been addressed to one or both of these approaches. Two lines of analysis have been paramount in that regard. One line starts with the post-modern work inspired by Foucault and others, and is represented for instance by the writings of Rob Walker. It then winds itself through the Habermasian critical theory exemplified by the work of Andrew Linklater, and finally culminates in the constructivist literature mainly identified with Alexander Wendt's work. The goal of that literature is to show that a series of assumptions about the nature of knowledge, identity, and interest underlie both realism and liberalism, and that these assumptions are historically specific in that they stem from particular historical and intellectual developments. The logic of power, human identity, rationality, and suchlike, which the realists and the liberals build on all these starting premises, are thus themselves historically contingent. What they present as universal elements of international politics on the basis of that logic remains, in that sense, nothing more than the effect of particular circumstances and conditions.

In counterpoint, another line of critique addressed to the realist and liberal literature draws on Marx's analysis of the material underpinnings of political and social power. It extends through the consideration of the global expansion of capitalism put forward by Wallerstein and others. It then ends up with Cox's neo-Gramscian exploration of the extent to which the organization of production and of other material forces shapes current conceptions of world order. This literature puts most of its emphasis on the material and economic configurations which support forms of international politics, rather than on the ideational factors of knowledge and identity underscored by the constructivists. The objective of this approach is to show how the organization of production gives power to certain social groups in world politics and how these groups, in turn, aim to propound understandings of world order and international politics which sustain these structures of production and economic development from which their power is derived. Here again, the idea is to show that what is taken by the mainstream literature to be universal and natural characteristics of international politics corresponds in reality to particular visions of world order, put forward by specific social groups in order to sustain and legitimize their power precisely by presenting it as natural and uncontroversial.

Two points about all these critiques of realism and liberalism are essential in the context of the logic of this book. First, these critiques express, in effect, a dissatisfaction with the universalism that lies at the heart of realism and liberalism. They aim to show that the language of international studies, and the universals upon which this language is predicated, can be unraveled to reveal prior structures of material and ideational factors which are historically contingent and specific to given historical and social developments. Furthermore, these approaches to international affairs claim that it is the forces they study that allow us to see how the universals of international politics can be reduced to an unending series of specific moments and circumstances. By looking at international affairs the way they do, they tell us, we will be able to see the particular and the specific in international affairs.

The second point is just as important. The opening up of the universals contained in the mainstream literature that these critiques offer is just that – only a reassessment of the underpinnings of these specific conceptions of what is universal in international affairs – and it remains limited to the elements that have given rise to these understandings of universality in world affairs. These critiques only operate backwards, so to speak, from the universals contained in the current literature. What those critiques cannot do, then, is integrate in their logic what these universals miss about international politics in the non-Western world. This leads to a crucial problem. This literature presupposes that it speaks to the contextual nature of all international politics because it accepts in its own premises, as will be shown here, that the mainstream literature has already covered everything that needs to be covered in global international politics. It implicitly posits, therefore, that there is no need for a critique of what is left outside the purported universals of the mainstream literature. In that sense, this literature is also very much, in the end, about universals. It speaks a language of particulars, but it always assumes that what it says about the specificity of international politics pertains to all of international politics throughout the globe. Because it remains caught in this assumption of universality, as will also be shown, it often misses how the non-Western world requires other ways of defining the specificity of its international politics.

The first element of this literature, constructivism, finds its source in the post-modern literature. Post-modernism, in the way it has been used in international studies in recent years, stems most directly from the work of Michel Foucault and Jacques Derrida. Through his calls for "une archéologie de la connaissance" and of "une généalogie du pouvoir" (the development of an archaeology of knowledge and of a genealogy of power), Foucault aimed to make visible the ways in which knowledge and truth are constituted rather than given, and how this construction is eminently social, in that it corresponds to specific social settings and to the power structures underlying these settings. Ontology, he claimed, remains circumscribed by epistemology: there can be no truth in itself, because truth and knowledge are always reflections of the processes through which they were constructed. There can be no universals, then – no universal and timeless truths. There can only be interpretations of what is true, and these interpretations will always remain captive of the specifics of time and place in which they were formulated.[1]

For its part, Jacques Derrida's work revolved around a study of the relationship between language and meaning. Derrida suggested that the categories of language and thinking, through which the world is understood and explained, never result from a transparent apprehension, by the mind, of the world as it is. Instead, categories of thought result from "une intertextualité," an interface between a subjective perspective on the world and the construction of meanings of the world that this perspective allows. Derrida argued that the concepts and categories through which the world is read and interpreted must thus be "deconstructed": if meaning resides in language itself, rather than in an immanent reality external to language, then the construction of the categories through which meaning appears must be opened up and shown to proceed from particular standpoints and perspectives. Here again, then, notions of the universal are simply artifice. They are given credence only because they stand within a bounded and self-legitimizing discourse, which allows them to appear to be universal to those who share this language and the worldview it supports.[2]

Many specialists have drawn on this notion that the construction of knowledge determines what is known and said about the world – that epistemology frames ontology and normativity – in order to attempt to open up the ontological and normative tenets underlying international studies. The work of Richard Ashley,[3] for example, or that of David Campbell[4] can be mentioned in this context. It is Rob Walker, however, who has provided the most penetrating post-modern critique of international studies, for instance in his *Inside/outside: International Relations as Political Theory*.[5]

Walker wants us to see that the basic claims which structure the distinction between domestic and international politics can be questioned. The foundational categories of international politics and the constant reverberation of an assumed distinction between politics inside and outside the state that animates them can then be reconfigured, Walker tell us, in ways that allow for a much more fluid interplay between sovereign and international spaces, domestic and international politics, and, ultimately, citizen and human being. Inserting this sense of the construction of knowledge and discourse within the basic language of international politics can thus lead to a radical alteration of the very logic of international politics itself. Opening these categories, showing how they stem from the particulars of a specific research agenda rather than from the discovery of immanent truths, can reopen our "political imagination"[6] and give us the intellectual space necessary to contemplate new forms of political community and interaction, which will alter the way in which international politics is conceptualized and conducted.

This is, then, where a first attempt to offer a counterpoint to the language of universals at the core of international studies can be found. In echo to the post-modern writings of Foucault and Derrida, universals cannot exist: international politics cannot be founded on universal realities, which pertain to the entire realm of international affairs, irrespective of time and place. On the contrary, nothing is ever set in international politics. What we say, what we think about international life – those things are always a function of specific discourses and perspectives about the realities we are trying to describe. These can change, and these changes will in turn alter the very nature of what we see as being fundamental to international affairs. From this standpoint, international politics can only be about the specific: it can only be about particular perspectives resulting from specific attitudes to the world, which cannot be connected one to the other in ways that are not themselves historically and socially contingent. What we define as international politics, then, is no more than the confrontation of those particular perspectives; and there is no reality of international politics that exists outside of these discourses and perspectives.

This brings forth, however, a paradox which will be explored in greater detail later on. This sense of international politics as a world of particulars, this idea that international affairs is constituted by changing sequences of specific perspectives and discourses, contains within its own worldview an assumption of universality. *All* international politics has to be about particulars, if we follow this logic, because no one international reality, anywhere and at any time, can escape the specific perspectives and discourses that give rise to it. To put it differently, it is part of this logic that international politics throughout the entire globe can be opened up to the sort of analysis proposed here. Just as is the case with the realist and liberal approaches, which are more open about their claims to universality, one is confronted with this line of reasoning, then, to a form of analysis that also assumes that it speaks to all of international politics throughout the world.

This need to reduce all of international politics to a series of specific circumstances and discourses also underlies another literature, one which this time is articulated around the work of writers like Andrew Linklater, who attempt to introduce elements of Jürgen Habermas' critical theory into the language of international studies. Habermas' critical theory is part of the so-called second generation of writings associated with the Frankfurt School. First-generation writers, most prominently Max Horkheimer, had based their work on two central premises. Drawing on Marx's historical materialism, these thinkers had argued that knowledge is always contingent upon existing material realities and on social and historical contexts. They had also all maintained, however, that knowledge could as well provide a critique of this prevailing order – a distinction between what is and what ought to be – and that intellectual inquiry could show how social orders more conducive to human freedom and contentment should be built. Since Habermas published his main works (between the late 1970s and the mid-1990s), this two-fold concern, with the state of knowledge in the material world and with the ability of knowledge to transform this material world, had evolved into a series of reflections that, today, form the basis of much of what is called "critical theory" in international studies. Through an ethics of discourse and communication, Habermas argued, human beings can envisage frameworks of dialogue which at first draw from their embeddedness in the historically and socially contingent structure of differentiation and conflict. These frameworks of dialogue, however, will also bring to light the possibility of less distorted forms of contact between human beings – precisely because of the manifold frustrations and restrictions entailed by such discussions about the apparent limits to human freedom and mutual understanding. In this search for an open-ended and inclusive space for discussion about eradicating factors of difference and conflict, Habermas suggested, a universal underlying rationality will surface that will then be recognized by all as the best criterion by which this discussion should be guided and judged. As we discuss our differences, our shared need to understand each other will also provide, in counterpoint to what separates us, a common rallying point.[7]

Habermas thus proposes to us an epistemology of particulars, insofar as knowledge can never be abstracted from the forms of shared rationality, which are determined by changing social realities and structures of interaction. But there is also in Habermas an attempt to uncover the universal of rationality that lies behind all these manifestations of the particular. His communicative rationality assumes that all human beings can take part in a dialogue about what unites them and what separates them. Furthermore, this inclusive dialogue will lead to a mutual recognition of the freedom and rationality that animates all human beings, universally; and, in its celebration of the universal of human rationality, it will offset the particular and the different in human affairs.

Thus there is here a marked contrast with post-modernism. Habermas wants to oppose, to the skepticism of post-modernism vis-à-vis grand narratives of human rationality and human progress, a renewed expression of the Kantian faith in the possibility of rationality and progress in human affairs. He also wants to underscore the fact that, behind the endless spiral toward the particular, brought forward by the post-moderns and by their rejection of any universal sense of meaning or knowledge, lays one universal: that of human beings rationally trying to understand their world through the confrontation of the diversity of perspectives and contexts they each bring to that process of ever growing mutual understanding.

This is precisely where Habermas becomes valuable to those who bring his notion of critical theory within international studies. The best known of these authors remains, as was mentioned earlier, Andrew Linklater. The titles of his books convey their intellectual lineage: *Men and Citizens in the Theory of International Relations;*[8] *Beyond Realism and Marxism: Critical Theory and International Relations;*[9] *The Transformation of Political Community: Ethical Foundation of the Post-Westphalian Era.*[10] Linklater attempts to show how Habermas' insights can provide a potent critique of mainstream international studies. He draws from Habermas a recognition of the artificiality, the sheer contextuality, of the different rationalities and discourses which comprise international affairs. He also echoes, however, the Habermasian suggestion that these different perspectives and rationalities are all underlain by a widespread common desire to make rational sense out of international politics. This can provide the basis for a dialogue that emphasizes the shared rationality and identity of all individuals above the differences and tensions imposed on them by state-driven worldviews. It is thus possible for a renewed commitment to forging the global human community foreseen through this type of dialogue to emerge out of the critique of the way in which existing international politics supports the divisions between "citizens" to the detriment of the links that unite all "men."[11]

Linklater thus brings to the discourse of international politics the same tension between the universal and the particular introduced by Habermas in his work. International politics can be seen, he argues, as a series of shared rationalities and perspectives which justify certain forms of behavior and expectations in the conduct of world politics. Understandings of international affairs, then, need always to be seen as particular to a given context. They are significant for those who study or partake in international politics only within the bounded realities these people establish through a discourse and a perspective they share. There cannot be, then, universals of international politics. Realist thinking, for example, may appear to be a persistent feature of international affairs, but it is only so because of the continued legitimacy given to it by its supporters, not because it corresponds to some universal and unchanging character of international politics. What also matters, though, is the universality of the search for meaning and rationality in international affairs. This profoundly human quest will always provide the basis for an inclusive and open-ended search for models of international politics which favor human freedom and rationality, and it will always serve, as well, as a critique of the models and behaviors of international affairs that impede this global search for freedom and rationality.

This return to the universality of human rationality is what sets apart the post-modern and critical streams in international studies. The two approaches nevertheless share a common point, which is central to the

argument pursued here. Just like post-modernism, the Habermasian critical theory exemplified by the work of Linklater assumes that it speaks to
all of international politics throughout the globe. The underlying rationality of human beings which Linklater attempts to draw out is possessed by
all humans, wherever they live. The conflicts of perspectives and discourses
which shape the evolution of international politics can always bring to light
this underlying human rationality, wherever they take place. And nothing
in all of international politics, in this sense, can stand beyond the dynamics
of change and progress painted by this approach.

The impact that this entire post-modern and critical literature has had on
international studies is felt most intensely at the moment within constructivism. This is an approach which represents in many regards the leading
edge of the discipline at this point. This approach, whose greatest champion
is probably Alexander Wendt, attempts to find what Wendt describes as a *via
media*[12] between, on the one hand, the post-modern and critical literature
just surveyed, and, on the other hand, more traditional accounts of international affairs, related most often to realist worldviews. Constructivism
endeavors, in this sense, to determine how far it is possible to reduce international relations to specific constructs of rationality and knowledge, and,
conversely, to what extent more concrete elements of state power and force
represent universal factors of international life, which retain an autonomous
influence whatever is known or thought about them. This effort to determine what can change in international politics through alterations in the
world of ideas and what, on the contrary, remains constant because it is
impervious to these changes is now a central element in any discussion
of current developments in international studies. There are certainly many
authors who try to push the work of Wendt in new directions – the writings
of Maja Zehfuss,[13] for instance, or those of Bill McSweeney[14] come to mind –
but he remains the key writer with whom this question is associated.[15]

It is in a widely read book, *Social Theory of International Politics*, that Wendt
presents his views on the role that ideas and material forces play in shaping international politics and on how this process entails a pluralist and
changing understanding of international politics rather than a fixed and universalist one.[16] For Wendt, the starting point of any analysis of international
affairs is the recognition that states must be seen for what they are: independent agents able to set in motion specific consequences in the international
environment. This is so because the state, although it comes together and
sustains its existence through a multitude of processes, still constitutes a
self-referential actor when it comes to the control of the means of violence.
Control of the means of violence, in turn, represents one of the key channels through which all the material forces underlying international politics
can be secured and controlled. This is the "essential state," or the "state-
as-such."[17] It corresponds to a centralized and unitary "institutional–legal
order [that determines] the norms, rules, and principles 'by which conflict is

handled, society is ruled, and social relations are governed.' "[18] International politics, then, cannot be reduced "all the way down,"[19] as he puts it, to the interplay of ideas, knowledge, and perspective. States have a reality that endures, whatever is said or thought about them. This is one side of the *via media* that Wendt is attempting to set down between traditional approaches in international studies and the critiques addressed to these approaches by the likes of Walker and Linklater. State and the use they make of violence cannot be deconstructed "all the way down," Wendt claims, to suggest that they arise only on the basis of specific configurations of ideas and perceptions. On the contrary, states retain at all times a material reality, and they set in motion effects in the material world, all of which escape this sort of analysis.

The other side of this *via media* concerns the role that ideas do have in shaping and influencing international politics. Wendt claims that the "structures of human association are determined primarily by shared ideas rather than material forces; and the identities of and interests of purposive actors are constructed by these shared ideas rather than given by nature."[20] It is mostly the ideas we have about ourselves and others, Wendt wants us to understand, that determine the structures of interaction we establish with those around us. It is not the distribution of material means that constructs these structures of interaction, it is instead the "distribution of knowledge"[21] and the configuration of ideas we have about each other. Furthermore, our "identities and interests" – how we see ourselves and how we choose to interact with others – are not "given by nature," but are themselves part of the constant construction and reconstruction of these broader ideational structures. This is the "constructivist" strain in Wendt's work. The material world exists. However, we do give the world identity, meaning, and logic. These identities, these meanings, and these logics are not fixed, and they can thus be reconstructed in ways that will change how we see ourselves, others, and the world we share.

For Wendt, then, "the character of international life is determined by the beliefs and expectations that states have about each other, and these are constituted largely by social rather than material structures."[22] The element of violent anarchy, which many in international studies take as a given, is in fact constructed through "the beliefs and expectations that states have about each other." These are "constituted by social structures" of ideas and knowledge with which states form their notions of self-identity and their understanding of how they should interact with other states. International anarchy and violence can thus give way to more cooperative and non-violent frameworks if states develop new visions of their role in international affairs.

This is where Wendt's understanding of the particular in world affairs comes through. The power over the material world given to the state through its control of organized violence represents a constant element in international politics. This is the "universal state," the "state-as-such," which remains at all times and everywhere a distinctive feature of international politics. What this all means, however, remains highly contextual. The way in which violence and its threat are used can vary widely over time and space, depending on the identities and modes of interaction states set up for themselves and for other states. States and violence do remain constant elements of world politics, whatever we may think of them, but ideas and identities do construct much of international politics, and they do so in a manner that gives international life a highly contingent and provisional character. International life, then, is a realm of particulars rather than one of universals: it remains, at all times, what is produced through this construction and reconstruction of shared ideas.

This understanding of what is specific in international politics is now extremely influential. The notion that international politics can be, as Wendt puts it, "what states make of it" has become part of the vernacular of international studies. The article from which this phrase is drawn is certainly one of the most quoted writings of the past few years.[23] The core assumption here is that the world of ideas and knowledge is important to the constitution of international affairs because it is through specific understanding of other states – of their nature, identities, and agendas – that each one determines how it will act toward the others. The nature of international politics, in that sense, is never set. It follows the movements and changes within those beliefs and ideas that underlie the actions of states as they interact with each other. Thus, when students and specialists of international affairs want to think about the way in which international life can reflect the specific interplay of particular forces and circumstances, this is very often the sort of image they have in mind nowadays.

The crucial point, though, is that this way of thinking brings back students and specialists of international studies to a strongly universalist perspective. The state, in this logic, is reduced to what is understood to be its simplest expression: an institution able to centralize and control violence. In that sense, its nature remains fixed throughout time and space: the state, we know, will always be at least that – an institution able to control violence. And identity, we also know, is at all times malleable in the way described by the constructivists. To that extent, then, we know that the dynamics ascribed to the nature of the state and the dynamics of identity in the constructivist literature are also present at all times, throughout all of international politics. Constructivists, in sum, believe that the nature of international politics is never set and can always change; but they also assume that it will always change in the way they emphasize.

The problem studied in this book, however, is still present with this type of argument. When post-modern, critical, or constructivist authors develop their case, they do so on the basis of their critique of more mainstream approaches in international studies. But these mainstream approaches overlook a lot when it comes to the non-Western world. Critiques of these approaches also overlook sizeable problems, then, because they are structured as a response to this incomplete account of global international life. In fact they compound this truncated view of the world as they conduct what amounts only to a further inquiry into Western-centric intellectual constructs. This feature will be explored in detail in the second part of the book. The recent attempts to move away from the universals of mainstream international studies in order to develop a more nuanced understanding of the specifics of international life in different contexts have missed much when it comes to non-Western international politics. An altogether different way of marking out what can be particular about international politics must be developed if one is hoping to capture what is truly particular about the international affairs of these parts of the world. This must be done if the increasing role of the non-Western world in global politics is to be assessed properly.

One very last element needs to be considered, however, before this entire analysis can be presented. This is the post-Marxist literature. Like the series of writings just examined, this literature holds that international politics should be understood in terms of an ever-evolving and varied interplay of shifting political and social developments. It proceeds this time, though, from the core assumption that it is material factors rather than ideational ones that underlie these patterns of constant change in international affairs. These writings follow from an engagement with the questions raised by Marx about the material organization of the world – particularly as it unfolds through the realms of production, work, and economic relations – and about the extent to which these material underpinnings determine variable modes of evolutions in politics and society. It is by bringing to light how such dynamics of uneven and varied material change characterize international politics that this literature aims to challenge the assumptions of immutability and universality central to the mainstream realist and liberal literature and to substitute in their place a worldview marked by a concern with the specific and the contextual in international affairs.

A starting point of this literature is the world-system theory most often associated with the work of Immanuel Wallerstein. In a series of works which first gained acclaim in the 1970s and 1980s, Wallerstein presents his views on the "capitalist world-economy"[24] and on the way in which an analysis of world capitalism undermines both realist and liberal understandings of international politics. For Wallerstein, the world has now become integrated by capitalism. We live in a world-economy where there exists only a "single division of labor, but multiple polities and cultures."[25] Who we are, what we can and cannot do is influenced to a degree by our relations with these "polities and cultures," but much more by our place in that worldwide "single division of labor."

Wallerstein thus paints a picture of the global economy that in many ways resembles the critiques of mainstream economic theory also put forward in the 1970s by a number of writers, many of whom were associated with the so-called "Dependency school."[26] There are global structures of capitalist accumulation, which traverse all countries throughout the globe and perpetuate patterns of exploitation and injustice that favor the advanced economies of the North to the detriment of all other regions of the world. This global capitalist architecture, in the words of Cardoso and Faletto, "engenders specific relations between internal growth and external ties."[27] The possibility of growth outside the core economies of the North is stunted by "external ties," which these regions cannot avoid with financial, production, and trade processes and which always act to their disadvantage.

This is the critique of mainstream economics that comes most forcefully out of this literature. Development is not a neutral and autonomous process, which can be duplicated everywhere it is set in motion. It comes out of specific circumstances, which prevailed at one point in the North – the industrial revolution, for instance, and the way it intersected with the availability of primary resources set forth by the colonial machinery. It cannot, then, be duplicated in the South, because these conditions are absent or different there, and indeed because the North maintains in place structures of exploitation, such as the extraction of primary resources at a low exchange rate, which underlie its own continued growth.

Here then, in counterpoint to realism, the organization of the economy precedes and shapes the organization of violence. States behave and relate to each other, before anything else, in terms of the particular place they occupy in the global capitalist structures. In dispute with liberal arguments, the workings of markets and their influence on political life or, more profoundly, the space available for human emancipation in politics or economics always remain a function of the countervailing forces exercised by these global capitalist structures. In this sense, the key critique addressed to mainstream international studies by this line of thinking is that its core elements are developed as if this underlying reality of global capitalism did not exist. This is wrong, according to this approach. There should not be talk of the state or of the market *per se*, because the very nature of state and market structures changes depending on where they are in the global economy. The character of the state and of the market, the alliances they build between them or among other social actors, and the relationships they form with global political and economic actors are simply not the same at the core and in the more peripheral regions of the world-economy. A language of international politics which fails to acknowledge these differences and merely speaks of "the state" or "the market" implies that there is similarity amongst all states and markets, where in fact there is great diversity and change, depending on location within the global economy.

This sets up, here again, an understanding of international politics where a language of universals is dangerously mistaken. All international realities are different one from the other, depending on their situation within the global political economy. From this perspective, where one looks when studying international politics will determine what one sees: the very character of state to state relations, or of market and state interactions, for example, will be widely divergent as one moves from the core to the peripheral parts of the globe. Also, when one looks at international politics matters a great deal. The workings of the global economy are always historically constituted and do allow some measure of change and development in some states of the periphery. The moment in time used as a point of entry in the study of the international interactions of these states will have an impact on what is said about the issue.[28] Thus the very nature of global economy is such that all the elements which comprise mainstream understandings of international politics – the state, the market, and so on – must be seen in terms of where they stand in these particular intersections of space and time.

The logic that underlies these claims and allows Wallerstein to think that they speak to the very nature of global politics draws most directly, as was mentioned before, on the Marxist tradition. Marx's own claims about the impact of the capitalist mode of production on world politics are quite well known. The anchoring point in his work is that the way in which we act in the physical world determines what we can and cannot do, who we can and cannot be. "As individuals express their life," he argues,

> so they are. What they are, therefore, coincides with what they produce, *what* they produce, and *how* they produce. The nature of individuals thus depends on the material conditions which determine their production.[29]

Production is the pivot around which human life revolves. Human beings produce their world, and this world then defines them: "as individuals express their life, so they are." Marx directs his attention, in this context, to the dominant mode of production, capitalism, and to its consequences in the world, mainly at the political, economic, and social levels. The fundamental character of capitalism is its exploitative nature and the extent to which these exploitative economic relations then translate into political, social, and ideological arrangements that sustain and legitimize them. Another feature of capitalism is its propensity for global expansion: the search for new sources of profit leads to an ever-going integration of additional resources and workers from all possible parts of the world.

It is by following this same logic that Wallerstein can arrive at the conclusions he reaches regarding the global reach of capitalism and its impact on all international politics. Marxist theory assumes that the material conditions of production create the central foundations of society, which then determine all else in the social space. Nothing in that space, it is posited here, can escape the sway of the material configurations created by the circumstances of production and by economic relations, and these material configurations will always have the same effects of subjugation on political and ideational structures. All societies throughout the world, then, will suffer the same fate. There aren't any social realities which can escape an entanglement with underlying material situations, and this entanglement will always lead to the same results. Wallerstein starts with similar assumptions and arrives at the same conclusions. For him, too, capitalism always captures all other realities within the social space and brings all of them under its control. This is his belief that behind all "polities and cultures" lies "a single division of labor," in echo to the *Communist Manifesto*'s idea that "capitalism compels all nations to adopt its mode of production" and thus "creates a world after its own image."[30]

In this case again, therefore, one finds an approach which endeavors to substitute to the universals of mainstream international studies a concern with the specific and the circumstantial in international affairs, but which also returns, in fact, to a language of universals precisely as it does that. Wallerstein assumes that explanations of international politics which, like realism or liberalism, focus on factors other than capitalism will always be wrong throughout all of world affairs. The elements which they study, such as the state or the liberal market, can never have the explanatory power ascribed to them by these paradigms because, all the time and everywhere, they will only reflect the underlying movements of capitalism and production. Conversely, Wallerstein claims that international politics should always be understood as a series of settings and circumstances within the global capitalist economy: no element of international affairs, anywhere or at any time, can escape the grasp of global capitalism, and all segments of international politics will thus be defined by the position they occupy within this global capitalist structure.

This line of thinking has been quite influential. Now, however, it most often meshes with another approach: post-Marxism. This is an approach that attempts to redefine the role of production in international affairs in light of the other axes of exploitation and fragmentation, which act at cross-purposes with it in world politics.[31] The writings of someone like Theda Skocpol, and her attempts to underscore the "autonomy of the state" within the global capitalist system, are certainly well known in that regard.[32] It is Robert Cox, though, who probably remains the thinker who has pushed the furthest this kind of analysis. His work has spawned what is frequently called the "neo-Gramscian approach to global politics," a phrase drawn from his use of Gramsci's work. Here again, other authors can be mentioned – the work of Stephen Gill, for example, is widely recognized.[33] The work of Cox, though, serves as a constant point of reference.[34]

Cox's most famous and widely read work is *Production, Power, and World Order*.[35] He opens up his argumentation in this book with an outlook which follows directly from the Marxist tradition when he notes that the "premise taken as a guide to inquiry" is that "power relations in societies and in world politics [need to be considered] from the angle of power relations in production."[36] This is an appropriate starting point in the study of world politics, Cox continues, because "production creates the material basis for all forms of social existence, and the ways in which human efforts are combined in productive processes affect all other aspects of social life, including the polity."[37] The interrelationship between production and power is, then, the central focus of this study of world politics, because "production generates the capacity to exercise power, but power determines the manner in which production takes place."[38]

Cox, however, adds in this approach two elements that are more specific to his thinking. First, he wants to consider the role that ideas and ideologies play in lending legitimacy to models of world order. In that context, he parallels to some extent the work of many writers – for instance those associated with the Frankfurt School, who hold that ideology is never neutral and springs at all times from the configurations of the material power which underlie it. Cox is also concerned, though, with the reverse relationship. How do ideas enter into a mutually constitutive rapport with the material world, he asks, and how do they establish the vocabulary of norms, values, and goals, through which the material aspects of society are set in place and then accepted as legitimate and normal ways of the world? It is there that Cox draws from the work of Antonio Gramsci.[39] For Gramsci, the power that economic elites hold over workers is not only a matter of coercion and repression, as traditional Marxist views would hold, but also a matter of consent. These elites, through the control they exercise over the main channels of intellectual and cultural discourse, are able to present the order they dominate as natural, as something which springs from the inherent order of things, and which must therefore be accepted by all as such. Capitalism, for instance, is presented by these groups not as a system of domination and exploitation of many by a few, but rather as the most normal, the most natural way of organizing production and society – hence a way that should be seen as such by all. For Cox, this is central. Global capitalism maintains itself in place not only through the organization of the material capacities it entails, but also through the organization of the ideas and values it brings to bear on structures of global political and economic governance. The way in which this is done is also crucially important. Global elites are able to build consent for the order they dominate when they are able to substitute the universal for the particular in accepted views of society – when they are able, in other words, to take what remains a particular arrangement of social and economic mechanisms, which benefits a very specific group of people, and to present it as something natural, which is the only possible way of organizing economics, politics, and society so as to favor everybody. This is what the supporters of global capitalism have been able to do over the past decades, according to Cox. And this explains, in his view, the continued power of the global capitalist system.

The second element Cox adds to the study of the role played by the forces of production in shaping international politics is a broadened understanding of the material factors at play in that process. For him, again in parallel with Gramsci, the civil society which animates social relations below the state represents a cohesive structure that both embodies and reproduces the values and institutions necessary to the perpetuation of the dominating order. In addition, the state is not simply a reflection of underlying economic structures. It has a necessary and specific role in the upholding of the social order linked to those economic structures: it is the "primary focus of social struggles"[40] and, as such, it must continually reconfigure all these struggles in ways that can be reconciled with the basic tenets and dynamics of the existing order. Furthermore, the state is also the "basic entity"[41] of international politics. It maintains a more strategic agenda, rooted in the constant need to interact with other states in military, political, and diplomatic terms. It must also always fulfill this agenda, though, in a manner that will not contradict or undermine the dominant economic order. Finally, international institutions help also to maintain this existing order, as they "embody the rules which facilitate the expansion of hegemonic world orders [and they] ideologically legitimate the norms" of this order.[42]

On that basis, Cox claims that the tension between the universal and the particular is constitutive of the very nature of international politics. This is what he means when he uses the phrase "limited totalities"[43] to illustrate his take on global international politics. International politics is socially and historically constructed in a series of particular moments, defined by the interaction of specific interests. These "limited" and specific interests, though, define themselves as "totalities." The capitalist system, for instance, serves the interests of a minority in global politics. It endures, however, by presenting itself as a universally valid system which is the only suitable and natural order for the organization of all of the global political economy. The complex of national and international institutions which participate in the process of global political and economic governance then support this vision of world order through rules and practices that fit its core values.

Cox's understanding of the nature of international politics then provides the standpoint from which he offers his critique of mainstream international studies. For him, as he notes in remarks frequently quoted, conceptual frameworks such as realism and liberalism do not take into account how

> theory is always *for* someone and *for* some purpose. All theories have a perspective [and these] perspectives derive from a position in time and space, specifically social and political time and space.[44]

Realists and liberals, to put it differently, do not acknowledge that they are working from within specific "limited totalities." They do not recognize that their objects of study – the workings of the state or of the market, for instance, in the international realm – cannot be understood independently of the "social and political time and space" in which they are considered, and that their own insights are always circumscribed by the fact that they arise from a specific "perspective," a given "purpose," set by a particular "position" in those circumstances of time and space. The language of universals they adopt when they talk of the state or of the market in the singular – rather than in the plural, which would be needed to convey the different realities these concepts can represent in changing "social and political time and spaces" – obfuscates how that language stems from one particular understanding of the universal, an understanding embedded in specific historical and social conditions. These approaches, Cox argues, are therefore "taking a form of thought derived from a particular phase of history (and thus from a particular structure of social relations) and assuming it to be universally valid."[45]

From all these claims there arises, nevertheless, their certainty that they always capture the specificity of international politics in all contexts, and at all times. Here again, an approach focused on the tensions between the particular and the universal winds up arguing that it speaks to all of international politics and that no other approach is ever needed if one is to explain international life. The elements of capitalism, civil society, state, ideology, and the like, which comprise post-Marxism, are supposed always to explain international politics. By their very nature, the different material and ideational forces that run through this explanation can only be amalgamated in the way shown here. World politics, then, will always be explained through the factors put forward by this approach and through the type of interaction between these elements that it describes. International politics will remain a world of moments and change, a world of the particular, but at all times it will be possible to understand this reality of the particular in international affairs from the perspective proposed here – and not, for instance, from the perspective of other meanings of the particular involved in post-modern or constructivist writings.

The argument advanced in this book, however, holds that this sort of logic also fails to reflect fully the nature of international politics in the non-Western world. As will be shown in upcoming chapters, the core tenets that anchor the Marxist analysis are often quite problematic in those parts of the world. It is not the case, for instance, that the organization of production precedes and shapes other social phenomena: it is instead the organization of violence that shapes production and other forms of social relations. There has to be, then, a conceptual shift, which is difficult to operate within the Marxist worldview. By the time the literature moves on to the neo-Gramscian approach, this problem is magnified. The forms of rationality which emerge in the contexts of violence often found in the non-Western world, for example, can lead to understandings of the self and others, of identity and plurality, that affect the tension between the universal and the particular in ways unforeseen by this approach. As was the case with the literature extending from post-modernism to constructivism, then, the line of reasoning going from Marxism to neo-Gramsian works well as a critique of mainstream international studies, and it certainly raises important questions regarding the universals that lie at the heart of realism and liberalism. When it is confronted with the international politics of the non-Western world, however, this line of reasoning loses some of its resonance. A new sense of the particular must be found, then – one that remains somewhat different from what these approaches set forth. As will also be shown, this entails, in turn, the need to reconsider what the universal and the more contextual factors that frame global international politics are. This is how the specific nature of the forms of international politics now emerging out of the non-Western world, and their impact on the character of global politics, will be captured by international studies.

At the end of this survey one is thus left with a fundamental problem. The edifice of approaches that comprise international studies seems quite solid, so to say, from the inside. Realism is based on a series of coextensive assumptions, which give it an unyielding sense that it speaks to all of international politics. Liberalism attempts to provide a counterpoint to realism and, in the process, it brings together a series of assumptions which also give it a sense of having a universal scope. In response to this assumption of a universal scope, which is prevalent in both realism and liberalism, another way of looking at international politics has developed, one that emphasizes how these universals can be unraveled and made to reveal more specific configurations of ideas and material circumstances. Constructivism is central to these efforts, and it highlights the role of ideas in the construction of international politics. In counterpoint, post-Marxism emphasizes the role that material forces play in the series of factors which underlie the changing nature of all international politics.

The issue, though, is that these approaches and debates can appear quite a bit more problematic from the outside, as it were – that is, from the standpoint of the non-Western world. All of them do have an internal coherence: they rest on self-reinforcing assumptions, and each one then ushers in the next, as a response. From the perspective of the non-Western world, however, this can appear to be a self-enclosed discussion, which leaves aside many of the realities that give the international politics of this world its specific character. Realism and liberalism, the two key approaches used in international studies, work from an assumption of universality which leads them to forego a study of the specific character of international life in the non-Western world. The approaches that attempt to critique this assumption of universality end up returning to it themselves, by positing that the way they unpack the language of mainstream international studies resonates through all of global politics. In all of this, the specificity of the non-Western world – what it might be, and how to capture it fully – is not considered.

Worse still, the issue *cannot* be considered. The logic of the different approaches that comprise international studies entails a belief that they speak to all of international politics throughout the world. One cannot simply propose, then, that new elements should be integrated in all these approaches if one is to make them more inclusive of the realities of the non-Western world. The very logic of such approaches militates against this idea: they cannot claim, at the same time, that they speak to all of international politics and that they fail to address the international politics of some parts of the world. In this perspective, there is an additional level of difficulty which must be addressed, if international studies is to understand better the non-Western world and its impact on global politics. It is these different issues that are addressed in the second part of this book.

Part II

What Do We Overlook? International Politics in the Non-Western World

4
Violence, Rationality, and the State

Any discussion of the non-Western world starts with a question which seems simple enough: Where is it? Which parts of the world do we have in mind when we use that rubric? And the usual answer points to a number of predictable geographic areas: Africa, the Middle East, Latin America, or Asia. The discussion must then turn, however, to a rather more complex question: *what* is the non-Western world? What are its key characteristics? And how do these characteristics make it different from the Western world? This is where things get more ambiguous.

A discussion of the non-Western world can often be a discussion of modernization and development: the West is modern and developed, and the non-Western world is less so. Thinking in those terms, however, creates enormous problems. One of these problems, obviously, is that this approach leads to undifferentiated explanations where much more nuanced ones are needed. The West is seen, in this view, as having followed one model of development, when in fact it has followed many. In counterpoint, the non-Western world is seen as catching up to a Western model of development while, in reality, this model might well not even exist in such a pure form in any part of the Western world. More profoundly, thinking in those terms also defines the Western experience of modernization and development as the sole standard by which any other trajectory of development should be judged or explained, thus blocking out any sense of the non-Western world which could be, as it were, more non-Western.

Beyond all of this, the problem with thinking about the non-Western world might simply be that this requires in the first place an assumption that there is a radical difference between the West and the "rest." This might be a difficult case to make. As Pinar Bilgin has argued in an important essay,

> "Western" and "non-Western" experiences as well as their various explanations have, over the years, clashed and fused in so many ways that "non-Western" ways of thinking about and doing world politics are not always devoid of "Western" concepts and theories. The reverse may also

be true. What we have come to think of as "Western" [worldviews on international politics] may contain "non-Western" as well as "Western" input, notwithstanding prevalent disciplinary representations [in international studies], which often sterilize the history of the "West" by leaving out "non-Western" challenges, interventions, and contributions.[1]

To that extent, thinking about the non-Western world might entail a sense of difference and distance from the West, when in fact – the essay quotes Bhabha this time – we are talking about things that are "almost the same, but not quite."[2]

While acknowledging this degree of ambiguity, it is still possible, however, to identify a series of questions and themes which must be addressed in any such discussion. Asking how the state was shaped by the colonial experience, for instance, how these dynamics played themselves out in different parts of, say, Africa or Asia, and how these processes have influenced the evolution of state behavior on the international stage over the years – all these questions cannot be avoided in any discussion of this sort. The goal is not to claim, in other words, that all that needs to be said about the non-Western world has been said, or that the very essence of what constitutes the non-Western world has somehow been captured in a given set of explanations. The goal, instead, is to underscore how some problems, some dilemmas, open important lines of inquiry into this very question of what constitutes the non-Western world, while recognizing that this is a discussion which remains lively and open-ended.

It is also certainly possible, then, to turn toward international studies and ask whether or not the discipline takes these issues on board. For instance, do the debates about the nature of the state that occupy international studies as a discipline (to continue with the example just mentioned) deal with the way the state has developed in certain parts of the world as a result of the colonial experience? This is, after all, the key question. Can international studies learn to explain a world where global politics is shaped to an unprecedented extent by forces, actors, and agendas coming out of different parts of the non-Western world? Can the discipline discuss how it should identify and explain these elements? Can it know how to integrate this discussion into its study of current global politics? The hope, here again, should not be to arrive at a point where it is possible to assume that all that needs to be said about the non-Western world has been said, or that its underlying essence has been captured in a given series of insights. The point should be instead to recognize how, at least, some questions open interesting points of entry for the discipline as it gets into this entire discussion about the way forward, given current shifts in global politics.

This certainly corresponds to the approach adopted in this second part of the book. This part of the text is focused on a fundamental issue: what does international studies, as a discipline, fail to see when it comes to the international politics of the non-Western world? What stands beyond the current scope of the discipline? What, then, should be brought in international studies if the Western-centric aspects of the discipline are to be forced open, so to speak, in order to let a broader understanding of the nature of international politics throughout the entire world develop within its core approaches and concepts? The point is not to claim that all that is specific about the non-Western world has been outlined or, indeed, that the very quandary of how to capture that specificity has been solved in some definitive way. What this second part of the text does suggest, though, is that the questions raised here cannot be addressed without at least engaging in some fashion the issues put forward in these pages. There is a large literature on these matters, with a number of approaches and debates. It is possible, though, to identify cross-cutting themes within that literature and to arrive at the sense that some issues simply must be part of that discussion. Cases drawn from Asia are used throughout these sections of the book to illustrate the arguments put forward. Here again, the issue is not that Asia explains all that needs to be explained about the non-Western world. However, no discussion of the non-Western world – its nature and its role in current global politics – can proceed without reference to Asia. To that extent, the examples provided here can be instructive.

Throughout this entire discussion, another question is also raised in parallel with all these elements: can the issues and themes surveyed here in relation to the non-Western world actually be brought in international studies in order to make the discipline less Western-centric? After all, this is the goal. International studies overlooks many issues when it comes to the international politics of the non-Western world. We should identify these issues and bring them in the workings of the discipline. We will then have a form of international studies that is much more global in its outlook and in the sort of analysis it puts forward. Indeed, this is the form of international studies that we must now strive to attain, given the evolution of global politics. If we live in a world that is less and less Western-centric, we need an approach to international affairs that is also less Western-centric than has been the case in the past, and this is the way to achieve that objective.

What this second part of the book also emphasizes, though, is the extent of the challenge involved in bringing about this type of dialogue between international studies and the literature that is more closely focused on the international politics of the non-Western world. International studies, as was explained in the first part of the book, assumes that it speaks to all of international politics throughout the world. In counterpoint, the literature considered in this second part of the text takes for granted that this approach to international affairs remains, in its very nature, completely misguided. The underlying logics at play in the two approaches that need to be brought together in a dialogue cannot be reconciled. In fact, they may prevent this dialogue from taking place at all. This is precisely the challenge that must be tackled, though, if international studies is now to address the global politics associated with the "rise of the rest." Ways of dealing with this challenge are presented in the third part of the book. Before they can be introduced, however, the full scope and nature of the problem at hand must be explained. This is also what is done in this second part of the text.

What, then, are some of the key issues and questions that must be taken into account in any consideration of the international politics of the non-Western world? And how are these issues and questions overlooked by international studies as the discipline stands at the moment? Reflections on these questions usually start with a discussion about realism – because of the pre-eminence of the realist approach in the literature and, most obviously, in the habits of thought that guide policy circles at international level. These reflections are usually structured around critiques of the two central components of the realist tradition: the line extending from Machiavelli to Morgenthau and the classical realists, which looks at the character of violence and rationality in international politics; and the line going from Hobbes to Waltz and the neo-realists, which focuses more on the nature of state and inter-state structures to explain international politics.

One starting point for these reflections is the extent to which the non-Western world can often remain a place of violence. The control over the means of organized violence, seen in the West as the hallmark of the state, can be lacking, or be tenuous at best. There can be sizeable zones of utter lawlessness and brutality in the outlying areas of a given state, secessionist or guerilla movements bringing recurrent bloodshed to the interior areas that that state is attempting to police more forcefully, or unremitting violence and intimidation from the marauding criminal gangs inhabiting large tracts of its urban centers.

This is a key feature of notions such as "inadequate stateness" or "quasi-states," put forward by Mohammed Ayoob[3] and Robert H. Jackson[4] respectively, which are intended to explain why violence can still be an overriding concern in the non-Western world. Two arguments are typically at the root of these explanations. First, in contrast to the process of monopolization of violence by the state depicted so famously by Tilly,[5] violence in the non-Western world can often remain scattered throughout all of society. There might be not be as much of an inside and of an outside, to use Walker's phrase,[6] between the domestic and the international: the state might remain too weak to extract violence from society completely and to establish a pacified domestic space, clearly demarcated from a more violent international one.

Second, as a result, violence might endure as the currency of power within the state, rather than more political or institutional means. Looking at the Western experience, one sees how the development of the state is coextensive with a series of institutions and practices that limit the use of physical coercion to exercise state power. In place of violence, power is then brought to bear on individuals and groups, through laws and administrative rules. Sheldon Wolin, for instance, describes this as the rise of constitutionalism, whereby efforts are made to

> restrict the application of violence by setting defined limits to power, by insisting on the observance of regularized procedures and by establishing strict methods for rendering those in power accountable for their actions. The paraphernalia of constitutionalism – the rule of law, due process, the separation of powers, checks and balances, and the system of individual rights, with its significant emphasis on privileges and "immunities" – [do] not eliminate power, but they [contribute] to its regularization, to eradicating that unpredictable, sheerly destructive quality that epitomizes all violence.[7]

The "paraphernalia of constitutionalism," however, is precisely what the state can often fail to develop fully in the non-Western world. In that context, there might not be an overarching and stable framework of "laws and rights" allowing the rearticulation of power away from violence and toward "regularized procedures" and "due process." Violence might escape the reach of these laws and rights and, because of their weakness, linger on as the most effective means of exercising power. The issue, then, is not only that violence might still remain present within the state, but also that it could constrain the emergence and exercise of other forms of power.

This is where the critique of realism must begin. Realism provides the starting point of a vast reflection on the nature of violence and the best responses to it in international studies. The crucial point made by many realists is that human rationality provides the key countervailing force against violence. A rational assessment of the presence of violence in all human affairs must be made. Then violence must be controlled and used. In that context violence will not disappear. At a minimum, though, it will support broader political objectives. Perhaps, in time, this will also allow non-violent forms of politics to develop and entrench themselves alongside these other forms of power, rooted more directly in the exercise or threat of violence. This is what Machiavelli tells us, and this is what Morgenthau and many of today's proponents of *realpolitik* believe.

For this to correspond to reality, though, some elements must already be in place. I can be the most rational person in the world. If I am in a zone of endemic conflict and I get killed tomorrow by a suicide bomber or a paramilitary militia, however, my ability to use my rationality to influence the nature and conduct of life around me will be, to say the least, severely curtailed. This speaks to the "economy of violence," to use Sheldon Wollin's phrase again,[8] which surrounds me as I attempt to deal with my world. Some people, for instance, may well have more means of violence at their disposal than I do, and this will determine my ability to use my rationality to act in the world.

I am always rational: the use of that rationality to control violence and to engage in other forms of politics is always limited, though, by factors that stand beyond my own rationality and go to a broader, and prior, "economy of violence." The realists, when they tell me to use my rationality to control violence around me, must thus take for granted that there is already in place an "economy of violence," which allows me to do that.

Realists, in this sense, tell well one part of the story. Obviously, human beings are rational agents who, when confronted by violence, engage in calculations which can often make violence appear as a valid and effective instrument of power. They do not tell as well, though, the second part of the story. All of this requires a prior organization of violence. Means of violence must be available to me, and in a way that eludes others around me, if I am to be able to use violence effectively to pursue my objectives. And this organization of violence entails, in turn, what could be termed an organization of agency. It is not simply because I want to use violence to exercise power that I can do so. There is an organization of violence which stands beyond my own agency and limits the way it can be deployed in the world.

Confronting realism to the realities of the non-Western world, however, immediately leads to the idea that it is this second part of the story that should be given more emphasis. Intra-state violence can remain a crucial problem in the non-Western world. Addressing this problem, though, requires an engagement with questions of state-building, institution-building, and the like, which are not readily identifiable if one focuses only on the connection between human agency and the control of violence. There is more to the problem of violence. An "economy of violence" is already in place, which structures what can and cannot be done about violence, how it can and cannot be used, and who can or cannot use it. This "economy of violence" evolves in counterpoint to the ability of the state to control violence, or to the extent of its failure to do so. This is where the notions of "inadequate stateness" and "quasi-stateness" put forward by Ayoob and Jackson ultimately push the reflection.

This all means, quite simply, that understanding violence in the non-Western world requires a study of the nature of the state just as much as it entails a study of the series of calculations and strategies that always surround the use of violence. This also ultimately means, though, that approaches which are usually opposed to each other must be brought together. The rational agent of Machiavelli and Morgenthau must be linked up with the more structural and state-centred elements observed by Hobbes and Waltz: realism and neo-realism, in a word, must be connected in some fashion. Clearly, the issue is not limited to the politics of the non-Western world. The atrocious bloodshed which marked the fragmentation of the former Yugoslavia, for example, can be traced back precisely to this tension between patterns of state failure and generalized violence. The specific trajectories of development of the state in the non-Western world add a number of particular dimensions to these questions in those parts of the world, as will be shown in the course of this discussion. Most importantly, this also leads to a series of considerations about the resolution of long-standing conflicts in the non-Western world, as will be shown in the third part of the book, in the sections dealing with the image and models we should have in mind as we think about some of the most pressing issues in current global politics.

It was important, though, to bring in this issue of violence at the outset of the discussion for two reasons. First, the possible presence of sustained violence in some parts of the non-Western world must be kept in mind even when working with approaches to international politics that might not focus on the issue as much as realism does. To give an example that will be explored in further detail later on, theories of development often study patterns of trade and production to explain the dynamics of economic growth. In doing so, however, they circumvent the problem of violence. Or, rather, they assume that violence has been stamped out and that other forces now determine the nature of economic growth. The reality in many parts of the non-Western world, though, is that violence still precedes and shapes economic development. From the commerce of blood diamonds in parts of Africa to the human trafficking prevalent in many regions of Southeast Asia, it is the organization of violence – the use of sheer human brutality and the "economy of violence" it brings about – that allows broader patterns of trade and production to emerge and then sustain themselves. Determining, then, where violence is, who controls it, how this does connect to other social dynamics – those are questions which to some extent must be asked at the beginning of any theory of international politics if it is to capture the full reality of what is happening in the non-Western world. A discussion such as this one, which is concerned with the applicability of different approaches to international politics to the realities of the non-Western world, must thus proceed while keeping in mind this issue.

Keeping in mind the question of violence while the discussion proceeds further is also important for a second reason. Why do some approaches to international politics assume that they can circumvent the issue of violence and focus on other dynamics of development and politics? Very often, it is because they use as the starting point of their own analysis arguments from other approaches, which themselves take for granted that the problem of violence can be addressed and resolved successfully. To use another example, which will be studied later on, the Kantian liberals look at the rational individual depicted by Machiavelli and the realists and at the ability of this individual to control and use violence. They then push that rational individual and his control over violence in new directions, arguing for instance that values and rights can guide his actions just as much as the strategic calculations associated with control over violence. The issue, though, is that, if the realists themselves overlook some of the factors involved in the control of violence – for instance, the role that more structural factors linked to state development also play in the movement away from violence – a cascading effect will follow. The liberals who import some of the realist assumption in their own argument will miss part of the picture, the approaches which build on liberalism to develop their own logic will then duplicate this oversight, and so on. Following some of these sequences, as is done here, can thus help us understand why some approaches in international politics do not address fully all the dimensions of the issue of violence in the non-Western world, how that oversight skews their logic, and how it should be addressed.

Violence, most fortunately, is not always a factor in the non-Western world – far from it. However, as was just suggested, the question of violence, the way it might affect, in many instances, other factors, must at least be raised if we are to understand the full array of issues that determine the international politics of those parts of the world. The discussion can now move, though, to a second element, which, this time, is always part of the studies devoted to the international politics of the non-Western world: the state. What is specific about state development in those parts of the world, these writings ask, and how do these factors affect international behavior? How is this problem often missed by international studies as the discipline stands now?

This is a critique which is most often addressed to neo-realism. As Stephanie G. Neuman notes in her introduction to *International Relations Theory and the Third World*,[9] Waltz and the neo-realists work on the basis of a fundamental assumption: that there is a "difference between domestic and international politics which 'turns on the distinction between politics conducted in a condition of settled rules and politics conducted in a condition of anarchy.' "[10] This is the well-known logic espoused by Waltz and his followers. Violence compels individuals to create the state. The "war of all against all" described by Hobbes requires the creation of the "Leviathan," an institution able to monopolize violence within its own apparatus and pacify the rest of society in the process. This creates spaces within the state where non-violent politics is the norm; but it also creates, however, gaps between states, where violence is not controlled and thus remains a constant determinant affecting all political relations. This is the primary factor, which shapes all others in international affairs and lets us know that international politics will, at all times and everywhere, remain a function of this underlying trait. It is by drawing on this logic that someone like David Singer, Neuman further remarks, can then profess that there is "only one international system 'on and around the planet Earth' "[11] and be seen to encapsulate, as he makes that claim, a patent premise shared by generations of international relations scholars. Clearly, though, Neuman and others will want to respond that there are dissimilar sorts of international politics "on planet Earth," and that this is missed in the logic put forward by Waltz and the neo-realists.

These objections typically revolve around two arguments. First, the neo-realist idea that a distinction exists between the inside and the outside of the state when it comes to the organization and regulation of violence is taken to task. This argument usually begins with a reminder of the history and character of the state in the non-Western world. As Ayoob notes, the development of the non-Western state should be seen, before anything else, as unfolding within "colonially constructed boundaries," which force

> diverse and dissatisfied elements [...] to remain within their postcolonial boundaries while at the same time encouraging those elements to make political, administrative, and economic demands that the state[...] cannot begin to satisfy, either because [it lacks] the capabilities or because doing so could jeopardize [its] territorial integrity.[12]

This, in turn, leads to a

> lack of internal cohesion, in terms of both great economic and social disparities and major ethnic and regional fissures; lack of unconditional legitimacy of state boundaries, state institutions, and governing elites; and easy susceptibility to internal and inter-state conflict.[13]

The state in the non-Western world was created from the outside, during the colonial period. It compelled different ethnic and social groups to cohabit in a common administrative and political structure, while it divided, with its imposed borders, societies which had a previous coherence and a unity of their own. What amounts still to an artificial assemblage is short, then, of "internal cohesion and legitimacy," and it cannot do much to address the issue without "jeopardizing its territorial integrity."

In the non-Western world, violent conflicts thus happen most often in a space which is "both internal and external," as Ayoob puts it.[14] Major "ethnic fissures" created by "dissatisfaction with colonial and post-colonial boundaries" will lead one ethnic group to be at war with a state from the inside, within the nominal borders of that state. This ethnic group will receive military training and support from other members of the same group – who live, though, on the outside, within the formal territory of a neighboring state. The movement back and forth of troops and military equipment will in many cases be happening without the consent of that neighboring state because it might not itself fully control its own territory. The state where the ethnic conflict is unfolding will mount, in response, military interventions that will occur outside its own borders and also, so to say, within the neighboring state rather than against it. The goal will be to engage militarily groups situated inside the borders of that neighboring state without, however, going to war against it: indeed, its political support will be required to sanction these operations within its borders.

The spaces where violent conflict occurs here are thus quite unlike those imagined by the neo-realists. The inside of the state, as was said a moment ago, can be a place of violence. That violence, furthermore, will happen at once inside and outside the state: the state will often reach beyond its borders to address a conflict which is happening, in fact, within its own territory. And the inter-state realm, the space between the state divided by ethnic war and its neighbor, might also witness the emergence of mechanisms of political cooperation aimed at lessening the violence within these two states. The outside of the state, in that context, might come to be the space where peace develops and is protected by the state, whereas the domestic space is the one where violence and war endure. The reality would then be the reverse of the core image the neo-realists have in mind: in such cases, the state would build peace outside its borders, only to wage war better inside of them.

Simply thinking of two spaces – one inside the state, where violence does not dominate politics, and one outside, where violence prevails – totally overlooks all of this. A good part of the neo-realist logic flows from this assumed contrast between two political spaces created by opposed "ordering principles," to use Waltz's expression[15]: an internal space, ordered by the control of violence, which exists in tension with an inter-state space, on the outside of that pacified domestic realm, where order is established through anarchy and violence. Such a logic cannot comprehend the dislocated areas of violence and peace of the non-Western world, where in fact Waltz's two "ordering principles" often share the same space. Violent disarray and a more pacified order can be at the same time, in that world, part of the space internal to the state, and part, as well, of the space outside the state. The inside and the outside of the state, in reverse to what the neo-realist logic can envisage, can thus possess common traits rather than stand in total opposition one from the other.

The second key argument regarding the blind-spots of the neo-realist literature vis-à-vis the non-Western world concerns the use of notions of rationality and agency in that literature. The motor that drives neo-realism is a minimal key assumption: rational human beings, when confronted by generalized violence, will have no choice but to establish the Leviathan, a structure which will guarantee non-violent social relations within its boundaries. The presumed nature of the state and of the inter-state realm then follows from this assumption. What this fails to address, though, is the question of how that rationality can be deployed in a world where violence is endemic. This is where the discussion connects with the preceding remarks on violence. The exercise of rationality in a context of violence is not something that simply happens. A specific organization of violence is a necessary prerequisite to the emergence of rationality as an instrument of social and political power. It is precisely this organization of violence that is frequently absent or incomplete in the non-Western world. The logic of neo-realism cannot see that: it posits the presence of rationality and works from there on, without reflecting on the prior developments, which led to what constitutes the starting point in its argument.

Why does the neo-realist logic lead to these problems? As was shown in the first part of the book, to understand the way the neo-realist logic is employed now, one first has to go back to the series of claims and postulates set up by Hobbes centuries ago. This is still the source on which neo-realism draws in order to establish the veracity of its claims today. Hobbes' argument follows from the tension he sees between the fact that "every one is governed by his own Reason" and the fact that everyone still has to deal with the "condition of Man," which entails the possibility of a "Warre of every one against every one."[16] Consent given to the creation of the Leviathan is the single possible answer to that situation. The "only way" for human beings to protect themselves from the "injuries of one another," Hobbes continues, is to "conferre all their power and strength upon one Man, or upon one Assembly of men, that may reduce all their Will, by plurality of voices, unto one Will," which will in turn protect "common peace and safety."[17] This is the "principle of organization"[18] of social life that Kenneth Waltz seizes upon to anchor the whole neo-realist logic. Violence demands a response from rational individuals. This will be the state, which will establish a "monopoly over the *legitimate* use of violence" enabling it to have "public agents organized to prevent and to counter the private use of force."[19] As a consequence, two distinct sorts of politics and two "ordering principles" take shape: a "national system," where "citizens need not prepare to defend themselves," and an "international system," which will be instead one of "self-help," where recourse to force will often be the sole means of protecting oneself.[20]

Thinking along these lines prevents one, first of all, from understanding correctly the process of state formation in the non-Western world. In the neo-realist view, the creation of the state grows out of decision and consent, as human beings "conferre their power to one Assembly" and agree on a new "principle of organization," which will lend "legitimacy" to the state as it sets itself up to "counter the private use of force." In the non-Western world, though, the state is imposed from the outside: it grows out of administrative spaces forced upon populations by outside actors during the colonial era. It is the result, as Ayoob put it a moment ago, of "colonially constructed boundaries," which still testify today to the imposition of a will external to that of the populations they now encircle. This sets up a tension between the logic of neo-realism and the actual original trajectory of development of the state.

The premises of neo-realism also account for the second element it fails to capture in non-Western international politics – the extent to which its understanding of rationality and agency conceals the prior developments necessary to the exercise of rationality in a context of violence. "Every one is governed by his own reason," claims Hobbes. Waltz follows the same path, as was shown earlier, when he also starts with the postulate that all individuals are rational and then asks how they are bound to act, as rational agents, in an environment of violence. This is his well-known use of the language of economics, where politics can be compared to the interactions set by the market. The "individual unit acts for itself," Waltz contends, and politics follows from the "coaction of like units [out of which] emerges a structure that affects and constrains all of them."[21] In all of this, the issue of possible prerequisites to the exercise of human rationality and agency in a context of violence is overlooked. Someone like Waltz begins with the image of the rational human being painted by economics – the rational agent faced with the "coactions" of politics, similar to the clash of individual agencies set by open market conditions. He then places that rational agent in a context of violence and asks how that agent will behave. The prior developments that allow that rational agent to have agency, so to say, in a world of violence, are not part of that equation.

The problem, however, is that one cannot simply add these new elements to the logic of neo-realism. The neo-realist approach is embedded in assumptions about its universal scope that prevent it, if it is to remain coherent with itself, from incorporating in its worldview these sorts of issues. Hobbes, as Macpherson remarked earlier, is a "mechanical philosopher."[22] There is a chain of causes and consequences in the *Leviathan* that can only lead to the same results, all the time and everywhere. All human beings are rational – "every one is governed by his own Reason." They are all confronted by a world where violence is possible – it is the "condition of Man" to endure a possible "Warre of every one against every one." Just as two chemical elements, when brought together, will always cause the same reaction to occur, these two realities will continually lead to a similar end result. All individuals will want to "conferre their power upon one Assembly of men," to find "common peace and safety." This is, as Hobbes declares, the "only way." The logic, in its "mechanical" certainty, cannot ever deviate: the same causes will at all times lead to the same consequences. Waltz and the neo-realists follow the same sequences of causes and effects. Individuals are all moved by the same basic rationality, they are "like units." From the "coaction" of these like entities will come about the "structures that will affect and constrain them," and these structures will always resemble one another, because they will all stem from the same triggers and sources. This is why we know with certainty that the "ordering principles" entailed by these structures will also be identical everywhere and at all times: the domestic space circumscribed by the state will always have certain rules, and the international realm, outside the state, will also always have its own rules. Indeed, this is why we can know, as Waltz claims, that there is "an enduring character to international politics which accounts for the striking sameness in the quality of international life through the millennia."[23]

It is this "mechanical" quality of the neo-realist argument that leads to its universalism. Human rationality can only ever want to conquer blind violence. Its response – the creation of the state through a "common will" – can only ever be the same, and then result in the same type of inter-state life "trough the millennia." Once the sequence of arguments is set in motion, it can only lead to the same conclusion – and this, all the time and everywhere. The idea, then, that factors *other* than rationality and agency come into play in the control of violence, and then in the construction of the state, cannot be accommodated in this logic. Here, on the contrary, it is assumed that it is rational agency, and nothing else, that accounts for the structures which frame society and protect it from violence. The idea, furthermore, that domestic and international spaces can intermingle one with the other is also something that cannot be integrated in the argument. Here the inside and the outside of the state can only ever be well demarcated and totally different one from the other, because of the chains of causes and consequences which give rise to these two distinct spaces. The issues that must be raised if the nature of state formation and the inter-state relations in the non-Western world are to be understood properly cannot, then, become part of that logic: the interlocking postulates on which it is based render those issues invisible, if not absurd.

Asia provides concrete examples of these problems. Observers of the international politics of the region often comment on the degree to which it proceeds, within spaces and with rationales quite dissimilar from those considered by the neo-realists. Alagappa, for instance, notes that the

> three most acute conflicts in Asia – between Taiwan and China, between North and South Korea, and between India and Pakistan – are outcomes of conflicting political imaginations that have become sharpened and entrenched by military competition, both local and global.[24]

These instances of conflicts amid "divided Nation-States," as is the case between China and Taiwan, and of conflicts involving "post-partition States," as is the case between India and Pakistan, and also between North and South Korea, involve, at their core, "rival national self-conceptions" and "conflicting ideas about the identity of the nation-state." [25] Those are not conflicts, then, taking place within a space clearly delineated by the lines separating domestic and international politics. Quite the contrary, these conflicts are about the very definition of where those lines should stand and what they mean. They are not, in other words, unfolding in spaces marked by a clear distinction between the inside and the outside of the state: these conflicts are about *denying* that distinction and bringing the outside, whether it be Taiwan or Kashmir, inside. There is, of course, "military competition, both local and global," which has "entrenched" these conflicts in the international politics of Asia in ways that are clearly understood by the neo-realists. But the point is that these conflicts also stem from "political imaginations" and unsettled state "self-identities" that remain unseen in the neo-realist logic, and that yet play a fundamental role in their evolution and nature. China, for example, simply does not look at Taiwan the way it would at any other state with which it could fight an eventual war. This is missed in the neo-realist assumption of a unique "ordering principle" guiding all inter-state interactions.

What was described earlier as the intermingling of these "ordering principles" – which the neo-realists see as always distinct one from the other – is also exemplified by Southeast Asia. This is a part of the world where zones of internal turmoil and fighting have always had cross-borders dimensions. Muslim unrest in Southern Thailand, for instance, cannot be explained without reference to the fact that people in that area identify themselves more closely with the Islamic community across the border, in Malaysia, than with the rest of the Thai population. Terrorist attacks can be sponsored and receive logistical support from groups based beyond the Thai border, on Malaysian soil. In that context, Thailand has endeavored to build a relationship with Malaysia that will guarantee Kuala Lumpur's support in its effort to eradicate Muslim terrorism within its own territory. Southeast Asia, in fact, is full of such examples of states coming together and building security relations essentially intended to deal with internal threats of violence and disorder.

The language of regional security itself reflects that reality. When the Indonesian government speaks of defending national security through the promotion of national resilience (*Ketahanan Nasional*), it links that policy agenda with the broader aspects of regional stability or unrest likely to impinge upon that process. National resilience, an official document claims, thus revolves around the "ability to develop national strength to face and overcome all manners of threats, *internal and external, direct or indirect.*"[26] National resilience and, just as much, regional resilience are, in that approach, part of Indonesia's national security. To give another example, Malaysia's definition of comprehensive security underscores the elements of internal economic and social developments connected earlier here to the concept, but it also puts emphasis on the idea that this process requires political stability in its neighbors, and thus efforts to ensure that degree of regional stability. Noordin Sopiee, one of the most celebrated Malaysian analysts of international politics in Southeast Asia, once noted in that regard, for instance, that Malaysia's security entailed a "commitment to the territorial integrity of [...] Thailand," and the "building of mutual trust, confidence, and goodwill between the ASEAN states."[27] Insurgencies in neighboring countries, quite simply, can jeopardize Malaysia's stability and security, he was saying, and Kuala Lumpur must thus endeavor to "commit to the territorial integrity of these countries" and "build the mutual regional trust and confidence" necessary to achieve that goal.

There is, in all of this, the acknowledgment that the state can never really establish a boundary between internal and external instability. Violence carries through borders, so to speak, and states remain unable to stop it at their periphery. In such a context, the answer to internal instability must be at once international and domestic: the "building of trust" must occur between regional states if it is to take place at all in domestic society, and sustainable security is to be forthcoming within the state. The two discrete "ordering principles" that the neo-realists link in a very clear-cut fashion to domestic and international politics – rational social convergence here, and violent anarchy there – thus fuse together closely in this case, and this in both domestic and international spaces. The premises through which the neo-realist literature looks at international politics, then, and the importance it assigns to the disjuncture of these two discrete "ordering principles," fail to reveal fully the character of international politics in those parts of the world.

5
Politics, Economics, and Self-Identity

All of this, in turn, has a vast impact on the liberal literature and its ability to explain the international politics of the non-Western world. As the remark by Tim Dunne quoted earlier emphasizes, liberalism in international studies has developed by positioning itself as the "historical alternative" to realism.[1] Liberalism is a response, a counter-argument, to the claims of realism. The approach looks at realist assertions about rationality, violence, and the state; it proposes a new take on these realities, one that calls attention to other possibilities held in the human mind when dealing with violence; and it highlights how society and the market can counter-balance the state in defining the role and scope of violence in international politics.

This is, however, precisely why the questions raised in this book must be brought to bear on the liberal literature. Liberalism considers the claims of realism and then responds to them. If these claims miss a part of the picture of the non-Western world, then liberalism, in counterpoint to these claims, is bound to overlook the same realities too. Moreover, the specific additional elements put forward by the liberals to structure their response to the realists – the nature of the individual, society, and the market – must be made to match, quite evidently, the character of these realities in the non-Western world. The notions of individual and society first described for the liberals by Kant, which animate their thinking to this day, and also the understandings of the individual and of the market painted by Smith, which still course through liberal literature – each one of these must be brought in line with its actual makeup in the non-Western parts of the world. And then, in that logic, the way in which these specific aspects of the individual, of society, and of the market shape international politics in the non-Western world must be integrated in the liberal literature.

This brings into play, at a first level, the critiques levelled at the Kantian brand of liberalism by observers of the international politics of the non-Western world. Kantian liberalism assumes that there is a rationality inherent in human beings, which allows them to interact on the basis of mutually recognized rights and moral imperatives, instead of them constantly confronting one another in contests of power or violence. The development of these frameworks of rights and morality will, over time, establish broader and broader social networks that will, in turn, limit the ability of states to conduct wars. A human community will emerge through that process, which will not permit itself to be led to violence and division by state-driven loyalties and interests. This is the line of thinking that informs today, for instance, the work of civil society advocates and of proponents of a wide array of social movements.

From the perspective of the non-Western world, however, one finds a series of questions in that way of thinking. First, is this a correct understanding of the associational spaces through which individuals interact with one another in non-Western parts of the world, and of the way in which the social networks that stem from these associational spaces can then influence state and inter-state comportments? The fundamental fact about the state in the non-Western world, as was argued in the comments about the realist literature presented above, is that it was initiated from the outside, during the colonial period, and superimposed on pre-existing social formations. How this carries into deficiencies within the liberal approach has to do with the delineation of the private and the public spheres, which came to be in that process of state-building. Certainly, the development of a public and political space did occur, and was supported by the creation of a series of governmental and administrative structures charged with the macro-organization of society. In counterpart, Western notions of individual empowerment were indeed propounded, and then embraced, by large segments of the population. Systems of rights intended to articulate and defend the value and power of the individual did come into existence in that process – obviously, in certain places more than in others – and ensured that a private sphere of voluntary association and opinion emerged, in counterpoint to the public sphere embodied in the state and its various agencies. The relationship between the private and the public, in that sense, did come to resemble somewhat the "paraphernalia of constitutionalism" described by Wolin. The notion that the individual as such precedes in importance and logic the political and the public and possesses a rationality and self-identity that should be protected from the state and other public institutions through a system of rights and laws did gain currency in the non-Western world. To that extent, then, the story told by the liberals holds sway here too. The individual, undeniably, has been recognized as being endowed with rights, and these rights have translated into new modes of political and state governance more consonant with the protection and expression of such rights.

But there is more to the story; and this is where problems arise. There are other ways of establishing the divide between the private and the public, between the individual and the state, in the non-Western world – ways that are not conveyed by this depiction of the facts. The "entrenched primordial attachments," to use Lee Hock Guan's phrase,[2] which were in place before the development of the state and revolved most often around ethnic or ethno-religious forms of community and identity still traverse the politics, formal and informal, of non-Western societies. The sense of belonging to a particular ethnic group, for instance, remains even now the key prism through which social differentiations are established and social and political roles are ascribed. This is a world where, for instance, individuals often define themselves in terms of religious beliefs before they think of themselves as citizens of a given state. The politics of the Islamic world, to give an example, cannot be understood without reference to that fact.

This leads to another issue: the sense of self-identity of the individual might be more closely intertwined with the identity of the ethnic or religious group to which that individual belongs than the liberal model will allow. As Partha Chatterjee's work on "post-colonial democracy" implies,[3] the rights that an individual recognizes as her own are very much a part of a negotiation with a more ancient sense of community and with a broader social identity, against which she situates those demands for rights that she can call her own. In many cases, the "tyranny of the cousins" – to quote now Ernest Gellner[4] – might involve a communitarian sense of self, which will essentially conflate the pursuit of individual rights with that of greater affirmation of the group's identity.

The consequence of this situation has to do with the sort of rapport that the individual can then establish with the state in such a context. The relationship with the state often takes place here completely outside the institutional frameworks set in place by the "paraphernalia of constitutionalism." It takes place outside of these institutional frameworks in a literal sense, through the manifold informal links of kinship and through the personal networks through which so much of the relationship between society and the state unfolds in the non-Western world. This is the "relative autonomy of civil society" vis-à-vis the state described by Chua Beng Huat.[5] This engagement of the state by the individual takes place outside of these frameworks because, more profoundly, it has a different meaning here. It is not, as the Kantian liberals would have it, about the expression of an individual self-identity that should be acknowledged and acted upon by the state. It is, on the contrary, a recognition that the individual must subsume his own identity within that of broader ethnic or religious groupings if he is to have any power in the public sphere, or in the state itself. This is where, in the end, there is a line between the private and the public in the non-Western world that is drawn in different places, so to say, by comparison with the one taken for granted in the Kantian logic. Here the private sphere centered around the individual is incomplete if it does not invest itself in commitments to larger, more public, ethno-religious identities. It is this larger, more communal identity that leads then to a negotiation of rights with public institutions like the state and its agencies.

This all means that there are frameworks of rights intended to enlarge the ambit of human rationality and identity in the non-Western world, and that they do influence the behavior of the state. What this also means, though, is that these frameworks of rights act in ways that are completely missed by Kantian liberalism. The sense of self-identity to be enshrined in these systems of rights is focused on the need to express an allegiance to a broader ethnic or religious grouping, not an autonomous human identity distinct from that group. In fact, these ethno-religious identities might well be understood as a more valid, a more legitimate way of defining human identity and human nature.

It is these particular frameworks of rights – and this is the fundamental point – that often provide the basis for the claims addressed by the individual, and by society more broadly, to the state. The defense of ethno-religious interests and ideologies, to put it plainly, becomes a core preoccupation of the state, and this is seen as a most appropriate response of the state to – again – the legitimate demands of the individual. Furthermore, these demands are exercised through extra-constitutional channels of kinship and personal networks that give them an immediate and direct voice within policy circles. Ethno-religious concerns, in that context, are not marginal to public life. On the contrary, they *are* public life, a constant and inescapable point of focus for the activities of the state and for its relation to society. Moreover, the nature of international politics in the non-Western world is such that these ethno-religious demands are also exercised on the state from the outside. The spaces occupied by ethno-religious groups remain here, to use Ayoob's phrase once again, "both internal and external" to the state, as was shown in the previous section on realism. They often straddle borders established during the colonial era, or they even come to constitute what Nancy Fraser and others have termed "diasporic public spheres"[6] – social spaces where communal ties and identities are strong, but which do not correspond to the social spaces demarcated by sovereign states. In this international environment, ethno-religious demands for recognition will be addressed to the state from outside its borders, but in ways just as insistent as if they came from within its national space.

This is where there are factors present in the interrelationship between social systems of rights, on the one hand, and, on the other, state and inter-state behaviors – factors that bring added elements to the story told by Kantian liberalism. There are systems of individual rights in the non-Western world, and they do look a lot like the "paraphernalia of constitutionalism" found in the West: civil and political liberties achieved through a recognition of the rights and self-identity that should be ascribed to all human beings. There is, however, in addition to that, a sense that individual rights cannot be autonomous from more communal rights and that indeed individual rights are to be attained through the promotion of communal rights that escape the purview of the individual. These rights act at cross-purposes with those championed by liberalism: they work from a logic of differences between ethno-religious groups, instead of building on the postulate of the universality of human self-identity propounded by the liberals. The state, for its part, does feel constrained in its behavior by the rights and demands of the individual, as the liberal paradigm would have it. It is also quick to respond, however, to this language of communal rights and fundamental plurality of identity between human beings. It is these communal rights that inform in large part its behavior, either domestically or internationally. The state operates in an international environment where the promotion of these more communal and ethno-religious rights is bound to remain a core element of its foreign policy, given the presence of ethno-religious groups with which it identifies outside of its borders – groups that will require of the state that it concern itself with the defense of these sorts of rights on its international agenda.

What is missing from the liberal perspective in this context, then, is any grasp of the interplay between all these different elements. There is an understanding of rights and individual identity within Kantian liberalism, but one which focuses on a certain understanding of human self-identity and thus fails to acknowledge the other conceptions of self-identity, which are also at play in the way individuals define themselves and their relation to society and to the state in the non-Western world. The constant processes of negotiation, so to speak, between these different understandings of human self-identity, and the role that these processes play in evolving conceptions of human identity and human rights in the non-Western world are not part of the liberal outlook on these questions. How this fluid negotiation of self-identities then carries forward – in shifting demands addressed by the individual and by society to the state, some emanating from the "paraphernalia of constitutionalism," and others from extra-constitutional channels rooted in more ethnically or religiously driven self-identities – is also missing from that outlook. How the nature of the state in the non-Western world also influences, in turn, the state's responses to these different demands, and the extent to which each state will be allowed to drive its foreign policy agenda, are also neglected problems here. All these elements play within the liberal logic that connects systems of rights and state behavior, and yet they are not recognized by it. Without starting the analysis earlier, and without looking at how state and society came into their own in the non-Western world, these elements are bound to remain ignored in that logic.

Kantian liberalism misses these points. Kant, as was shown earlier, sets out in a series of major works the argumentation that still underlies this approach: the *Critique of Pure Reason*, which, along with the *Critique of Practical Reason*, asserts the primacy of rationality in human affairs; the *Idea for a Universal History from a Cosmopolitan Point of View*, dealing with the impact of human rationality on the nature of politics and political institutions; and *Perpetual Peace: A Philosophical Sketch*, a consideration of the impact of these reflections on understandings of the nature of international politics. In the two *Critiques*, he lays out the epistemological and normative considerations that place human rationality and human identity at the very core of liberalism. It is not "our knowledge [that] must conform" to the world, he says, it is instead the world "[that] must conform to our modes of cognition."[7] The way we think, the way we use our rationality as human beings, creates our world and gives it its character. And, Kant continues, it is the "determination of the will that alone makes maxims really moral and gives them a moral worth." This is what should be the "real incentive for action."[8] Our rationality gives us freedom of choice and behavior. Through the exercise of that freedom we can opt for individual and social choices that will make our world moral and good. Our rationality will push us ever further in that direction by allowing us to see that this moral world is in our grasp, precisely because of our inherent rationality and of the ability this gives us to shape our world. This will bring about a more moral world, because our rationality will compel us to recognize the rationality in others – this recognition of the rationality of all individuals will demonstrate the need to fashion our individual and social choices in ways that let us treat them in a respectful and moral manner precisely because of the rationality inherent in each of them.

The ontological postulates put forward by Kant – his vision of domestic and international politics – follow from these ideas. In *Idea for a Universal History from a Cosmopolitan Point of View* he notes how the search for rationality and morality, intrinsic to all individuals, will "force them to obey a will that is universally valid, and under which each can be free."[9] This is the search for a democratic social environment, which then must be supported by a state which itself will be democratic. "The history of mankind can be seen," Kant continues, "as the realization of Nature's secret plan to bring forth a perfectly constituted state as the only condition in which the capacities of mankind can be fully developed."[10] This ushers in his famous three articles in *Perpetual Peace*, where he explains that democracy will bring democratic states, which in turn will want to act democratically and morally on the international stage, which then will produce a democratic and moral international environment where the rights and rationality of all individuals will be recognized as a matter of course.

The sequence central to Kantian liberalism is thus set forth forcefully here: human rationality, which leads to democratic states, which then leads to peaceful and moral international politics. As was shown here before, people like Michael Doyle and the other proponents of the democratic peace theory follow in their work the same sequence of postulates – what Doyle calls the "Kantian road to peace."[11] An inner sense of the rationality that animates human beings and of the rights that follow from this rationality leads, Doyle tells us, to "habits of respect for individual rights"[12] in democratic social settings. This process triggers a push for states to behave in a way that respects such rights and the values espoused by citizens. Lastly, this situation brings about, in inter-state relations, an environment where contacts are marked by a search for "consensual and just [...] accommodation"[13] rather than by violence and the exercise of raw power. This sequence must also work, Doyle claims, outside the Western world. The democratic community, which is mainly based around Western countries, must enlarge the ambit of the "liberal zone of peace" there as well. This is to be done through a three-fold strategy of "inspiration, instigation, and intervention:[14] Western countries must "inspire" the people of the non-Western world to demand the protection of their human rights; they must "instigate" programs of legal and political reforms that will make non-Western states more responsive to these demands; and they must certainly consider "intervening," through force if necessary, if non-Western states themselves use violence to block the democratic aspirations of their citizens. Rights will emerge through that process as the core driver of politics in the non-Western world, states in turn will be compelled to respect these rights in their international behavior, and the non-Western world, then, will arrive at a model of international politics similar to the one which now prevails in the Western "liberal zone of peace."

The same logical sequence is found in the work of the proponents of "cosmopolitan democracy," who follow Kant through the implications of his writings on the nature of global politics and global governance. David Held talks about the "empowering rights and obligations" of individuals, which "cut across all [...] sites of power, whether rooted in politics, economics, or culture."[15] Pushed forward by these "rights and obligations," there should now be a movement toward a "cosmopolitan model of democracy"[16] where local, state, and global institutions will be moved at all times by the need to respect democratic rights. Richard Falk, for his part, looks at how "moral purpose and values" can usher in a "people-oriented model of politics" that will provide a "unifying ideology" for global politics.[17] In all the instances it is assumed that this should involve the non-Western world: rights "cut across all sites of power" and they bring all individuals throughout the entire world in that universal search for a democratic model of global governance.

What is left out here, then, when it comes to the non-Western world? First, Kantian liberalism assumes that rationality can always force the world to "conform" to it. In many such cases of violence and war, however, this might be going too far. As was shown here in the discussion of realism, rationality can sometimes be confronted by an "economy of violence" that restricts the ways in which it can be used to transform the world. This is one instance where liberalism repeats some of the oversights of realism.

But then what is missing in Kantian liberalism is also – and more importantly – the recognition of a sense of the self rooted in more communal ethnic or religious identities, and of the rights and demands which follow from these other definitions of the individual and from his position in the private–public continuum. Rights can be couched in a language of difference, not in one of identity shared among all human beings. It is these definitions of rights, absent from Kantian logic, that often inform the political constructs and state institutions of the non-Western world. This leads to another blind spot in the Kantian logic. These other definitions of rights often shape the international behavior of the state in the non-Western world as much as the notions of rights depicted by the liberals do; and yet this is not part of the liberal argumentation. In other words, the point is not that individual rights and demands for democratic domestic and international governance do not influence the behavior of states in the non-Western world. They do. The point is rather that there are other, dissimilar definitions of rights also at play in that process, and that the liberal logic cannot account for them or integrate them into its claims about international politics.

Can these issues, in that context, simply be incorporated into the Kantian logic? This is where the universalism at the core of the approach sets up formidable obstacles. Kantian liberalism operates within a language of universals. The "freedom of the will," Kant says in the *Idea for a Universal History from a Cosmopolitan Point of View*, is "determined by universal laws."[18] Human beings are rational, and this *a priori*[19] of human rationality exists outside of circumstances and social or political context. Rationality always gives humans "freedom" from the world and, indeed, it gives them the freedom to change that world. To put it differently, human beings cannot not be rational and free to change their world – this is a "universal law." This universality of reason then sets up, by way of consequence, the universality of the political possibilities opened up by rationality. We are all rational and, therefore, we can all recognize the rationality in all others. Building a good, a moral–political community centered on the mutual recognition of our common human rationality is thus always a possibility, irrespective, again, of circumstances and context. The universalism of Kant's ontology then follows from these postulates. We know that we can always expand the ambit of such communities from the domestic to the inter-state, and then to the global levels, because we know that we will be appealing to a combination of rationality, free will, and mutual respect, which is present at all times and everywhere in human beings.

It is from this universalism that contemporary Kantian liberals derive their certainty about the universality of their prescription. Doyle, because he gathers along the "Kantian road to peace" the assumptions about the universality of human rationality and morality contained in Kant's writings, can then assume that his advice about the enlargement of the "liberal zone of peace" to more global dimensions will always work. Held or Falk, because they take from Kant the idea that the rights and rationality of the individual "cut across all sites of power" and constitute a "global unifying ideology," can then assume that their prescriptions about global politics have universal validity.

This universalism prevents, however, the consideration of the issues raised here. One cannot argue that rationality is present as an *a priori* in all human beings, in all circumstances, and claim that human beings can always recognize each other's rationality and each other's rights, and then see how there are forms of self-identity and self rationality in the non-Western world that lead to a logic of communal ethnic and religious rights, which contradict, in fact, the notion of a shared universal human identity. One cannot maintain that the understanding of rights propounded by the liberals can always act as an agent of change in international politics in the way envisaged by Kantian liberalism, and then admit that there might be other definitions of rights in some parts of the world – definitions that act at cross-purposes from that process and push it in different directions from those imagined by Kant and his followers. Just as was the case with realism, in other words, the universalism underlying liberalism prevents the consideration of many of the issues that must be taken into account if the international politics of the non-Western world is to be fully understood.

Here again, Asia provides illustrations of these problems. Many have tried in recent years to move the security paradigm dominating the region away from its core focus on state security and closer to the sort of broader model suggested by the liberal approach. The concept of cooperative security was introduced in the region by academics and non-governmental groups as part of that process. Their goal was to institute a series of so-called "track-two" channels of diplomacy in the region, in contrast to the formal, or "track-one," diplomatic architecture. These more informal conduits between academics, business people, non-governmental organizations, and the like would allow for the international politics of Asia to be considered in a way that would not be limited to state-centric perspectives. In the long run, it was hoped, they would open up the foreign policy process of regional states to much wider inputs, which would allow the insertion of the security concerns of these different groups into the security discourse of their respective states.[20] The main framework through which this track-two approach progressed was the Council for Security Cooperation in the Asia Pacific (CSCAP), which remains active to this day.[21]

Moreover, to the notion of cooperative security was soon added the concept of human security. The idea, this time, was that track-two groups should make the promotion of the basic rights, well-being, and physical safety of the individual a key component of their vision of regional security. This was part of the wider reorientation of the global security discourse proposed in the mid-to-late 1990s by a multitude of actors – perhaps chiefly among them the Canadian government and a number of Canadian academics.[22] The basic assumption underlying this project was that the conflicts of the post–Cold War era had to do, most fundamentally, with conditions of injustice, poverty, and violence affecting the individual. Social dislocation, widespread famine, or endemic destitution, for instance, were much more likely to cause conflicts than inter-state rivalries. It was precisely these factors, in fact, that could now lead to war: civil unrest or ethnic strife, for instance, could always be expected to expand beyond state boundaries and to create tensions and conflict between neighboring states. The answer was to make the safety of the individual the cornerstone of international security: if the security of the individual was ensured through a web of institutions and rights guaranteeing his freedom, safety, and advancement in a just and democratic environment, then the tensions most likely to lead to international conflict would subside. Human security, in a word, was a prerequisite to international security. It is this argument that, today, offers the proponents of human security in Asia the main line of the reasoning they use in their critique of the pre-eminence of the notion of comprehensive security in the Asian diplomatic and security discourse.[23]

This draws heavily from Kantian liberalism. Track-two groups contend that international politics in Asia should not be structured only around the needs and concerns of the state. The social level and that of the individual should be prime considerations in the conduct of international affairs. Indeed these groups have created numerous channels of interaction and debate with so-called "track-three" networks – civil society organizations and human rights groups – in order to portray themselves as proper representatives of the will and concerns of broad segments of the population in many Asian states.[24] That project is most often guided by the agenda encapsulated in the notion of human security – which shows that the rights and security of the individual speak to a much more profound source of legitimacy than the rights and security of the state, and that international politics, if it is to be legitimate itself, must draw from the former rather than from the latter.

However, none of these groups – and this is the key point – would suggest that the pursuit of this agenda can totally abstract itself from the issues raised here. Rizal Sukma, for instance, is one of the most astute participants in these track-two exchanges. He notes that "human security cannot be achieved without [...] a degree of political stability."[25] Putting the individual at the center of the domestic and international behavior of the state requires, before this is accomplished, that the conditions allowing the individual to be a politically salient site of power already be in place. If, as an example, violence remains the only true currency of power within the state, the notion of agency of the individual and the idea that this agency carries with it a potent form of political power will not carry much weight. Pressing the notions of individual rights and power enshrined in the concept of human security will not, in that context, resonate strongly enough to force political change in that direction.

To push the argument further, there are conditions of political development and "stability" that are necessary to any progress toward human security and, more broadly, to the realization of the goals entailed by Kantian liberalism. This is what is meant by Mely Caballero-Anthony, another observer of these track-two discussions, when she speaks of the need to bring discussions of human security "into a coherent security framework."[26]

Simply talking about human security leaves one blind to some of the conditions which are essential to the introduction and implementation of the concept in the international politics of Asia. Civil society, in a context like that of Asia, must look at the nature of the state in the region, its current makeup and its past trajectory of development, and it must engage state actors accordingly, if it is to move forward. Civil society, in a word, must help build the sort of state that will then be able to engage civil society.

Another issue is that the image guiding these track-two groups is not merely that of a unified democratic civil society at the domestic level, which connects to other democratic forces through a regional transnational civil society and then forces the state, through pressures from above and from below, to abide by the values and rights it upholds. Looking at Southeast Asia, for instance, one sees different sorts of democratic civil societies. The nature of democracy in a country like, say, Malaysia cannot be understood without immediate reference to the extent to which democratic institutions there are deeply interwoven with the ethnic and ethno-religious identities of the ethnic Malays against the Chinese and Indian population. The character of democracy in Indonesia, to give another example, cannot be studied without looking at the importance of Islam in shaping the nature of democratic identities, which are to be protected and expressed by the state. The identity of the democratic individual pressing for the further development of democratic institutions does not stand aside from these other forms of ethnic or communal identities. Quite to the contrary, in fact: these different forms of identity are intertwined, or each reinforces the other.[27] This means that, when the state engages democratic groups on issues of security and rights, it is those forms of democracy that will be at play. The state can, for instance, openly favor entrenched Malay identities in its reading of the security *problématique* affecting the country – in its discourse on, say, who constitutes a threat and why – and yet it may still argue that it is responding to pressures and forms of identity widely and democratically recognized as legitimate.

This is where the tensions with Kantian liberalism become most evident. The state in Southeast Asia is often faced now with democratic pressures driving it toward new forms of international action, more clearly articulated on the promotion and defense of liberal values. This much matches the liberal logic. What must also be understood, however, is that, within these democratic pressures, the state can also still favor different forms of non-liberal ethnic and ethno-religious identities, which are very much a part of the democratic identity defended by individuals and civil society groups in their relationship with the state. And this, in turn, will often push the state toward forms of behavior that will remain at odds with the liberal logic. This is the problem that needs to be recognized, track-two groups in Southeast Asia would argue, if one wants to grasp how states in the region actually respond to democratization within their borders and to the pressures it puts on them to behave, at the international level, in a way that is consonant with liberal assumptions. Liberalism as it is formulated now, however, cannot integrate these issues within its own logic.

This brings the discussion to the second fundamental component in the liberal approach: the liberalism propounded by Smith and his followers, which is based on the idea that it is market dynamics, rather than any other type of social relations, that constitutes the dominant factor now shaping the nature and evolution of international politics. Smith's liberalism, as was seen before, is a response to realism, but also to Kantian liberalism. Like all forms of liberalism, it questions realism and asks whether it is true or not that issues of violence and inter-state competition must always remain the crux of all international relations. It distances itself from Kantian liberalism, however, by assuming that there is a structural component to the full expression of human rationality and freedom. There must be, as we saw Smith put it earlier, an "impartial spectator,"[28] who will guarantee that the freedom and rationality of everyone is ensured at all times. This is what the market can accomplish: it can impose conditions that force all individuals to respect the freedom and rationality of all others. Because the market will then speak to a level of individual and social legitimacy which can only supersede the artificial machinations of governments and politicians, it will be seen by all as the better arbiter of social relations, in opposition to the state and to any political and social agenda that state actors might champion. This is why, in the long term, market relations are bound to displace inter-state relations as the primary point of reference in international affairs for an ever-growing number of individuals and societies. In turn, this can be expected to produce an international environment where the common interest in peaceful and rational economic exchanges brought on by the market will largely replace the violence and divisiveness associated with a more state-driven perspective. To this day, this is the case argued by the followers of Smith, from the functionalists to the more recent proponents of complex interdependence.

Does this really capture what goes on in the non-Western world? In the first instance, it should be noted that the remarks made about Kantian liberalism a moment ago are also pertinent here. Smith's logic assumes a constant and mutual recognition of a common rationality and identity among all human beings. Each of us, Smith believes, recognizes the rationality of all others. This is how we know for sure that a system like the market, which operates precisely through this mutual recognition of the freedom and rationality of all individuals, will work. The image, in this perspective, is that of a seamless terrain where identical rationalities extend from the local to the national and then to the global level: we are all rational in the same fashion, and we all know that all others also know it. This is why, if we let mechanisms like the market draw on our common rationality, we can build ever expanding communities, which will not be hampered by the more artificial and irrational antagonisms entailed by the state system. What the consideration of Kantian liberalism presented above demonstrates, however, is that this image misses much of the nature of self-rationality and self-identity in the non-Western world. Any sense of the self in those parts of the world, as was explained, is often hard to detach from broader ethno-religious constructs that instill the belief in a plurality of self-rationalities and self-identities in human beings as they relate to each other, whether in their own states or across borders. It is the tensions, the sense of profound differences between varied human communities created by these more communal identities that will persistently shape much of the way in which individuals perceive their relationship with others. It is, then, this understanding of the self and others that will enter into the construction of market relations and of their use in international politics. When Smith and his followers imagine a seamless mutual recognition of identical self-rationalities throughout all social spaces, and when they go from there to a conceptualization of the market and of state–market relations, they fail to acknowledge this point.

A second problem concerns the one element that Smith's liberalism adds to the discussion – its understanding of the market – and how many realities this particular understanding of market forces overlooks when the non-Western world is at stake. There is, quite plainly, an enormous literature explaining how market dynamics unfold from the perspective of the non-Western world. It is certainly possible, though, to divide that literature according to the two central issues which it aims to underscore. The first issue is the series of processes through which the economies of the non-Western world have been integrated into the global economy, most notably during the colonial period, and the impact of these phenomena on the nature of market dynamics in that part of the world today. The so-called Dependency School has been the most closely associated with these questions. The classic work associated with this approach is *Dependency and Development in Latin America*, by Cardoso and Faletto.[29] Although, as is made clear by the title, the focus of this work was the relationship of Latin American countries to global economy, it set in motion a vast intellectual reflection on the dynamics of economic development of the non-Western world itself. The work of Peter Evans – most notably his *Dependent Development* – is perhaps the clearest example of this process.[30] The basic claims made by the Dependency School are usefully summarized by Stephan Haggard when he suggests that

> two underlying theoretical assumptions characterize work in the dependency tradition. First, the international economy is conceived as a hierarchically ordered system of dominance. As in a stratified social system, various mechanisms, both political and economic, exist through which inequality is reproduced. Second, the character of the periphery's development has largely been of function of the way in which it was incorporated into the international division of labor. This "postulate of

external dominance" holds that external factors are responsible for the distortions that characterize the economies of the developing world.[31]

No matter what theoretical perspective one might care to adopt, the claim is made here, a crucial point cannot be denied: many of the economic transformations that brought non-Western countries within the ambit of the world economy were instigated and sustained not from within these societies, but from the outside, by the colonial powers as they extended their control over the "periphery's development" and integrated it into an "international division of labor." This division of labor forced non-Western countries to focus their development on certain economic sectors – exports of food like coffee or fruits, for example, or of raw materials like timber – where demand and prices are still most often controlled by the West. This means that the development of peripheral countries, to this day, cannot be understood outside of their amalgamation within this much broader global economic architecture, which regulates prices, consumer demand, and trade patterns – and, in truth, outside of their dependence on it. Moreover, this global architecture is maintained in place by a series of "mechanisms, both political and economic," ranging from international financial and banking institutions to trade and exchange barriers operated by the large Western economies, which sustain a "hierarchically ordered system of dominance" greatly more aligned with the interests of the West than with those of the non-Western world. There is thus, in the latter, a "postulate of external dominance" – a constant appreciation that the market, exactly as was the case with the state, was created in the non-Western world from the outside, and was, in a way, intended to address the needs and interests of outside actors rather than those of local populations.

These writings have sparked, in counterpoint, the growth of a literature concerned with the second central problem considered in the works devoted to the economics of the non-Western world: how is development in fact possible in the conditions of "external dominance" painted by Dependency theory? The answer given has had to do, more often than not, with the relationship between the state and the market, and more generally between politics and economics in the non-Western world. The names of Peter Evans and Stephan Haggard can surely be mentioned in this context again,[32] precisely because the intent of both was to add to the dependency paradigm the notions of political will and choice, which are marginalized in that literature. Most of the work, though, came out of studies specifically devoted to the so-called East Asian miracle, because the spectacular development of countries like Japan or South Korea in the post–World War II period raised with the greatest acuity, it seemed, the questions of how development was possible at the periphery of the West and what role exactly a strong centralized state could play in the development process. The work of Frederic C. Deyo is emblematic of that literature, his published collection

The Political Economy of the New Asian Industrialism[33] being probably his best-known work, although others, for instance his *Dependent Development and Industrial Order: An Asian Case Study*,[34] also stand out.

This is where, evidently, the discussion connects to the idea that Asia can provide examples of some of the issues discussed in this text. The key point of entry into the process of development studied in this literature is the success of the export-oriented industrialization strategy pursued in the post-war period by states like Japan, South Korea, and Taiwan. This strategy was centered, as Richard E. Barrett and Soomi Chin put it in the collection edited by Deyo, "on rapid growth in volume of trade and especially of manufactured exports relative to growth in gross domestic product."[35] The idea was to focus production on certain sectors – the automobile and electronics sector, for example, in the case of Japan; to support them through a series of protectionist and fiscal measures; and then to carry out sustained policies of expansion of these sectors on foreign markets. But the crucial point, made time and again in that literature, is that this was, above all, a strategy: a machinery had to be in place with the power to implement and enforce this economic agenda and with the social and political sway to have it accepted by most segments of society. This is where an analysis of the state and of its relationship with society at large and with the market comes into play within this literature, to explain the sort of economic development witnessed in East Asia since World War II.

Three factors are usually brought to light in this sort of analysis. First, there is what Bruce Cumings calls the relationship of the state and market in "world time."[36] A strong state must be there to engineer the series of protectionist measures needed in order to foster the growth of the different sectors targeted for expansion and to modulate the influx of foreign investments funds necessary to finance the intensification of production in these sectors. This requires that a coherent and far-reaching bureaucratic apparatus be in place before foreign multinationals and foreign investment capital implant themselves within the national economy. Therefore it matters a great deal where the state stands, "in world time," within the broader trajectory of the development and movement of global financial and trade flows. A second factor is the nature of the relationship between state, industry, and finance within the national space. The state must be able to control fiscal and financial levers in order to establish a sustainable policy of subsidization of certain industrial sectors; and this entails, in turn, the centralization and coordination of financial institutions and industrial conglomerates under mechanisms dominated by the state. Chalmers Johnson, for instance, has shown to great effect how the success of the Japanese economy in the post-war period was predicated on a truly national form of planning, where the state created coalitions of interests with financial institutions and centralized industrial conglomerates (the famed *zaibatsu*),[37] and then steered them through the different phases of Japan's economic development. A third factor is the nature of the relationship between the state and, this time, society at large. The state, in the context just described, will build its legitimacy mainly on its ability to deliver economic development to its population. Legitimacy, then, will not be defined in terms of the capacity of the state to respond to popular demands and to embody the will of the majority. On the contrary, the state will want to be seen as excluding itself from the movement to and fro of various social and political interest groups, in order to be able to claim that it responds only to economic imperatives for the greater benefit of the national economy, which it is supposed to defend above all else.[38]

Where this all matters for the argument presented in this book is in the way the images of the market and state which come out of this sort of analysis are completely at odds with the ones contained in the liberal literature. For the liberals, the market is the vehicle through which the freedom of the individual and that of society can be built and defended against the dominance of the state. Here, on the contrary, the market does not exist in opposition to the state, but as an extension of it. Economic development is a function of the situation of the state in "world time" within global financial, trade, and production patterns. Economic actors derive their strength from the extent to which they conform to state-sponsored and state-driven strategies of growth. The state, in its interaction with the market, does not find itself confronted with a popular will, built out of the free expression of individuals and socials groups. On the contrary, it uses the degree to which it is embedded in the economy so as to reduce the space opened to the expression of democratic freedoms. Indeed it defines its very legitimacy through its ability to ignore social priorities other than those which are closely aligned with the imperatives of economic development. The importance of each of these elements will obviously change from one part to the next within the non-Western world. The roles of the state emphasized in the literature on East Asia only point, quite evidently, to factors that should be studied if development in Latin America or Africa is to be understood with some insight.[39] The importance of these factors will also change, of course, over time. To take an example, the role of the state in Japanese economy is certainly not what it used to be twenty years ago. The fundamental issue, though, is that any analysis of the interaction between the state and the market in the non-Western world is impossible without at least a consideration of the elements just raised, and that the liberal perspective, because of its assumptions about the state and the market, cannot enter into this type of study and remain coherent within its own logic.

This means, in turn, that liberalism can only be uncertain of the veracity of its argumentation when it uses its understanding of the market and of the state to build a set of claims about international politics, and then tries to apply these claims to the non-Western world. The cornerstone of the whole liberal literature inspired by Smith – the notion that the market creates a realm of human freedom, which stands apart from the vagaries of state-driven politics and can influence their evolution – is bound to miss much here, because the understandings of the state and of the market it brings together in its logic are themselves erroneous, or offer a poor fit with the realities of the non-Western world. Also, as was seen earlier, the other component in that equation, the understanding of a human rationality, which underlies the entire liberal line of analysis, overlooks many of the features of human self-rationality and self-identity in the non-Western world. In this perspective, the whole logical sequence followed by Smith and his followers – human rationality, which leads to the market, which then leads to a certain type of international politics – must then be handled with extreme prudence in the non-Western world.

The issue, moreover, is that the liberalism of Smith and his contemporary followers does not have within its own set of claims the instruments allowing it to resolve these problems. For Smith, as was shown in the first part of the book, the nature of human self-identity and human rationality is immutable. We all know what it is because we all possess it, and we all know that all others around us also do. As human beings, we share, as Smith said in a passage from the *Theory of Moral Sentiments* quoted earlier, "a general fellow-feeling which we have with every other man, merely because he is our fellow creature."[40] This is why all we need to regulate our interactions is an "impartial spectator" – something or someone who will not interfere, but in fact will facilitate, the free expression of our rationality and our mutual recognition that each of us has the right, before anything else, to this unfettered expression of our intrinsic rationality. The market provides such an impartial structure. It enforces our freedom: it compels us to act on the basis of our free volition and choices, and it forces us to recognize the right of all others to act in the same way. The famed "invisible hand" of the market will, of course, drive each individual to pursue as fiercely as possible his own interest. It is, however, precisely this pursuit, by each one of us, of our individual interest that will make the market work as an instrument of freedom and rationality: my constant search for what is best for me will be the most palpable demonstration there can be that I live in a system that allows me to act according to my rationality and free will, and that each individual living with me in that system is accorded the same freedom.

It is on the basis of these arguments that Smith then turns to the relationship between the market and the state. There is a connection between human rationality and self-identity and the market, Smith contends, which simply cannot be duplicated by the relationship between the individual and the state. By its nature, the market embodies the most common and basic rationality of all individuals. On the contrary, states and governments, also by their very nature, proceed from an attempt to control human rationality according to the wishes and interests of the select few who wield political power at any given time. This is why the market is natural and legitimate, and the state, unnatural and illegitimate. We know this to be true because our experience of the world – the free exercise of our individual will, which we witness in the market economy and see kept in check by the state and its agencies – tells us every day that it is. We also know that this speaks to an even greater moral truth: the social institutions which protect human rationality and freedom are superior to those which do not, and the market is thus inherently better, more principled, and more just than the state in that regard. What choices are best for the individual, Smith says in the *Wealth of Nations*, "he can judge much better than any statesman or lawgiver can do for him."[41] This tells us, finally, why we should strive for an international order, built on the workings of the market rather than on those of the state. The market can help build an international life that draws its energy and purpose from the rationality, freedom, and hence legitimacy it can bring to bear on inter-state affairs. The state, for its part, can only deny these aspirations in its self-driven and unrelenting quest for power on the global stage.

As we also saw earlier, this is, as well, the route followed by later proponents of functionalism and complex interdependence in order to arrive at the idea that market forces can change international politics. Ernst B. Haas, one of the leading exponents of these notions, argued that functionalists "are interested in identifying those aspects of human needs and desires that exist and clamor for attention outside the realm of the political."[42] There is a human identity, a primordial structure of "needs and desires," which exists on its own, "outside the realm of the political." These "commonly experienced"[43] needs and desires are best expressed in the economic realm, "outside" of the "political," because it is there that individuals can truly act according to their own volition and self-interests. In turn, this brings about a recognition – in the words of David Mitrany, the other leading figure of the functionalist literature – that there are "common habits and interests," which are felt through this engagement in the market and which entail the "natural growth of common activities and common administrative agencies."[44] The freedom afforded to all by the market is thus enshrined in the construction of a social order supported by "activities and agencies" intended, precisely, to protect the freedom of all in society. This is a "natural growth" and it happens simply because of the very nature of human needs and through the necessity that all individuals feel to build a social order which respects and protects these needs.

This worldview, then, shapes the perspective of this literature on the state and the character of current international politics. The state, as Robert O. Keohane and Joseph S. Nye put it, is now overtaken by "multiple channels which connect societies" through the expansion of the market and the array of administrative agencies set up to regulate its global reach.[45] This interdependence at the social and human level is brought about by the pressures and movements of the economy. It exposes a common humanity, formed by shared interests and needs. This common humanity, in turn, undermines the legitimacy of the state and of the divisions it creates between human beings. International politics, in that sense, cannot remain caught up in these divisions. As Mitrany puts it, in this "lies the prospect [...] of making frontiers meaningless"[46] and of forging a global humanity able to move slowly beyond the state-driven conflicts of the past.

It is the very nature of these claims, however, that prevents them from capturing the realities of non-Western international politics underscored here. The engine which drives the entire line of reasoning within this literature is the notion that there is a basic common identity, which is always apparent to all of us as human beings. This is Smith's "general fellow-feeling which we have with every other man," echoed in the contemporary literature by Haas' notion of "human needs and desires" that are evident to any observer once we abstract the artifices of the "political realm." It is because of this common human identity, mutually recognized by all individuals, that the idea of the market then makes sense: we know that everyone is alike, we also know that everyone knows this, and we can thus build a system which will work because of this mutually recognized need to express our common identity and aspirations. The problem, though, is that thinking this way cannot coexist with the inquiry into the construction of human identity, which is needed, as was said earlier, to understand the international politics of the non-Western world. One cannot, in all logic, believe that human identity is inherently set in all human beings, and then ask about the political and social processes through which identity is developed and about how this can lead in fact to different self-understandings of human identity. More to the point, this line of thinking certainly cannot allow the idea that such self-understandings of human identity may lead to very stringent and harsh divisions among human beings, divisions of the sort found in the non-Western world because of the importance of ethno-religious affiliations in the makeup of individual self-identity. One cannot assume that individuals will always recognize in each other a common identity, a "general fellow-feeling," and then ask how this correlates with definitions of human identity which, as a central part of their configuration, negate that common identity between different social groups.

The same problem arises with the conceptualization of the market, which is at the core of this literature. For Smith and his contemporary followers, the market is different from all other social institutions because it is the only one that is crafted from the free exercise of human rationality. It is merely an "impartial spectator," meant only to facilitate the expression of the individual's will and rationality. Its power is put into effect through an "invisible hand," which helps and pushes the individual forward as she seeks to fulfill her self-interest. This is in opposition to the state, which is far from being "impartial" or "invisible" in the pursuit of its own narrow and politically charged interests, and thus stands in the way of the free expression of the individual's rationality and self-interest. This is what the contemporary proponents of this approach take from the canon established by Smith: a sense that the market creates a zone of autonomy for the individual, where she can act according to a rationality and a set of interests which she herself defines, at a distance from the broader and more contrived agenda pursued by the state. It is there, "outside the political," that a commonality of "needs and desires" among all human beings can become apparent and serve as the rallying cry for the construction of a global human community, unhindered by the divisions and conflicts created by the state.

These claims, though, overlook what was said earlier about the nature of the market in the non-Western world. However distant or close one might choose to be vis-à-vis the literature on dependency, the fact remains that it poses questions which at least must be raised when one considers the dynamics of development outside the Western world: to what extent is development controlled by outside actors and institutions with their own interests, rather than the non-Western world, at the center of their preoccupations? In what measure, then, can the market in the non-Western world be defined through a language of autonomy, self-interest, and self-identity? The liberal literature cannot begin to consider these questions, in spite of their importance. One cannot see the market as resulting from the interaction of autonomous and free wills, and also enquire about the degree to which it is the reverse – a space where autonomy is denied and self-interest is suppressed. Furthermore, one cannot think of the market as constructed from the inside, so to speak, from the interplay of free individual wills that make it come alive, and then also believe that the market is in fact constructed from the outside, through the action of more structural forces which stand above the purview of the will and rationality of the individuals caught in its development.

The same can be said about the understanding of the state prevalent in the liberalism inspired by Smith. For Smith, the market drains power and legitimacy away from the state. We want the life that the market gives to us much more than the repressed freedom and meager autonomy that the state allows us to enjoy, and we thus question the legitimacy of the state as much as we emphasize that of the market. This is also a notion that resonates to this day in the current liberal literature on these questions. It is in our economic life much more than in our political one, many contemporary authors suggest, that we are able to express freely our identity and self-interest. Over time, it is thus in the economic realm, and not in the political one, that we will want to build our lives and social affiliations and to imbue them with a legitimacy superior to that we reserve for the state and the social identities it creates. This is where Keohane and Nye, for instance, talk about the "multiple channels which connect societies" and question, in the process, the ruptures between these societies generated by the actions of states. All these ideas, however, are difficult to reconcile with the arguments just outlined with regard to the nature of the state in the non-Western world.

Models of development outside the Western world often make for a situation where the state itself is part of the market: it is through the guidance exercised by the state bureaucracy that economic activity develops and expands. Also, the state, more frequently than not, defines its legitimacy and power precisely through its ability to deliver economic development to its population. Thinking in terms of a market that stands opposed to the state and offers a zone of autonomy from its power does not allow one to investigate how the exact reverse is often happening in the non-Western world, and how the state and the market are often intertwined. Moreover, assuming that the market creates a new realm of legitimacy, which stands opposed to the one inhabited by the state, totally overlooks the ways in which the legitimacy of the market in the non-Western world often adds to the state's legitimacy and power, instead of subtracting from it.

Is it possible for liberalism simply to take these problems on board within its own argumentation? The problem, in this case again, is that there is an inherent universalism in this literature, which precludes its fully considering these problems if it is to remain coherent with itself. This universalism, as was shown before, is ingrained in the ontological, epistemological, and normative claims made by Smith and his followers. In terms of ontology, the nature of human identity is assumed to be fixed. It is inscribed in what makes us human beings, and it is always recognized as such through the "general fellow-feeling we have with every other man." The nature of the market, then, is also immutable. It is always the same because the forces that constitute it, the thirst for freedom and rationality to be found in all individuals, always remain the same themselves and are always bound to come together in this one mutual agreement – that all they need to guide their interaction is an "impartial spectator," which will both recognize and safeguard this universal thirst for freedom and rationality. Smith's epistemology follows from these considerations. We can know that what he says is true, he tells us, because our own experience of the world will always bring us to conclusions which are similar to his own. "Our continual observations upon the conduct of others," he informs us in the *Wealth of Nations*, "insensibly lead us to form to ourselves certain general rules concerning what is fit and proper either to be done or to be avoided."[47] I will want to express my freedom and rationality, and I will come to expect, "in the conduct of others," the sort of behavior that will allow me to do that. This will lead me "insensibly," without a reflection deeper than that provided by my need for freedom and the corresponding requirement for a social framework which respects this need, to the market, in the same way that Smith's reflection also led him to an embrace of market dynamics. We can know that these are "general rules" because our own personal encounters with society, our own "continual observations of others," will always lead us to them. Finally, the normative component of Smith's argumentation is also part of these claims. The market is morally good for him, because it is the direct and unmediated expression of the most evident of moral goods, the unbound expression of human rationality and freedom – it will always be good because it will always express these elements. And this will lead, then, to a relationship between the individual, the market, and the state, which will always be the same. The market will always appear moral and natural to the individual, and the state, in comparison, will not. This is how we can know that the market will always win more adherents and, by way of consequence, we can question the validity and legitimacy of the state.

More contemporary proponents of this logic follow it to the same conclusions. We all have "needs and desires," as Haas puts it, which we know are basic and natural to each of us. The market is constructed by these "needs and desires," and it will thus always possess the same fundamental qualities, because it springs from realities which are themselves unchanging and universal. The most central of these qualities, the ability of the market to promote human freedom, will then always make it a preferred alternative to those other institutions, like the state, which restrict or deter the individual's freedom and self-interest. One element always leads to the next in this sequence. It is this inevitable logic that allows us to believe that the interaction between individuals, markets, and states will induce at all times the changes in international politics studied in various configurations of functionalism, of complex interdependence, and of the commercial peace thesis. This is why, for instance, Haas can say that his work and that of those who also espouse its logic point to the construction of a "true world community"[48] – the dynamics he underscores can only, by their very nature, speak to universal truths and to the politics of the "world community."

As was shown earlier, the ontological, epistemological, and normative underpinnings of these claims also mirror Smith's own set of assumptions. We know that these claims encapsulate a global truth, because they stem from fixed realities – the individual's self-interest and his need to pursue that self-interest as freely as possible – which remain prevalent wherever in the world one might care to open up the analysis. We know that the rules and principles pointed out in this literature are universally correct, because they follow logically from what cannot be doubted in any context: our own need, as individuals, to promote our self-interest, and the recognition that all others around us can only feel the same way. This is Haas' idea that his theories are built upon what is "commonly experienced"[49] by all of us, in parallel with Smith's contention that the truth of his work is demonstrated by our "continual observation" of ourselves and others. And we also know, finally, how universal the morality of these theories is, because they connect directly to the most fundamental and natural aspirations of all human beings throughout the globe.

There is in this literature, therefore, a sequence extending from the individual to the market and then to the state, which cannot be changed. It corresponds to postulates which are assumed to have universal value and which thus cannot be modified and made to take into account the other approaches and realities underscored here in the discussion of non-Western international politics. One cannot hope to substitute, in that sense, the understandings of individual identity or of market and state realities discussed here for those contained in that sequence, because its very logic militates against such an exchange.

6
The Construction of Difference in International Affairs

What about the two other approaches that have framed the development of international studies in recent years – constructivism and post-Marxism? How well do they sum up the character of international politics in the non-Western world? After all, the status of these more recent approaches is different from that of those that have been considered so far in this part of the book. They are meant, precisely, to capture what is specific and unique to the different contexts of space, time, and historical and social circumstances in which international life manifests itself. Both perspectives, as was shown earlier, were developed to counter the universalism of realism and liberalism. Their key goal is to show that international politics can only be understood through a logic of the particular, which underscores how contingent international politics always remains. Do these approaches give us, then, the tools necessary to understand the specificity of international politics in the non-Western world? And, if they fail to do this, what follows from that situation? To what extent can we find, in international studies, a language of the particular that will allow us to address the specificity of international politics in the non-Western world?

The first approach that should be considered in this light is constructivism. The approach, as was explained in the first part of the book, assembles its core claims from three sets of arguments. First, it draws on post-modernism. Writers like Foucault and Derrida are used to demonstrate the degree to which the world exists through the meanings we assign to it. Social realities are not given, but rather constructed and reconstructed constantly, through the changing processes of thought and discourse with which we constitute these realities, invest legitimacy in them, or instead question their worth and power. Epistemology precedes ontology: the choices we make, what we opt to emphasize or marginalize in our engagement with the world we inhabit will shape that world. The state, then, and the inter-state realm, someone like Rob Walker will argue, can be seen as the result of an often unquestioned sequence of assumptions and discourses about the nature of sovereignty, politics, and the like. These assumptions, however, can be questioned and recast, and this can set in motion a reappraisal and reconstitution of the very nature of international politics. In this case, again, epistemology can drive ontological change: a new way of looking at these issues can reorient their very nature.

A second set of arguments also underlies constructivism, and it is drawn this time from Habermasian critical theory. The recasting of social realities, Habermas contends, is indeed possible through the critique of existing discourses and logics of the social. This critique, though, will always remain embedded in the structures of dialogue through which we come to formulate it. Communicative rationality, to use his phrase, makes change possible; but it also frames the conditions in which that critique will be considered, as well as the strategies and goals associated with it. To put it differently, change is an inter-subjective process, and it cannot escape the limits brought to bear on it by the different sorts of rationalities and self-identities that enter into it. Habermas also wants to underscore, though, that this inter-subjective process of dialogue and confrontation is bound to uncover points of convergence as much as points of divergence. A common humanity, a collective human identity, will emerge in that context, which will then guide the construction of new social forms, which are more democratic and legitimate because they stand closer to that underlying shared humanity in all of us. He clearly connects, there, with Kant's views. Andrew Linklater and others, as was shown before, bring these arguments to international studies. As citizens of different states, we participate in the dialogues, as well as in the clashes of identities and rationalities, which are a function of inter-state relations. This process of interface between different citizenries and communities, however, can lead to something else. We can use it to bring to light the shared humanity and rationality that unites us all as human beings, and we can then build on this recognition of our common humanity, to reevaluate the divisions and conflicts entailed by the state system. We can thus, in truth, reinvent international life, to make it more democratic and rational and more closely aligned with our shared humanity.

The chief architect of constructivism, Wendt, then adds a third element to complete the sequence of arguments at the center of the paradigm. This is realism and, in particular, its focus on the state. Wendt contends that the realists are correct when they argue that the state always remains an actor in international politics. Its ability to control violence, wage war, and manage resources endows it with agency, the ability to operate in the world in ways that cannot be ascribed to the prior developments that gave rise to it. This is where it is ontology's turn to determine epistemology. It is "not ideas all the way down," as Wendt says. The state cannot be unraveled away in terms of the discourses and presuppositions underlying it, because it has a sway of its own, which escapes these other factors. The state has a reality, an ontological presence, which limits and shapes the changes that can be brought to bear on it by movements in the world of ideas. A middle way, a *via media*, must therefore be found. Ideas and discourses do shape the nature of international politics, as post-modernism and Habermasian critical theory would have it. They shape how states define their own identity, the identity of other states, and the nature of the international relations entailed by both of these elements. This does not mean, however, that the state disappears entirely in the world of ideas: it has its specific existence, which sets limits to what changes in ideas can do to it.

At the mid-point of these arguments, then, a new picture of international politics emerges. States, of course, remain pivotal actors in international affairs. The nature of their relationships, however, and by extension the very character of the international realm are never fixed. The state and social identities informing international behavior are malleable, the discourses and assumptions about the essential features of international life can be modi-fied, and changes at these levels can imbue international politics with an entirely new character. A movement away from a politics of conflict and toward a recognition of common aspirations and common rationality is pos-sible. That is why this literature insists so much on this aspect of socialization in international politics. The nature of international life is not set, but rather constructed and changed through an eminently social process, whereby the assumptions, discourses, and identities that drive international affairs are internalized by states and other actors. This is why, moreover, this literature is adamant that international politics should not be depicted in terms of universals, but rather in terms of particulars. International life is contingent, changing, and can never exist outside the circumstances of identity and dis-course through which it arises. It is only by studying these circumstances that one will be able to understand it.

To what extent, though, does this line of thinking allow a perceptive understanding of the international politics of the non-Western world? The first problem is that this approach, like the ones considered before, uses other bodies of literature in international studies as the starting point of its own argumentation. The series of lacunæ present in these other seg-ments of the literature when it comes to the non-Western world are thus in turn duplicated in these writings. This is particularly the case here because post-modernism, Habermasian critical theory, and finally constructivism are, more than anything else, responses to the arguments contained in mainstream international studies. The ambit of the questions they ask is circumscribed by the problems they find in these mainstream approaches. What is missing in those more mainstream approaches with regards to the non-Western world is thus also lacking in their own analyses.

The post-modern literature, which sets in motion the logical sequence that culminates with constructivism, starts with one simple claim. Our world is constituted through the ideas we have of it, this literature argues, and through the meanings we assign to it. If we change our way of thinking, we can also change our world. The violence that is at the core of so much of international politics, for instance, can be rethought when it comes to our understanding of its place in the international realm, and become much more marginal than it is now. However, the key point, as was shown before, is that this notion, that human rationality can always influence the nature of violence around it or even do away with violence, follows from a particular series of developments. A specific "economy of violence" must be in place for this to be possible. These developments are not always present in the non-Western world, which in turn undermines some of the validity of the approach.

The second movement in the constructivist logic draws on Habermasian critical theory. The crucial claim, in this context, is that human beings enter into inter-subjective dialogues, which carry the accumulated differences of identity and perspective entailed by the diversity of the human experience, but which also push them to recognize in each other a common rationality and identity. This is where Kantian liberalism is reintroduced in the constructivist literature. We are divided by our allegiances to states, but we can find strategies of engagement with each other that will celebrate, rather than deny, the shared human spirit traversing all political demarcations. Cooperation and mutual understanding, in that sense, can become the norm in international affairs. As was shown in the discussion of Kantian liberalism, though, matters of self-identity and self-rationality in the non-Western world frequently escape that sort of logic. The line between the identity of the self and communal ethno-religious identities often remains ambiguous, and this leads to a sense of self-identity that cannot be disentangled from communal affiliations. The confrontation of these communal identities, then, does not reveal a prior and shared human rationality. It merely reinforces, on the contrary, the recognition of fundamental differences between human groups and the absence of an underlying human identity common to all of them. It is this denial of human universality, as was also shown, which then informs the construction of understandings of international politics. Kantian liberalism overlooks these issues. As Habermasian critical theory and the literature in international studies it has inspired develop further the Kantian argumentation, then, they replicate the same mistake and fail to address these questions.

The last element within the sequence of claims leading to the constructivist worldview is Wendt's return to the state. Wendt gives that much to the realist: the state does exist on its own, as an agent distinct from all the other forces operating in international affairs, and capable of influencing these other forces. The state, as a consequence, must remain central to any analysis of international affairs. It is possible to follow the post-modern and Habermasian literature and suggest, beyond realism, that the nature of international politics can be reconfigured in ways that make it less violent and tense. It is not possible, though, to discount the limits that states, as independent agents, will set in that process. As was shown, however, in the previous comments on the extent to which the realist take on the state is problematic when it comes to the non-Western world, this leads to some oversights. The distinction between a pacified internal space and a violent outside space is the crucial criterion used by the realists to situate the line separating the state from its environment. This line demarcates a self-contained entity, which is then to be studied in terms of the agency it can exercise within the broader world. In the non-Western world, however, the spaces occupied by violence and peace can be quite different. There is often continued violence within the state, rather than outside of it. States, moreover, will time and again want to foster peaceful relations with their neighbors the better to carry on the wars they wage within their borders, for instance in order to ensure that insurgents do not receive supplies or political support from groups situated in other adjacent states. Peace, in that context, is built outside the state, while war remains present within it. The spaces separating violence and peace, in that sense, are quite different from those envisaged by the realists: these spaces, in fact, are often intermingled. To trace a line around the state and to imagine that this line divides two fundamentally different spaces is thus inaccurate. To suggest, next, that it is this line that circumscribes the state as an entity endowed with agency is, then, also highly problematic. The entire ontology at play here, the sense of the basic entities that constitute reality, might thus have to be recast. The realists do not see that. Wendt, when he brings the realist definition of the state within the constructivist logic, transmits, inside of that logic, the same oversights.

The problem lies, in other words, in the very way this literature formulates the *problématique* it aims to study. This is a literature that attempts to dismantle, so to speak, realism and liberalism, in order to show the elements and logics constitutive of these approaches. All of this, the writers working in that approach contend, can be rearranged or reconstructed in different ways. Post-modern authors focus on the notion of rationality contained in realism and then argue that it can be reoriented in new ways, which change its relationship to violence. Writers inspired by Habermas trace back the notion of human identity contained in mainstream international studies, chiefly in liberalism, to show how it can be redeployed in international politics in a manner more conducive to the creation of communities emphasizing our common identity as human beings, instead of our disparities as citizens of different states. Those writers closer to the work of Wendt attempt to reduce the state to its lowest common denominator – its control of violence – to see how that one basic unit can interact in varying ways with its environment according to the insights put forward by post-modern and Habermasian authors. It is because these primary elements – rationality, identity, the state – can be reconfigured in different ways, this literature contends, that international politics should be seen in terms of particulars. Different ways of constructing these elements, and dissimilarities within their character in diverse settings, will bring about distinctive and quite specific international orders, according to the manifold variations they can provide. International politics, then, is never fixed. It is a varied and ever changing realm, shifting in nature in response to the constant rearticulations of all these elements.

What is striking in this literature, however, is its assumption that one can *always* study variations of these elements, and alterations within them, and understand the manifold discourses and practices possible in international politics. This literature posits that this is true because it positions itself as a critique of mainstream international studies. It considers the categories and postulates upon which realism and liberalism have been built, and it then opens them up to analysis, to show that they are fluid and can be rearranged in different ways. However – and this is the issue – mainstream approaches miss much of what is happening within the non-Western world. The agenda of inquiry that comes out of the process of opening up categories used within these approaches – rationality, identity, the state, and so forth – is thus itself part of the problem. Its very nature follows from previous intellectual developments, which overlooked the non-Western world. Can it now describe what is particular about it?

What has been shown here is that, on the contrary, this research agenda, focused on the search for what is particular in global politics, must itself be opened up to analysis. One cannot simply take for granted, for instance, the impact of rationality on violence because realism does so, and then take that as a point of departure. Instead, one must ask how the influence of rationality in a world of violence comes about in the first place. The same can be said about identity and the state: these very categories of intellectual inquiry must themselves be opened up to a study of the processes that led to their creation. It is only if all of this is done that a proper means of analysis of non-Western international politics can be uncovered. To put it differently, defining what is particular about the non-Western world requires another way of specifying the nature of the particular in international politics. What is said now about the particular in international politics is derived from a tradition of international studies that is itself, in a way, too particular to account for a large segment of global international politics.

This is echoed in writings that focus on the shortcomings of the constructivist literature and its conceptual bases when it comes to explanations of international politics in the non-Western world. These writings focus on two fundamental problems. The first is the notion of identity as it is used in constructivism. Identities can be reconfigured, the constructivists argue, and, through this process, the entire foundations upon which relations between human communities and states unfold can be rebuilt. Socialization into broader, and shared, identities can lead to a sense of *rapprochement* and convergence that will diminish the scope of conflict in international affairs. This is the Habermasian and Kantian heritage in constructivism. However, human and social identities in the non-Western world, as they figure in the construction of international politics, are not as malleable or prone to convergence as the constructivists would have it. In his text on "Identity and the Balance of Power in Asia" in *International Relations Theory and the Asia-Pacific*,[1] probably one of the best collections on the uses and limits of constructivism outside the Western world, Henry R. Nau suggests a phrase which is quite evocative of the issue: the "distribution of identity" and its impact on the politics of identity.[2] The human and social identities that inform international behavior are always multiple. For instance, we are always, as Linklater says, both human beings and citizens. It is a particular configuration of these multiple identities, a given balance between them, that sets the one overall identity that will predominate in a specific context and influence international undertakings. It is a postulate of constructivism, through its Habermasian and Kantian lineage, that these identities can always be socialized and made to converge toward each other and that this convergence can at all times lead to less conflict-prone relations. Non-Western identities, though, are likely to settle on a different balance, one that underscores forms of identity quite at odds with those envisaged in Western liberalism. Part of the nature of these identities, moreover, might be precisely that they cannot merge with liberal understandings of human and social identity.

This is part of the case made by the body of literature that has devoted itself the most directly to the study of identity in the non-Western world: post-colonial studies. The post-colonial literature often presents, as its foundational text, *Orientalism*, by Edward W. Said.[3] Said claims that the "Orient" was constructed by the "Occident" and remains today subservient to it in the development of its own identity. "My contention," he says,

is that without examining Orientalism as a discourse [in the manner suggested by Michel Foucault's work], one cannot possibly understand the enormously systemic discipline by which European culture was able to manage – and even produce – the Orient politically, sociologically, militarily, scientifically, and imaginatively [...] Moreover, so authoritative a position did Orientalism have that I believe no one writing, thinking, or acting on the Orient could do so without taking account of the limitations on thought and action imposed by Orientalism. In brief, because of Orientalism, the Orient was not (and is not) a free subject of thought or action.[4]

The Orient, and by extension the non-Western world, was "managed" during the colonial era. This management was not only military and economic, it went to the root of the basic categories through which notions of society, self-identity, or politics were constructed in those parts of the world in that era. European culture was thus able to "produce" the non-Western world and to control it even "imaginatively." In that process, the non-Western world came to be marked out as the other part of a duality centered on the West.

The non-Western world was judged and characterized according to where it stood in relation to the Western world. Its nature was framed in the Western categories of state, market, and the like. More profoundly than that, though, its character was defined in the context of a binary opposition with the West. It was, quite simply, what the Western world was not: underdeveloped where the West was developed, uncultured where the West was the prototype of civilizational progress, and unable to determine its own destiny, whereas the West's control of itself and of the world was made evident through the *mission civilisatrice* it was conducting on all continents.

Because of that process through which the non-Western world was framed "imaginatively," and also because of the "authoritative position" this process then attained in political and academic circles throughout the globe, it is now impossible to characterize developments in the non-Western world without using a language that at least draws from the categories of thought established during the colonial era. One can certainly contest the discourse of development, for example, and claim that it follows from Western models, but what will be said will still be a response, a counter-argument, to categories that always remain problematic because they were imposed from the outside. There are thus "limitations on thought" imposed by the past. In that context, the non-Western world can never be totally "free of thought" – its very attempt to free itself from the categories of thought imposed by the West endlessly brings it back to these categories and to the loss of control over one's fate which they embody. This sort of argument has launched a vast research program on the way in which dynamics set in motion during the colonial era determine to this day the positioning of the non-Western world in definitions of rationality, legitimacy, or progress. The work of Prakash,[5] for instance, or the writings of Chakrabarty[6] can serve as examples in this context.

One of the most interesting problems surveyed in this literature is the construction of identity in the non-Western world. In the liberal model represented in constructivism by the Habermasian and Kantian approach to questions of identity, identity and agency are coextensive. It is our choices – our agency – that determine how we will define ourselves. This is why changes in our identity are possible, and the construction of a shared human identity is feasible. Conversely, we know that this agency is common to us all, and it thus serves as a rallying point in the development of this shared human identity. The issue, in the context painted for instance by Said, is that agency is often absent in definitions of the self. The categories of thought through which the self is circumscribed and characterized – notions of subjectivity, society, and the like – are perceived as being imposed by the colonial and post-colonial conceptual burdens he depicts, and thus as escaping agency.

Many have worked on these issues, although perhaps the writings of Gayatri Chakravorty Spivak are the most widely known.[7] Representations of the self, of one's history, of one's society, are seen as having been constituted and managed from the outside, in a manner reflecting the histories and interests of other, more dominant societies. Can the liberal model, then, work here? Can identity really be chosen and modified according to one's free will? And, if the definition even of one's own core identity cannot be traced back to the exercise of one's free will, what does that say about individual agency? Can it still constitute the focal point of the "subject's itinerary," to use Spivak's language,[8] as the liberals imagine it will? There again, a vast research program has developed, though the work of Wa Thiong'o,[9] or that of Minh-ha[10] can serve as examples.

   A key concern in that perspective, for instance, is the extent to which notions of race still underlie approaches to the construction of identity in the non-Western world. The work of Kwame Anthony Appiah,[11] for example, traces how the conceptions of race that framed the colonial project in Africa have been inscribed in social relations in the continent to such an extent that contemporary depictions of culture or belief systems now cannot circumvent them. Discussions of self-identity, in that context, often proceed from categories that restrict self-expression as much as they allow it: they reprise themes and debates inherited from the colonial era and reinforce them instead of challenging and dismantling them. The work of Paul Ahluwalia on the idea of *négritude* in African literary theory,[12] to give another example linked to these concerns, shows all the ambivalence that accompanies questions of self-identity in that literature and relates this ambivalence to the fact that any critique of the racial categories imposed by the colonialists in Africa ends up by putting those categories back, at the center of the project aimed at circumventing them.[13]

   This is where this literature connects to the issues discussed in this book. The constructivists, building on the conceptual lineage outlined here, envisage an agency that enables changes in identity. They then study how these changes in identity can play against each other in the development of mechanisms of socialization. In the non-Western world, however, the construction of identity often stands in tension with agency and, indeed, it can be articulated in terms that deny its possibility. The opening premise which allows the constructivist logic to develop is thus highly problematic in this context. Furthermore, in the constructivist writings agency also provides the end point, so to speak, of the processes of socialization. Socialization highlights common points of reference amongst the varied identities it brings in contact and, chiefly among them, a shared human agency. It is because of this shared agency that states and human communities can choose to move beyond conflict – this is why international politics always remains, in Wendt's phrase, "what they make of it." This is also, however, a premise which is problematic in the non-Western world. The confrontation of social identities between those parts of the world and the West has not revealed agency so much as its absence. Seeing agency, in that sense, as a common denominator amongst all spheres of international life, one that can always allow a forward movement in all these spheres, is mistaken too in this context.

At a second level, this all brings back in the equation the comments on identity made earlier. If there is no core element of human agency at the center of debates about identity, how else will self-identity be defined? The pull from more communal forms of identity – which emerges precisely, as was shown here, when notions of self-agency are at their weakest – is likely to be greater. As was also explained here, these forms of communal identities, rooted in ethnic or religious models of social affiliation, are much more likely to be unreceptive to any agenda of convergence between human or political communities. This is the problem with the issue of "distribution of identity" identified earlier by Nau: the distribution and configuration of models of identity do not correspond, in the non-Western world, to the dynamics of identity formation and socialization upon which the constructivists base their argument. In the end, then, the validity of the entire set of assumptions about identity at the center of the constructivist literature thus remains questionable in these parts of the world.

The second problem identified in critiques of constructivism written from the perspective of the non-Western world is more straightforward. It concerns the conception of the state in constructivist literature. Constructivists see the state as a self-contained agent, in the manner established by the realists. The state always remains an agent in international politics, they claim, because its control over violence, resources, and people allows it to act according to its own agenda and in ways that are independent from the other forces, which constitute or influence international affairs. It is states, as agents of their own evolution, that enter into processes of socialization and change the nature of international politics as a result. Many contest the applicability of that view of the state, however, when it comes to the non-Western world. Someone like Alastair Iain Johnston, for instance, who has done extensive work on constructivism in non-Western settings through his constructivist interpretations of Chinese foreign policy, notes that it might well be wrong to assume that agents of socialization have at all times "relatively unobstructed access to states and sub-state actors for diffusing normative understandings."[14] In the non-Western world, the state is often still being built. Institutional development might be sparse and uneven, and centralized control over large segments of the bureaucracy or the military, for example, might still be weak. In that context, it is not at all certain that the state will react as a unitary actor – as an agent – to the "normative understandings" underlying processes of socialization at the international level. Different "sub-state actors" might react differently to these international norms, and they might in fact prevent the state itself from acting on the basis of these norms. One cannot, then, simply assume the presence of the state, and examine how that state will behave within processes of socialization.

In the non-Western world, one must study the nature of the state and the circumstances of its development, because these factors will have an impact on the way in which it can enter into dynamics of socialization. Constructivism fails at the moment to enter into this sort of analysis.

These critiques of the constructivist literature thus bring back the point made earlier. The constructivists move certain pieces, so to say, on the theoretical chessboard. They show that identity should be a powerful element in the analysis of international politics, they demonstrate that the state is another element that matters in that analysis, and then that the interaction of these elements through processes of socialization underlies the evolution of international affairs. The problem is that the definition of these elements – identity and the state – is at odds with the nature of these realities in the non-Western world, and this skews the analysis in ways unforeseen by the constructivist logic. Constructivism draws these elements from the mainstream theoretical literature it aims to reassess. This mainstream literature itself, however, overlooks many of the realities of non-Western international politics, and these oversights then distort constructivism.

The problem is that this literature cannot move away from its current categories of analysis. By defining itself as a critique of mainstream international studies, it locks itself within the universalism prevalent within this mainstream literature. It does isolate some elements in the realist and liberal worldview, and then it reorients them for the development of new insights. Walker shows that the rationality underlying the mainstream theoretical discourse can be redirected toward the construction of new types of international politics. Linklater and Wendt illustrate how human identity and the state can be taken out of the series of postulates framing that mainstream discourse, and then redeployed in ways that challenge established views on international affairs. These people, however, still presuppose that these basic building blocks of rationality, identity, and the state are always present in international politics. They are bound to be, because they work on the basis of a body of literature that assumes that there is nothing beyond its scope. This is a core assumption of mainstream international studies: it is based, more than anything else, on the postulate that its arguments pertain to all of international politics. This is a problem for the approaches that position themselves as critiques of that mainstream literature. These critiques can unpack the basic building blocks of this literature and then reinterpret or reorient them, but they cannot go beyond that because, in a sense, there is nothing beyond that for these critiques. By working within the confines set by the problems of mainstream international studies, they miss what is missed by the mainstream literature, and no point of entry can be found, either in mainstream approaches or in its critiques, into a possible analysis of the realities absent from that entire debate. Defining the categories through which the specificity of the non-Western world can be studied requires, in that perspective, another method.

Asia provides, once again, an instructive example of these problems. Constructivism most certainly provides at the moment the fastest rising explanatory framework used to describe the international politics of the region. This has to do, evidently, with the increasing recognition of the paradigm itself in international studies. This popularity of the framework, moreover, can also undoubtedly be attributed to the extent with which it seems to fit the questions now at the top of the regional agenda. Will China become socialized in the ways and norms that define the global political architecture? Will the mechanisms and processes of international social- ization involved in these efforts reflect something resembling a Chinese identity, or a set of Chinese values? How will Asia's two other giants, India and Japan, draw from their own identities and values to influence the norms and values governing regional and global institutions? What kinds of norms are likely to drive these different developments, and how will they impact on existing norms in international affairs? Constructivism, with its focus on matters of identity, norms and socialization, seems ideally suited to answer these questions.

The issue, though, is that most of those using constructivism in an Asian context notice that the nature of Asia's international politics reveals some flaws in the approach itself. The work of Alastair Iain Johnston, for instance, has just been mentioned. Johnston has put forward the most detailed and insightful studies of China's international politics from a constructivist per- spective. However, a point he makes repeatedly, as was said a moment ago, is that the nature of the state in China is different from the notion of the state that anchors constructivism, and that this skews constructivist interpretations of China's international behavior. The centralization and institutionalization of power in the Chinese context has not occurred to the extent entailed by a unitary conception of the state. There are sub-spaces within the structure of the Chinese state, ranging from utter discrepancies between urban centers and the countryside, for instance, all the way to zones of political and ideological incommensurability between the military, the Communist Party, and local and national economic elites. These sub- spaces operate according to logics and agendas that are at times disparate, and at other times much more convergent. One cannot assume, then, that the processes of international socialization studied by the constructivists will always entail a "relatively unobstructed access to states and sub-state actors for the diffusion of normative understandings," to repeat Johnston's remark just cited. The point, to say things differently, is the need to ask *what* is being socialized in the processes described by the constructivists. It might well not be the state. Different sub-state groups may engage in processes of socialization that are, in fact, repudiated, ignored, or even countered by other sub-state groups with their own access to international levers of power. Constructivist explanations often fail to integrate these issues into their argument because they work from a unitary understanding of the state, which, by its nature, obfuscates them. A new understanding of the state, one that recognizes the varied paths of development that can be followed by the state in cases like China, must be substituted for that more unitary conception of state institutions and behavior, if the constructivist literature is to convey a correct understanding of these problems.

The work of someone like Amitav Acharya leads to the same conclusions. Acharya is a leading authority on the nature of regionalism in Southeast Asia, and he has been one of the main proponents of the idea that constructivism constitutes the best point of entry into the issue. For instance, one of his major works, *Constructing a Security Community in Southeast Asia*,[15] is devoted precisely to a constructivist analysis of the growth of the notion of security community among the members of the Association of Southeast Asian Nations (ASEAN). As he himself notes, raising issues of socialization and emergent regional identity brings forward interesting intellectual puzzles in Southeast Asia's case because of the sheer diversity of sociopolitical, economic, or religious backgrounds that characterize countries such as Indonesia, Thailand, Brunei, or Vietnam.

As he also quickly adds, though, constructivism experiences quite some difficulties when it is employed in Southeast Asia. It has three main advantages. It emphasizes the social construction of regions and regional security communities. It shows the "transformative impact of norms" in that process. And it thus "allows us to look beyond the impact of material forces in shaping international politics."[16] The set of postulates upon which constructivism is based imparts the approach, however, a "somewhat linear perspective,"[17] which superimposes on all contexts where it is used the same basic set of explanations about the nature of international socialization. If we truly want to understand the nature of socialization processes in Southeast Asia, Acharya contends, we need "a framework that incorporates, but goes beyond, the linear constructivist logic."[18]

The way to "go beyond" constructivism is to adopt a more "sociological approach."[19] This entails a clearer focus on the nature of the state in Southeast Asia and on its impact on the construction of regional institutions and regional identity there. Acharya has demonstrated, for instance, that the construction of a regional identity in Southeast Asia "has had much to do with conscious attempts by its leaders [...] to 'imagine,' delineate, and organize its political, economic, social and strategic space."[20] The elites, the "leaders," of Southeast Asia have "imagined," and then created, a regional identity that suits their own needs and reinforces their power. The fundamental norms of regional identity in Southeast Asia, for example the mutual refusals to criticize the politics of neighboring states, or the reluctance to engage issues of human rights and democracy in regional fora, were created by these elites to serve that objective. Here again, then, the question remains: what exactly is being socialized in these circumstances? Is it states *per se*, or the set of elites that have used processes of regionalization to bolster their power? How has that influenced the nature of the regionalization process in Southeast Asia? Conversely, what does this say about politics in Southeast Asia? What are the models of state development that give elites such power? What are the political institutions and practices that allow elites to behave this way and to use regional frameworks of socialization to buttress their power at the domestic level? What Acharya wants to underscore is that the first set of questions cannot be answered without reference to the second one. The analysis of regional socialization in Southeast Asia must encompass a study of the nature of the state there, of its development and of its particular character. It is this analysis, then, that can bring to light the true processes through which socialization occurs and the nature of that socialization. Constructivism misses that more "sociological" dimension of the nature of the state. It overlooks the multiple paths of development that can be followed by the state and, as a consequence, the impact that these varied models of development can have on the dynamics of socialization upon which it focuses its attention. This is why it remains locked in too "linear" a perspective.

This literature also brings to light problems with the notion of identity within constructivism. The work of Mely Caballero-Anthony, for example, can be cited again in this context, in particular as it relates to the "narratives" of identity in Southeast Asia.[21] Caballero-Anthony has developed a very perceptive constructivist analysis of the attempts by "societal forces" to integrate, within the discourse of regional security and identity in Southeast Asia, a stronger focus on issues of democracy, human rights, and human security. She has spent considerable time documenting, for instance, the role played by the ASEAN-Institutes for Strategic and International Studies (ASEAN-ISIS), a consortium of think-tanks with long-standing points of access to the official circles of ASEAN, in the promotion of a "new regionalism"[22] articulated on the defense of these values.

What this work underscores, however, is a strong tension between two types of identity. There is a sense of regional identity being developed in Southeast Asia that does correspond to the objectives pursued by groups like ASEAN-ISIS and others. The language of "civil society driven regionalism," and phrases like "a people-centered ASEAN," are undeniably gaining currency in the region.[23] Indeed, this language is in fact bringing into relief a common agenda, a shared aspiration for democracy and human rights, which are giving even greater impetus to current calls for a "new regionalism" and for a new regional identity in Southeast Asia. There is, however, something else. As was just said, elites in the region have instilled in its institutions and diplomatic practices a totally different sense of regional identity. The central notion driving these institutions and practices is precisely the idea that the region should not evolve on the basis of a common project. The continued defense of the principle of non-interference in the affairs of other states or the refusal to address issues of human rights are meant to enshrine the utmost respect for the national sovereignty of each state in Southeast Asia and, in a word, to stop there. Elites mutually recognize that regionalism will be little more than a reciprocated endorsement of the claim that nothing should stand above national sovereignty. This is also what constitutes regional identity in Southeast Asia: the constantly reiterated idea that the history and values of the region militate against any movement toward a sense of regional, rather than national, identity.

The problem with constructivism is that it can explain the first type of identity, but not the second one. Its liberal background leads it to assume that progress toward a mutual recognition of human identity, and the expression of that process in regional and international processes of socialization, are always a possibility. What the constructivist literature cannot integrate in its worldview, however, is a notion of identity that denies the very possibility of that progression. This is precisely, though, the situation in Southeast Asia. It is not that mechanisms of socialization have not yet emerged, it is rather that, according to a certain definition of regional identity, these mechanisms simply cannot emerge. That is what constructivism misses – the presence, sometimes, of forms of identity that stand outside of the series of claims that constructivism makes about identity and socialization. The evolution of regional identity in Southeast Asia is framed, at the moment, by the confrontation of different logics of identity and socialization, some that conform to constructivist claims and some that do not. As long as constructivism does not reexamine its understanding of identity and socialization, it will miss that second part of the story.

Thus the literature that looks at Asia from a constructivist perspective, to sum up, often echoes the problems identified here with the approach. It shows that the main categories upon which the constructivist literature relies in its explanations of international politics – the interplay between state behavior, identity, and socialization – must themselves be opened to further scrutiny. An analysis must be made to see how they have come to be in the non-Western world and what they actually entail in those countries. It is only once this is accomplished that the issues of socialization studied by the constructivists can be understood correctly when it comes to the specificities of regions like Asia. This is to say, conversely, that attempting to isolate these specificities and to work toward a concept of what is particular in different settings of international politics cannot really be done if one starts only with the categories used at the present time by constructivism. This means, moreover, that constructivism must move beyond its position as a critique of realism and liberalism, because it is that position that locks it into its current understanding of these issues of state behavior and human identity.

Finally, for this part of the book, the same sort of problem must be underscored regarding the other well-known body of literature that attempts at the moment to encapsulate the ever-changing character of international politics: post-Marxism. This literature proceeds from objectives that are similar to those pursued by constructivism. In this case, too, the goal is to demonstrate that the rhetoric of universality of large segments of literature in international studies should be questioned, and it should give way to understandings of international life that are much more sensitive to the shifting and varied forms through which global politics can be articulated in different historical or social circumstances. Post-Marxism, however, adopts an approach that is in direct counterpoint to the one at the heart of constructivism. Whereas constructivism looks at the world of ideas, identity, and discourse, to see how it impacts on the more material world of state power and behavior, post-Marxism reverses the logic and studies how the material world of state power and production defines international politics and the key concepts driving its evolution. Is this better? Does this approach allow a more insightful and complete understanding of the nature of international politics in the non-Western world?

This is a literature that, in its opening stance, is clearly influenced by Marx's work. The material world of production, trade, and financial exchanges, it is argued here, sets limits to patterns of global economic development and allows some elite classes in a group of core countries to control these patterns of development to their advantage. These elites can also intermingle with the different networks that control global political, economic, and financial institutions in a way that is not available to other groups. These select points of access allow those elites to influence the global political and economic architecture so as to make it favor their own interests to the detriment of all other groups and classes.

Where the post-Marxist literature goes beyond these arguments is in the so-called neo-Gramscian position defined by the work of Robert Cox, for instance, or that of Stephen Gill. Two elements are crucial in that context. One is the role played by ideology. Dominant economic elites – someone like Cox would suggest, in echo to Gramsci – rule not only the material world of production and raw authority, but also the ideational world of culture and discourse, for instance through their ability to control or influence the main media. Through these channels, economic elites can propound models of economic and political development that reinforce their position of power. The trick there is for these elites to present those models of development as natural, as part of the order of things, and thus as impossible to change. By describing capitalism, for example, as something that appeals to a universal human nature rather than as something that truly benefits much smaller segments of the global community, elites are able to portray capitalist development as innate to human development itself, and thus unchangeable. The other crucial element in this literature is an understanding of the material forces at play in global politics and global economics that is much broader than the one contained in the Marxist worldview. The state, principally, is seen as a source of self-directed power in the material world, because it is the site of political, economic, and social struggles that are independent from those generated by the forces of production and capitalism. There is always, therefore, a latent tension between the state and these forces. In a capitalist world economy, then, the state and its different national and international agencies must be brought on side by economic elite: it is only if its political and economic policies remain compatible with the broader goals of capitalist development that this model of global development will proceed unchallenged.

This is where a powerful sense of the particular in international politics emerges. Working on the basis of these arguments, observers of international affairs are immediately confronted to varied configurations of state, economic, and ideological forces, which are themselves constituted in different ways as one moves from a section of the global order to another. It appears, from such a perspective, that nothing is not particular in international politics. All international circumstances and events are always tied to a certain context and to a given interplay with other forces, which are themselves evolving and varied. The material world of production and capitalism, though, does occupy a prominent place in that worldview. It is to that extent that the post-Marxist literature aims to distance itself from the current constructivist moment in international studies. Is this, then, a better way to understand what is particular about the international politics of the non-Western world?

There is much in this approach that goes to what has been said in these pages about the nature of international politics in the non-Western world. Market forces, and indeed the very nature of production and economic life, are questioned in terms of the prior conditions that have given them the evolutionary path and character associated with them today. Fundamental distinctions between different parts of the world – for instance between the core of the world economy and more peripheral regions – are acknowledged and integrated in the analysis. This is exactly what was said here previously about market forces and about how they should be studied in the non-Western world. The survey of the different authors who have built on the dependency literature to develop a framework of analysis of economic development in the non-Western world, for instance, led precisely to an argument in favor of that approach. Further to the point, diverse sorts of interaction between the world economy and varied forms of state and ideological configurations throughout the world are then also recognized and made part of the study of these issues. This corresponds to what has been studied here.

One can still point, though, to some problems. The post-Marxist analysis proceeds, it must be noted, as if the problem of violence has already been settled. The power of the market, the power of the state, those are forms of power that emerge only once they are allowed to come forward by constraints on violence. If, as can be the case in some parts of the non-Western world, violence is still the primary currency of power, these other forms of power are jeopardized. If it is through violence that wealth is accumulated, for instance, then it is the logic of violence that must be understood in the study of economic empowerment, not the logic of global capitalist production studied by the post-Marxists. If the state has not been able to bring violence under control within its borders, then that state does not have the power to manage economic and social forces in the way ascribed to it by the post-Marxist literature. The social and political arrangements regarding violence, which then lead to the forms of state and production dynamics studied by post-Marxism, must be understood first, to see how they produce these forces or, indeed, how they can prevent their appearance. This must be an intrinsic part of the analysis if the real character of international politics in the non-Western world, and the forces that drive it, are to be uncovered.

The problem, in that sense, is that post-Marxism repeats the error made by constructivism. It positions itself as a critique of mainstream international studies. It demonstrates that the elements which serve as points of reference in mainstream international studies – notions of state, market, or ideology – must in fact be seen as fluid and varied. And it then invites students of international politics to see how the different possible permutations of these elements must lead them to an appreciation of the specificity and sheer contextuality of all international life. What is missing in that approach, though, is a sense of the specificity and contextuality created by elements that remain outside of the mainstream approaches that post-Marxism aims to critique. How violence, for instance, precedes politics and economics, and how it still shapes the power and nature of these realities – all of this is not considered well by mainstream international studies, and the oversight then duplicates itself in the counter-assessment that post-Marxism provides of that mainstream literature. Saying, as post-Marxism does, that diverse possible forms of the state or the market must be investigated and integrated in the analysis does not suffice. What precedes the state and the market, what in fact might well prevent them from playing the role specified for them in the post-Marxist logic, must also be part of the work done to understand international politics in the non-Western world.

The literature that attempts to move post-Marxism forward on the basis of specifically Asian experiences of international politics speaks to exactly these issues. The best recent text that could be mentioned in this regard is probably *Empire and Neoliberalism in Asia*, edited by Vedi R. Hadiz.[24] The introduction of the volume asserts its intention to study the "political project" behind the "US-led process of neoliberal economic globalization"[25] as it pertains to Asia, and it describes themes of research which mirror those favored by the post-Marxists. There is an added emphasis, however, on the "increasingly coercive character"[26] of the forms of power through which neoliberal economics are now managed throughout Asia since the events of September 11, 2001 and the beginning of the American war against terror.

This is certainly something that the post-Marxists would recognize. The state uses coercion and consent to manage society in ways that make it more amenable to the expansion of global capitalism in Asia, and a part of the coercive aspects of that equation involves the use of the security sector – the military and the police – to enforce social stability in times when the economic inequalities generated by capitalism could lead to widespread unrest. There are now increasingly authoritarian and brutal policies being enacted in Asia in conjunction with the US war against terror – mainly in Southeast Asia, since the region has emerged as the so-called second theatre in the war against terror – but these policies have simply made more apparent realities that were already in place. There is nothing in this, post-Marxists could suggest, that goes beyond what they cover in their analysis of international politics.

But there is more. The reorientation of the use of violence entailed by more brutal policies leads to nothing less than the questioning of the social contract upon which models of political and economic development are predicated. In a country like, say, the Philippines, the use of the military to control entire regions of the country in the name of the war against terror is changing the nature of the power that state institutions can wield vis-à-vis all segments of the population. In the "state-of-siege environments"[27] described by Garry Rodan and Kevin Hewison, the rights and obligations connecting the individual and the state are weakened, and violence becomes again one of the main currencies of power. This changes the nature of the state itself. It cannot present itself as an instrument of legitimacy in society, as it appears more and more as an instrument of repression. The state cannot, in that context, propound the language of individual rights and empowerment associated with liberal capitalism, and, just as much, it cannot characterize itself as a neutral and legitimate manager of economic forces.

This is somewhat different from what the post-Marxists would claim. There is evidence here that the reorganization of power toward more violent expressions in fact prevents the interrelationships between the state, the market, and ideology, from proceeding in the manner they predict. The logic of capitalism itself is compromised, and often resembles nothing more than the brutal acquisition of wealth by powerful oligarchies protected by private forces or by privileged access to the police and the military. The state does not act as a conduit facilitating and legitimizing the expansion of global capitalism within its territory. On the contrary, it protects the oligarchies with which it is associated against the rules of global capitalism, for instance by allowing nepotism to determine economic policies. It is through sheer force, rather than through ideology and discourse, that this situation is maintained in place.

This sort of case study thus shows something more than what would be expected according to post-Marxism. One sees here prior arrangements regarding violence, which sustained the workings of state institutions,

capitalist forces, and ideological constructs necessary to the different dynamics studied in the post-Marxist literature. Now that this arrangement is
changing course and violence is no longer evacuated from social relations,
all of politics, economics, and ideology are also changing accordingly, and
in ways that depart from the post-Marxist logic. It is this added factor of
explanation that needs to be brought in the post-Marxist literature, if the
latter is to describe fully the international politics at play here. Conversely,
this also shows that the route post-Marxism follows to arrive at an understanding of what is particular in each context of international affairs still
overlooks important factors when it comes to the non-Western world.

The issue, though, is that post-Marxism cannot consider fully these issues
if it remains within the ambit of its own premises. There is in this approach,
as was seen in the first part of the book, an assumption of totality: production and capitalism, and the interrelationships they generate with political
and ideological forces, constitute a totality, a world closed on itself, which
supports a particular conception of global order. Its key contention is that
the world of production and capitalism provides a point of entry into the
study of all possible such variants of international politics. It cannot argue
at the same time, in this sense, that other starting points in the analysis
might be needed to account for certain types of international politics.

More profoundly, this raises the issue of how a sense of the particular in
international affairs should be built. Does an approach that positions itself
as a response to the universals contained in the main approaches at the core
of international studies condemn itself to overlook what these approaches
also overlook? This is the true problem here, for both constructivism and
post-Marxism: where should the analysis start? Both approaches open their
analysis by responding to the assumption of universalism in much of international studies, and proceed forward from that point on. In doing so,
however, they miss a fair share of what actually constitutes the elements of
specificity of international life in the non-Western world. And yet the logic
of inquiry that they set in motion by proceeding in this way prevents them
from going back and integrating these missing elements into their analysis.

This brings the discussion, then, to the key point that has been argued
in this part of the book. It is certainly possible to identify a series of elements that must be part of any analysis of the international politics of
the non-Western world. The problem, though, is devising an approach to
international studies that allows the discipline to take these elements into
account. The very logic of the discipline – its search for what is universal
throughout all of global politics – makes that process impossible. Clearly,
there is at the moment an attempt to move away from this language of
universals in international studies: this is what current advances in the
constructivist and post-Marxist literature are all about. Even this literature,
however, is structured and positioned in such a way that it ends up dupli-
cating many of the oversights about the non-Western world which have

most often underlain the development of international studies as a field of study. This is a fundamental problem for the discipline. This also means, in counterpoint, that the literature focused on the international politics of the non-Western world continues to stand aside in all these debates. It puts forward insights and arguments that cannot be integrated in international studies because of the logic still driving the discipline. In that sense, we have in international studies, as was said in the introduction, people talking past each other because they simply cannot find a common language. And the problem is made even more acute by the fact that we would need a meaningful discussion on these questions now more than ever: this is what the "rise of the rest" and the growing impact of the non-Western world on the very nature of international politics requires from us at the moment. Perhaps, in this context, a new approach is needed.

Part III

What Now? Reinventing International Studies for the Post-Western World

7
Reinventing Realism: Power and Violence in the Post-Western World

What follows from all of this? There is, on the one hand, international studies. The discipline is admittedly Western-centric. It is quite difficult for it, though, to address that problem. Its logic rests on the idea that it always speaks a language of universals, which captures the reality of international affairs throughout the entire world. In that context, finding points of entry for a more detailed understanding of the international politics of the non-Western world remains a formidable challenge. The latest advances in the literature do demonstrate a growing rejection, among international relations scholars, of this language of universals. These efforts, though, have also failed to capture some of the key issues that define international life in the non-Western world. To that extent, the key problem posed by the emergence of the post-Western world to international studies as a discipline – how do we build a coherent conceptual framework that finally integrates the non-Western world in our explanations of current global politics? – is still unresolved.

On the other hand, there is a sizeable literature devoted specifically to international life in the non-Western world. This is a literature that, by its very logic, rejects the language of universals at the core of international studies. It insists instead on speaking a language of particulars and focuses its attention on the elements that give international life in the non-Western world its specific character. Precisely for that reason, though, this literature has failed to push international studies beyond its Western-centric bias. Indeed, the tensions between the languages and the logics at play are such that they make this process impossible. To that extent, this literature has also failed to push forward the development of the new models which are now needed to help us understand the rising impact of the non-Western world in current global politics.

So then: this language of universals will not do, and neither will this language of the particular. What is the solution? Perhaps someone like Laclau can be of some help here. Ernesto Laclau has made it his life's work to study the role played by notions of the universal and of the particular in definitions of rights, pluralism, and democracy.[1] All the debates on these issues, Laclau tells us, are essentially about the confrontation of frames of reference regarding what is universal and what is particular in society. Any discussion of social rights, for example, involves marking out the universal qualities we all share, then the particular qualities we possess because of our differences of language, religion, and the like, and then defining the way in which these two terms of reference should be reconciled one with the other. A problem immediately arises, though, which has been noted time and again by a wide variety of writers. The confrontation of claims about what is universal and what is particular in each of us quickly exposes the fluidity and, more than that, the artificiality, of these claims. What we say about these issues varies broadly according to differences in criteria and in social and historical circumstances, and this seems to negate the possibility of a reconciliation between all of us. Everything we argue about the universal and the particular appears, in the end, to be itself very particular to each of us. How can we, in that context, find a common terrain upon which to build a plural and democratic environment, where all of our perspectives and rights will be respected?

To address this problem, Laclau makes two fundamental points. We cannot surrender to this endless incommensurability between all of our perspectives, he claims, and speak only a language of the particular. This would be bad politics. It would prevent us from acting meaningfully in society. The broad constituencies and coalitions of interests necessary to any political progress would constantly dissolve if we did not accept the idea that some level of common identity unites us all. In fact this would be counterproductive. It would not allow the organization of groups able to promote the recognition of all our rights and specificities, and it would also, precisely because of that, cede all the political terrain to groups that are not as sensitive to, or concerned with, the defense of our rights and differences. This would also be bad theory. It is wrong, conceptually, to assume that universals can dissipate completely into a discussion of particulars. Particulars are always about universals. Any discussion of my ethnic, religious, or language rights assumes in fact a prior discussion of ethnicity, religion, or language in themselves. Those are not discussions about my situation only, but, much more, debates about what realities over-extend my own situation,[2] that of others beside me, and come to define all of our lives – those are discussions, in a word, about universals. Failing to acknowledge that in a discussion of the particular leads to a wrong formulation of the problem at hand.

It is when Laclau proposes a solution to that problem that he puts forward the second fundamental argument central to his line of reasoning: we should not jettison the universal, we should instead redefine it. There is such a thing, to quote this time Neil Lazarus, as the "necessity of universalism."[3] As human beings, we need debates about what surpasses our particularities and unites us. This is how we can come to define who we are, both as individuals and as societies. The search for universals is thus very much a "necessity." We should not, however, see these universals as fixed. This is not the Kantian pursuit of universals inscribed in the nature of human rationality and human identity. The search for the universal, Laclau tells us, should be just that: a constant search, a never ending discussion through which we debate what unites us all. It should be an unending process, rather than a point being reached at the end of that process. Our discussions about rights, for instance, should not rest on the hope that we will find unquestionable universal rights accepted once and for all by everyone. The politics of difference, which shapes so much of our lives now, will not permit that in any case. Discussions of rights, instead, should be about engaging in that process and knowing that it will never end, but that this is the only avenue we have where we can move forward in our discussion of individual and social rights. This is the image we should have in mind when we speak of universals. The particular, in that context, will also become different. It will no longer stand in opposition to the universal. On the contrary, it will inform the universal, it will shape it. The particular set of circumstances that define, for each of us, our rights and needs, for example, will inform and shape broader discussions about the very nature of rights and will ensure that this discussion remains anchored in the consideration of the particular circumstances in which rights need to be deployed and defended. This is how we can move beyond the problems associated with the universal and the particular: by thinking of both at the same time. We need a conception of the universal that is always sensitive to all the varied perspectives and circumstances that shape its creation, and we need an understanding of the particular that draws from within its own specificity broader lessons for our constant discussion on what unites and what separates all of us.[4]

This can be very instructive for the argument pursued in this book. The current problem of international studies is the problem of universals. The entire discipline was built around the assumption that it could address universal realities and problems in international affairs, realities and problems that pertained to all of international politics throughout the entire world. The issue now, however, is that the realities of non-Western international politics seem to escape these models. Or, at least, international studies is unsure of the extent to which it can really explain them. This changes completely the status of the discipline. Its *raison d'être* was to explain international politics – all of international politics. Do these new problems show that, in reality, the field is no more than a Western construct, unable to understand non-Western international affairs? Do all of us in the discipline need at this point to start again, so to say, and to elaborate new models of international affairs? Is this what the "rise of the rest" now requires of all of us in the field?

This is where Laclau becomes interesting. Given the failures of the language of universals at the core of international studies, should we now turn to a language of particulars? Is this what will bring the literature devoted to the non-Western world within the discipline, and allow us to explain the nature of the global politics created by the "rise of the rest"? Laclau warns us of the dangers of such an approach. This would be bad theory and bad politics. We have in international studies a "necessity of universalism," and now more than ever. As a discipline, we require for it, like for any other field of knowledge, a language of concepts and approaches that transcends the specifics of any of the particular situations we consider as we build that language. This speaks to the tensions between the universal and the particular in the construction of knowledge that Laclau puts to us. More than that, though, the "necessity of universalism" also has global political resonance now: if the "rise of the rest" undermines established conventions and worldviews about what is universal in global politics, it also calls for a new language of universals, which will allow some form of global discussion on the values and agendas that should define that new international order.

The problem, then, is not that international studies has so far spoken a language of universals. The problem is the nature of the universals it has inserted in that language. These universals have always been turned on themselves, so to speak. They have grown from debates within the discipline, and they have been maintained in place by inter-locking and self-referential assumptions. Precisely because of that, international studies has missed quite a lot and has been unable to address, or even recognize, all it was over-looking when it came to the non-Western world. What the discipline needs to do now, in this perspective, is to rebuild its universals, not to discard them. We need to integrate, quite obviously, what has been overlooked, as far as the non-Western world is concerned. Our definitions of the state, of the economy, and so on must include the way these realities have evolved in those parts of the world. Then, evidently, we will have a more global, a more universal language with which to give account of global interna-tional politics. Just as much, though, we must also move toward a new way of defining universals. If our old universals were turned toward themselves, then our new ones need to be turned outward, toward these realities that have so far been overlooked in international studies. This is where the sort of study conducted here becomes important. We need to determine precisely, in the interlocking assumptions of universality through which we look at the world, what are the elements preventing us from seeing the realities that have escaped our purview so far. Then we must reopen our discussion about these elements on the basis of the shortcomings and errors uncovered in that process. It is only if we go through this exercise that we will be able to endow the discipline with a sense of dynamism and openness as it seeks to build new universals, more receptive to some of the realities of global politics it has thus far misunderstood or overlooked.

This is what Laclau means when he says that, in fact, we have to move beyond distinctions between the universal and the particular and learn to combine the two. Our attempts to understand international politics do entail the need for categories of thought that encapsulate what constitutes international politics throughout the world. The fundamental organizing principle driving the elaboration of these concepts, though, must be the recognition that this should always remain a lively and open-ended process. We should at all times acknowledge that we miss a lot of what goes on throughout the world when we develop the concepts driving international studies. We should incorporate this sense of incompleteness, this sense of a specificity of particular problems and circumstances, which escapes our current understandings of global politics in our work. It is as we endeavor to identify and understand these elements missed by our current conceptual frameworks that our concepts of world politics will move forward and become more refined and more accurate.

This tells us, then, how the two main sets of literature studied in this book should be handled. It is important to draw upon international studies as a discipline. There is a number of fundamentally important questions there – regarding, for instance, the factors determining state behavior on the international stage, or the impact of economic interdependence on the character of international politics. It is also important to confront these insights with the reality of international politics in the non-Western world. Through this confrontation of different perspectives, of different insights, a richer understanding of the nature of international affairs throughout the whole world will emerge. This can only be beneficial as the "rise of the rest" puts the non-Western world at the center of global politics and demands, in counterpoint, the development of models and approaches that fit this new global reality. All of this is crucial and, indeed, it constitutes a key component of the analysis presented in this book.

The real problem, though, is elsewhere. The critical issue is not combining the insights of these different sets of literature: it is combining the opposite logics that animate each of them. The insights put forward by international studies are a function of the debates about the possibility of a language of universals in international affairs that have underlain the entire evolution of the discipline. Conversely, the insights put forward by the literature focused on the non-Western world arise from the belief that only a language of the particular is possible in international affairs, and that the debates which have framed the evolution of international studies have been self-enclosed exercises, neglectful of the nature of international life in those parts of the world. All these insights cannot be brought together, because they carry with them a broader set of interlocking logical sequences, which prevent this process from happening.

This is where the way of thinking about the universal and the particular just outlined becomes essential. It sets up an approach to the construction of international studies as a discipline that does away with the tension between the search for the universal and the search for the particular in international affairs, which is at the core of so many intractable debates at the moment. In this approach, on the contrary, both frames of analysis complement each other, they enrich each other. This approach to the construction of international studies, then, does provide the broad conceptual framework needed to connect literatures that have so far remained apart from each other. In this sense, there is here a project that is also fundamentally necessary for the reinvention of international studies – a project the discipline must now set in motion if it is to draw from all the literatures it must bring together in order to explain the new global politics created by the "rise of the rest."

What does this all mean in practice? This discussion should start with realism. In the optic of the questions raised here, the force of realism is two-fold. Realism, at a first level, puts forward arguments about the nature of violence and the nature of the state which have framed the entire development of international studies as a discipline: more often than not, other approaches have emerged essentially by developing critiques of these arguments and then following the logic of analysis set in motion in this way. At a second level, the force of realism also lies in its assumption that it speaks to universal realities. This has allowed realism to remain self-enclosed. If the tenets of realism explain international politics throughout the world, as realists have been able to claim on the basis of their core assumptions, why resort to other approaches, and why explore approaches that come out of the non-Western world? This assumption of a universal scope, in turn, has cascaded down within other approaches, which have positioned themselves as critiques of realism. Realism sets up questions that have worldwide relevance, proponents of these other approaches have been able to claim, and our critiques will then also speak to worldwide problems. This is why the discussion must start with realism. As was shown in the second part of the book, the literature focused on the non-Western world points out many oversights in realism. These oversights must be addressed – this is the goal of this part of the book. This process, however, must engage more than realism. It should start with realism and then carry through all these other approaches which position their own logic as a response to realism, in order to show how changing one part of the story in realism will change the story told by these other approaches as well. This also speaks to the assumption of universality that traverses realism. The self-enclosed universals of realism must give way to a more dynamic and open-ended search for what is actually global in global politics, as was just argued. How, then, it must also be asked, will that affect the understandings of the universal and of the particular found within the other approaches that position themselves as responses to realism?

One element that realism needs to integrate in its logic, if we follow to its conclusion the argument defended here, is a much more dynamic understanding of the relationship between rationality, agency, and violence. This is where realism starts. We live in a world of violence. We cannot change that. The only thing we can do is devise a model of action in the world, a form of agency and rationality, which will allow us to control violence to some extent. This is crucial. We must be willing to use violence. We must see it as an instrument of political power that always remains at our disposal. It is this willingness to use violence that will protect us in a world of conflict and brutality. Indeed, it is our control of violence that will allow us also to create spaces in society where other forms of power, non-violent ones this time, will emerge. Agency and rationality, in that context, must always remain connected to this understanding of violence. As rational actors, we should at all times be concerned with the calculations of means and ends that permit the control of violence in society. In fact we must recognize that rational action cannot exist outside of these calculations and of the precarious social calm they bring: any movement away from these calculations would entail, we know, a return to a situation of such chaos and brutality that rational discourse would have no influence whatsoever on it.

This is where realism gains its sense that it speaks to universal truths. According to this logic, there can be no other solution to the problem of violence. Either violence is reduced to an instrument of political power employed through the sort of instrumental rationality described by the realist logic, or else it will remain uncontrolled and swathe all social relations, in an unending cycle of brutality and bloodshed. The choice is never between different types of politics, different types of rationality; the choice, instead, is between this type of politics and rationality and sheer, unremitting violence. There can only be, in that view, one solution to the problem of violence, anywhere and at any time. This is how realists can know that what they propose does suit all of international politics throughout the globe.

What the second part of this book showed, however, is that this type of logic encounters significant problems when it is set against the nature of international politics in the non-Western world. The notion that violence can be reduced to an instrument of political power and stand alongside other means of non-violent power, the idea that human rationality and agency can always orchestrate this process – all of this is coextensive with a precise series of political, social, and institutional developments. In the non-Western world, these developments can sometimes be absent or remain quite precarious. Failed or failing states, for instance, are precisely about the tenuous nature of many of these developments. Realism, though, cannot integrate in its logic the idea that it needs to look beyond its understanding of human rationality and violence in order to understand issues of violence in the non-Western world. The realist logic assumes that all that is required to move away from unending violence is the intervention of human agency and rationality. That is always the only solution to the problem of violence. It cannot situate in that logic, then, the need to go beyond these factors, toward much more structural elements of social, political, and institutional development, to capture the whole array of dynamics involved in the control or lack of control of violence in the non-Western world. This is what is required to understand violence in those parts of the world; and yet realism cannot make this sort of broader study part of the equation because of the makeup of its starting assumptions.

This must be, then, the first element of an amended realism, better able to deal with the violence of the non-Western world. Realists must integrate in their work the idea that the relationship between human rationality and violence is not given so much as politically, socially, and institutionally constructed. This is the key necessary to unlock the solution realism needs to arrive at a worldview more inclusive of the international politics of the non-Western world. The sequence associated with the rise of the "paraphernalia of constitutionalism,"[5] described earlier here by Wolin, must become part of the vernacular of realism. Has the state built a framework of institutions and rights solid enough to contain violence and to allow means of non-violent power to emerge in society? Have these processes been completed, or are they still ongoing? Do violence and rationality, in that environment, even approximate the image that realism has of them? Realism, in a word, must abandon the assumption that it can always be sure that violence and rationality are as it depicts them. The key point, though, is that none of this can happen unless realism first moves away from its assumption of universality. It is this assumption that blocks any movement toward the consideration of these issues.

However, a realism that would substitute these questions in its logic as a matter of course, in place of its unvarying sense of universality, would look quite differently at the world. Asking about the processes through which the rational control of violence arises would, more often than not, bring realism quite close to where it stands at the moment. The answer, in most cases around the world, would be that the developments necessary for the emergence of these elements are in place, and that realism can thus proceed with its analysis of the way in which violence usually corresponds to the exercise of human agency and rational calculations. In many cases around the non-Western world, however, the answer would underscore that these developments are incomplete or unstable, and that realism must look beyond rational calculations of costs and benefits and more toward the factors presented here to explain violence in those parts of the world. This would then be a realism – and this is the crucial point – much better able to articulate a vision of what violence can be, and of how it must be understood, throughout the entire world.

This brings the argument back to what was said at the beginning of this chapter about universals. The point, for international studies, should not be to jettison all aspirations to universality. The point should be instead to attempt to build better universals, which are more representative of the international politics of the entire world. This is precisely what an amended realism could achieve, by replacing its current built-in assumptions about the universality of its views on violence and rationality with a more open-ended and dynamic comprehension of these issues, one of the sort proposed here. It was claimed earlier that this search for a revised approach to universality in international studies should always proceed, in the end, on the basis of an explicit engagement with as many particular contexts of international politics throughout the world as possible. What is suggested here would accomplish exactly that. It would compel realism, as part of its very outlook on the world, to put its views on violence to the test every time it is called upon to provide a framework of analysis in the non-Western world, and it would thus also force realism, in that context, to speak of the universality of violence and human rationality in a way that would respect the reality of these elements in those parts of the world.

The best example of what is proposed here in the context of current global politics is perhaps the series of operations of post-conflict reconstruction conducted by the international community in different parts of the non-Western world. These operations are evidence of exactly the type of problem just outlined. They involve the deployment, in the non-Western world, of models of peace and politics that find their origins in the Western world. The difficulties encountered by these operations – to be sure, their poor rate of success – would seem to indicate, moreover, that their logic overlooks or misunderstands some of the realities of the non-Western world that they are supposed to address. The solutions proposed here in view of those sorts of tensions might well, in this perspective, prove instructive for such international operations.

These operations of post-conflict reconstruction are based, it must be noted at the outset, on a very realist take on the costs and benefits of violence. There is continuing violence between a number of groups in a given country, to such an extent that the international community starts talking the language of failed states and endemic conflict and launches a vast operation of social and political reconstruction. Aid is brought in, so are large numbers of military troops and humanitarian workers, and a concerted long-term attempt to rebuild the state, the economy, and even society itself, is undertaken. The hope underlying these efforts is that a fundamental change will occur. Political objectives used to be pursued through violence. Now that new forms of non-violent power are emerging – the state is now a viable one, the economy is starting to develop – it is through the workings of these political, economic, and social channels, that politics will be decided. Violence will remain a possibility, but an ineffective one. The international community will support those who follow the new rules of the game, and so will the population at large. All of this rests on an image very familiar to the realists: that of rational actors, who can choose to use violence or not and who make this decision on the basis of the costs and benefits associated with each option.

What happens, though, on the ground, once these operations are set in motion? The logic driving these operations assumes that violence was a choice from the start for the different groups involved in the conflict for which the international community is now trying provide an end. In that perspective, these groups can decide to end the hostilities and to move toward the cessation of violence offered by external actors. The reality of the situation, though, is that these groups most often evolve in a context where all institutional barriers to violence – state institutions and the like – have been destroyed. In that context, violence is not so much chosen as forced upon all these groups: physical violence is a necessary condition of survival, not a preferred means of political power. This is not, then, an environment where one can merely make a decision to leave violence aside and to resort to non-violent means of power. These non-violent forms of power do not exist. These elements – the choice between violence and other forms of power, a rationality widespread enough in society to allow one to believe that it represents the arbiter of that choice – still must be created, then, *before* the logic of rational movement toward non-violence can have any resonance in this environment.

This is where these situations connect with the problems studied here. There is certainly, within these operations, an abiding concern with the broader social and institutional context in which conflict and violence take place. Indeed, these peace operations are very much about pushing forward the development of new social and political institutions. The problem, though, is that this process is often seen as standing aside, so to say, from the dynamics of conflict and violence. There is violence amongst these groups, the logic goes, but they could also choose to move their conflict within the less violent arenas of electoral politics, for instance, or of new forms of power-sharing. The choice is theirs. The question, though, is always whether or not the institutional, political, and social context, as it exists around these groups, allows at all the movement toward a reduced and controllable violence envisioned in this logic. This means, then, that the social context in which these actors operate must not be seen as being external to their calculations about violent and non-violent forms of politics. On the contrary, each must be seen as being imbricated in the other. And this speaks, in turn, to the need for a broader vision of the interaction between agency, rationality, and contexts of violence, of the sort proposed here, as these peace operations unfold.

This is undoubtedly a lesson that is being learned, as all these peace operations encounter endless difficulties. Extensive work on the international presence in Cambodia in the early 1990s, for instance, has been done in order to look at these issues. The total destruction of all state and institutional structures by the Khmer Rouge during the era of the Killing Fields brought about a situation where, for a long time, only violence constituted a true currency of power in the country. This represented a key obstacle, which prevented the international community from engineering a transition toward the rule of law and constitutional politics in the course of its presence there. To grasp fully the dimensions of the problem, though, one was required to look at the broad social and institutional context in which political actors evolved, and not merely at the calculations of interests and concerns that motivated them as they looked at that environment. This is how it was possible to understand fully the behavior of these groups during the intervention of the international community and its attempt to establish a new social contract in Cambodia, one that would finally bring about peace in the country. Caroline Hughes, for example, has done extensive research on this question.[6] Cambodia was one of the earliest of these broad peace operations, and it has thus been the object of a vast literature.[7] The same conclusions also come back time and again, though, in the more recent literature on the interventions in Iraq or Afghanistan.[8]

In counterpoint to these more practical considerations, this draws the argument back to the issue of how deeply we need to rethink international studies. Realism is now very often the starting point of reflections on rationality and violence in international affairs. Critiques of realism also often take the understanding of rationality or the understanding of violence at the core of the approach, and then develop their own arguments from that point forward. The point made here is that a new approach is needed to incorporate in all these reflections the series of issues considered in these pages. None of this can happen, though, if international studies itself does not change. The discipline is built around constant references, made in the classroom or in the most advanced of academic journals, to a number of authors embodying its main questions and dilemmas. It is these authors who inject in the field its sense of universalism. It is then this presumption, that the field already has in hand the instruments needed to explain all of international politics throughout the world, that hinders its ability to see or understand phenomena that lie outside of its worldview. It is thus, in the end, that entire canon of authors and core problems at the center of the field that must be amended somewhat, so that the broader understanding of these phenomena, proposed here, may become possible.

As regards the nature of violence and rationality, it is very much Machiavelli and Morgenthau who, as was shown in the first part of this book, constitute the constant points of reference on these issues in realism, and in the discipline itself. Their work underlies the basic images with which discussions on these issues are opened up in the field. Conversely, they also provide the most common starting point of perspectives that, like liberalism, attempt to develop alternative takes on these subjects. Through all of this, it is mainly these two authors who imbue debates on rationality and violence in the field with a deep-seated assumption of universality and with the sense that what is said about these questions always pertains to all of international politics. This is, then, where work must also be done. Machiavelli and Morgenthau need to be reassessed in ways that open up the self-enclosed, universalist discourse on violence and rationality they have instilled in international studies. It is once this is done that the discipline will have a better basis on which to integrate the issues studied here in relation to the non-Western world, issues that have so far escaped its purview precisely because it was turned inward, shut in within the bounds of its assumption of universality. In this light, the point is not, most obviously, that students and scholars of international studies should stop reading Machiavelli and Morgenthau. The point, instead, is to ask how Machiavelli and Morgenthau should be read now, how they should be used in international studies, so that they can now help the discipline develop insights into issues such as the nature of violence in the non-Western world and the global responses to it.

The way in which Machiavelli and Morgenthau instill universalist assumptions about violence and rationality within the language of international studies has to do with the solution they provide to the problem of violence. Machiavelli reminds us that we all have a choice: we can be "animals ruled by force," or we can be "men ruled by laws."[9] It is this opposition between these two options that sets up the universalism in Machiavelli's vision of the world. We can only be beasts or rational human beings. The nature of violence is such that no other alternative is open to us. Either we control it through our rationality and thus impose limits on its role within politics, or it will dominate all social relations and reduce political life to the exercise of violence by all of us acting as so many "animals." This is the only solution to the issue of violence, all the time and everywhere. If we try to act otherwise and do without this foremost concern with the control of violence, we will not arrive at a different type of politics, we will simply be caught in the absence of politics where all of social life will be shrunk to the operation and effects of widespread violence. It is by following an identical logic that Morgenthau can tell us, as well, that he speaks of dynamics which are "universal in time and in space"[10] when he brings forth the same issues.

Both Machiavelli and Morgenthau, then, surround this understanding of the nature, the ontology, of violence and rationality, with epistemological and normative considerations that buttress their views. In terms of epistemology, they posit that rationality must be the same, all the time and everywhere. Rationality emerges out of the control of violence. It gains credence and clout in social affairs only once violence has been contained by institutions like the state, and other forms of non-violent power have been given a chance to influence the course of society. Rationality, then, is exactly like politics. It exists, or it does not exist. There cannot be other types of rationality because it always arises in the same way, through the control of violence, and it always has the same nature – a dispassionate instrument, focused, before anything else, on engineering the diminution of violence necessary to its very existence. This universality of rationality in Machiavelli and Morgenthau then squares with their broader vision of the relationship between violence, politics, and rationality. If we know that rationality is always the same, all the time and everywhere, then we also know that it will always act in the same way in the organization of politics and in the management of violence: we know, then, that it will always give a similar character to politics and to the control of violence, and that it will thus bring these realities in line with the universalist vision that Machiavelli and Morgenthau have of them.

The same is true of their views on the role of normative considerations in international affairs. For both Machiavelli and Morgenthau, morality cannot exist outside of the control of violence. The channeling of violence within institutions like the state opens up in counterpoint spaces where not only rationality will arise, but also morality. It is in these spaces, where violence has been evacuated from social relations, that we can search, as rational human beings, for the best in all of us, instead of continuing to behave one toward the other like "animals only ruled by force." To that extent, and just as was the case with the nature of violence and rationality, we can also be sure that we know universal truths about morality. We know, for instance, that it will always exist only in the spaces marked out by the control of violence: outside of these spaces, where violence still rules all behavior, the pursuit of morality will never be a viable project. We also know that this pursuit of moral ideals should always remain circumscribed, at all times and everywhere, by the rational calculations needed to control violence in society: any moral design that would undermine these calculations could allow a return to violence and thus endanger the conditions necessary to its success.

In this case again, then, Machiavelli and Morgenthau add, with their vision of morality, another reinforcing layer to the conceptual construct that allows them to think that they address universal realities in international politics. This universality of morality, this universality of its limits in the face of violence, justifies everything they say about rationality, violence, and politics. Those are realities, they argue, which can never change. The only source of change that could possibly transcend and alter them would be the pursuit of broader moral ideals inscribed in our nature as human beings. Morality, though, can never exceed the bounds already set for it by these elements of violence, rationality, and politics. If the only source of change that could possibly alter these realities cannot do so, we can then know, in turn, that they will always remain the same, universally.

Machiavelli and Morgenthau thus use these series of self-reinforcing arguments to lock in place, so to speak, their overall sense that what they argue about violence and rationality carries universally throughout all of international affairs. Indeed, once one enters this logic, it is difficult to find a way out and see how it could miss much in the nature of violence and rationality in the non-Western world. That is why those who draw on that logic to address questions of violence in those parts of the world get caught, themselves, in a line of reasoning which leaves them ill-informed about many of the realities that they should integrate in their thinking.

This is where the call for a new reading of Machiavelli and Morgenthau, along the lines of what has been proposed here, imposes itself. The key problem outlined in the preceding sections of the book, when it comes to the non-Western world – the need for international studies to consider the more structural processes that connect with agency, rationality, and violence – remains invisible as long as one continues to abide by a conventional reading of these authors. It is this situation that must be kept in mind as one reads them in order to gain insights in matters of violence within these parts of the world. In this sense, students and scholars of international studies must learn, so to say, to flip around Machiavelli and Morgenthau. They cannot read in their work a mere description of the nature of violence and rationality, and then apply it to the international politics of the non-Western world. They must reverse the sequence and ask what social, political, and institutional developments precede the conceptions of violence and rationality contained in Machiavelli and Morgenthau and make them possible. They must then ask if the politics of the non-Western world always allows this movement toward conceptions of violence and rationality, which they now simply adopt as their starting point. This is how the issues brought forward in this book will become visible through a reading of Machiavelli and Morgenthau.

In fact, simply asking these questions would bring about in international studies much of the change of perspective proposed here. Machiavelli and Morgenthau often shape, right from the start, the phrases and images used in the field to describe issues of conflict and violence. Setting their work against a wider background – one asking how exactly understandings of violence and rationality come about – would take nothing away from them. They would still represent a crucial point of convergence, within the literature, for debates dealing with the problem of violence in international affairs and with the possible solutions that can be developed to deal with this problem. Engaging in these debates against this wider background would also underscore, however, the dynamics at the root of the specific tensions between violence and rationality in a setting like the non-Western world, and the extent to which they can come together in ways that are sometimes quite at odds with what can be gleaned from conventional readings of Machiavelli and Morgenthau.

Much has been made in these pages of the need for international studies to develop new universals. The field, it was argued, must not move only toward a study of the specifics of international politics in the non-Western world. Instead, it should craft a language of new universals, ones that are more inclusive of the forces that shape international politics in those parts of the world and that also connect with, and enrich, the broader themes of debate that have underlain international studies up to this point. As has been proposed here, this should be part of these new universals in international studies. The field needs a broader, a more universal outlook on the social and political factors involved in the construction of notions of rationality and violence in international affairs. This would provide it with an overarching framework explaining both the conceptions of rationality and violence now central to the field and those accounting for the nature of these realities in the non-Western world. That is how an understanding of the nature of violence and rationality in the non-Western world could become an integral part of international studies. The reading of Machiavelli and Morgenthau proposed here would help set in motion precisely that process.

The second element that should be discussed is the understanding of the state which realism injects in international studies. Indeed, a certain notion of the state is key to realism, and then also to the approaches that position themselves as critiques of the realist paradigm. How could this notion of the state be made more congruent with the international politics of the non-Western world? And how does that play into our understandings of global politics in the post-Western world created by the "rise of the rest"?

The vision of the state espoused by the realists comes in large part from a certain reading of the work of Hobbes and from later interpretations, associated, for instance, with the writings of Waltz. For Hobbes and Waltz, and for all the neo-realists who now use their work as the starting point of their own analysis, rationality is not enough to control violence. I can undoubtedly be rational, just like Machiavelli and Morgenthau want me to be, and then attempt to reduce the use of violence around me through cautious and rational thinking. The problem, however, is not me, it is the others around me. What if they decide to resort to indiscriminate and irrational violence, even though I am presenting the most rational of cases against it? The solution to that problem is the state. The state controls violence in society, essentially because it possesses more means of violence than anyone else, for instance through the police and military forces at its disposal, and it can thus punish those who would resort to violence irrationally or indiscriminately. With the state in place I can feel safe, since I know that others will not dare attack me, for fear of being themselves the victim of the greater violence that can be exercised by the state.

This vision of the state within the neo-realist canon then leads, in turn, to a specific view of international politics. The space within the state will become pacified, rational, and manageable. The space outside the state, though, where international politics is to unfold, will be exactly the reverse. This will be a space where violence is not controlled in any way and where, therefore, it remains the only arbiter of politics. The only "ordering principle" of international affairs, as Waltz puts it, [11] will thus remain violence itself. What transpires in international politics will always be the simple, direct result of the use or threat of violence. Nothing will affect international affairs more directly or more immediately.

We can be sure, the neo-realists also tell us, that this logic speaks to universal realities. Human beings are all rational. Everywhere, moreover, they are forced to accept the idea that violence is always a possibility in social relations, and that it could thus one day be used against them in some way or another. The only rational solution to that problem, always, is the creation of the state. The creation of the state, in turn, always brings about the same violent "ordering principle" in international affairs. There is an immutable sequence extending from the nature of human rationality and violence all the way to the nature of international politics, which lets us know that we are always right when we see that "ordering principle" as the best point of entry into the study of international politics, wherever we are on the globe.

This logic does not quite play itself out the way the neo-realists would have it, though, when it comes to the non-Western world. The problem has to do with the crucial element that the neo-realists wish to add to the discourse of international studies: an unswerving focus on the nature of the state and on its implication for international affairs. The vehement defense of this focus of study in the neo-realist literature stems from the two-step sequence at the core of its logic. Human rationality defines the state, it is claimed in this approach, and the state then defines international politics. Both elements of this sequence, however, are problematic in regard to the non-Western world. This is a part of the world where the state was created from the outside, through the manifold dislocations and recompositions that marked the colonial period. The state, then, is not the culmination of negotiations between free-willed individuals that the neo-realists envision. Its nature, instead, must be explained to a large extent by factors that stand outside the neo-realist logic: much more structural factors, linked to the economic and political dimensions of colonialism, which, in fact, often trumped the search for rational models of society in the array of dynamics underlying the constitution of the state.

How the state defines the nature of international politics must also be reexamined in the context of non-Western international politics. The neo-realist logic assumes a clear delineation between the inside of the state, where rational politics prevails, and the outside of the state, where it is violence instead that determines the "ordering principle," defining the relations at play in that space. In the non-Western world, though, the state often remains quite weak internally. There are dire ethnic or religious cleavages, for instance, which undermine its legitimacy and create zones of endemic tension, or even open conflict, within its borders. Violence, then, remains inside the state as much as outside of it. The state, moreover, often deals with these internal conflicts by forging regional security frameworks with other neighboring states, so that insurgents are denied freedom of movement or access to resources across their borders. The attempt to pacify social relations inside the state, in that sense, develops outside the state as much as it does within its own borders. The geography of violence, so to speak, is thus quite different from what the neo-realists imagine it to be. The clear delineation between radically different "ordering principles" of politics, as Waltz puts it, does not exist in this context. In both the space inside the state and the space outside of it, these "ordering principles" are in fact intermingled one with the other in ways that are at odds with the neo-realist logic. There might well be cases, for example, where the state develops a democratic life for some sectors of its population, while at the very same time it continues to use brute violence and repression against other segments of its population, and within its own borders.

It is these problems that must be taken into account if the particular geography of violence at play in the non-Western world is to be understood properly. It is all these factors, to put it differently, that one must keep in mind to explain adequately where violence is likely to occur, why it could be used, and what political purpose it would serve. Neo-realism, however, cannot simply take on these issues and then move forward within the bounds of its own logic. The universalism at the center of its worldview prevents that. This is where, therefore, work needs to be done now. A key component of this work must be the development within neo-realism of a much broader outlook on the nature of the state and on its impact on the character of international politics. The state is certainly the result of an effort to extirpate violence from social relations and to substitute for it a more rational and peaceful form of social interaction. It also needs to be acknowledged that in many parts of the world where the trajectory of state development has been set by the legacy of colonialism it is in fact factors quite different from this search for rationality and peaceful society that account for the nature of the state. Thinking in those terms would allow the neo-realists to get out of the logical *cul-de-sac* where they find themselves at the moment. They now work within a logic which leads them to assume that the only factor they need to consider in order to explain the nature of state, in whatever context, is human rationality and its response to violence. Recognizing right from the start of the analysis that the state is to be explained by a variety of factors influencing each other to diverse degrees in different parts of the world would force them to acknowledge, at the very core of their logic, that the form of the state, which they take at the moment to be universal, is in reality one among many possible routes to statehood. This is how the self-enclosed universalism underlying neo-realism when it comes to its view of the state could be opened up to the sort of broader perspective on state development proposed in these pages.

Certainly, this would immediately introduce in the neo-realist worldview the one key element it needs to bring on board if it is to understand better the international politics of the non-Western world: a more nuanced view of the geographies of violence at play in that part of the world. The neo-realists now look only at human rationality as the driver of state development. It is because of that focus on rationality as an object of analysis that they come to divide politics into two distinct spaces – one inside the state, where rationality can prevail, and the other outside the state, where it is violence instead that dictates rules of behavior. Integrating in neo-realism a broader perspective on factors other than rationality, which play in the construction of the state, would also underscore how these additional factors can create the mixed spaces described here earlier, where both rationality and violence cohabit one with the other, in ways not readily envisioned in the neo-realist logic. This would lead to a much more inclusive understanding of the nature of violence throughout the entire world. This, in the end, is the point. The idea defended in these pages is not that the neo-realists are always wrong when it comes to the non-Western world. There are, in those parts of the world, assertive states of the type described to us by neo-realism, states that interact one with the other almost solely on the basis of the means of violence they could engage in a possible confrontation. The point made here is that these states should also be seen for what they are: uncertain and incomplete structures, which often deal with violence through domestic and international arrangements that remain at cross-purpose with the neat division between the inside and the outside of the state depicted by the neo-realists. It is these arrangements and the additional logics of violence they produce, and the way they then intrude within the accounts of politics and violence at the international level painted for us by neo-realism, that must be figured out if the true nature of violence in non-Western international life is to be fully grasped. This is what is missing now in neo-realism. The approach proposed here, though, would allow neo-realists to remedy that situation.

This brings the argument to the case for new universals in international studies which has structured this part of the book. Neo-realism works on the basis of a language of universals. The state always establishes, it claims, a fundamental distinction between its inside, where rationality is the norm, and its outside, where violence dominates. In turn, this always gives the international realm its specific character. It is this assumption of universality that provides, then, the starting point of neo-realist thinking about international life. Yet it is also this sense of universality that prevents neo-realism from understanding correctly the nature of violence and of international life in the non-Western world. What is proposed in these pages is simply that the search for a global, a universal take on the state and violence should in fact revolve around a series of more open-ended questions: how, it should be asked, does the state deal with the problem of violence? What other factors, beyond the search for a rational and peaceful way of life, influence that process? And how do these other factors shape the "ordering principles" at the heart of the domestic and the international realms in ways that are different from what is envisioned at the moment by the neo-realists? Asking these more open-ended questions, instead of merely assuming that the state always deals with violence in the same way, would provide a much better standpoint from which to consider the nature of the state, that of violence, and that of international life – throughout the whole world. This is, in a word, the type of intellectual inquiry that could point at what is more truly universal about all these issues when one considers the entire globe. The neo-realist logic would still pertain to all these cases where its claims about the organization of the state and of violence at the international level do correspond to the reality of the situation. It would also be possible, however, to account for all these other cases in the non-Western world where the nature of violence and of international politics differs markedly from what is assumed in the neo-realist logic.

The concrete example which best illustrates this point is perhaps the rise of China. This issue is now often the most crucial question attached to the "rise of the rest" and to the challenges it poses for our understandings of current global politics. What is striking about these debates is the extent to which they rely on the language of neo-realism. As G. John Ikenberry notes in the introduction of the book he edited on the "future of the balance of power,"[12] these questions are mainly seen through the prism of the "most elegant and time-honored theory of international order: order is the result of balancing by states under conditions of anarchy to counter opposing power concentrations or threats."[13] In a world where international politics is ruled by nothing but "anarchy" and where China's rise amounts to an "opposing concentration of power," solutions must be found to either counter-balance or contain that new center of power, so that new frameworks of global stability can be put in place. This is neo-realism. States are self-enclosed entities that relate one to the other in terms of the anarchy that envelops all of them and then forces them to seek order only in the balancing and counter-balancing of raw power. This is also very much the universalism that underlies neo-realism. All states throughout the globe evolve within the same worldwide anarchic realm, which imposes, on every one of them, a similar need to engage in these strategies of balancing and counter-balancing of power capacities. Nothing else, then, needs to be known about China: it is a state and, like all states, it will abide by this universal logic. It is on that basis that foreign policy options for the United States and other Western states can be elaborated to deal with China's rise in power.

The problem, though, is that this sort of analysis misses much of what actually determines calculations of power balancing and counter-balancing in China's relations with East Asia and the wider world. Indeed, Ikenberry's book is about that issue: something more seems to enter into these calculations, in that part of the world and in other ones, beyond what is described in the neo-realist logic. This speaks to the issues covered in the second part of the book. Robert H. Jackson uses the phrase "negative sovereignty"[14] to designate these realities: states built from the outside, through the intervention of external powers, and which remain caught in a process of state-building and self-legitimization. These states do not always match the clear distinction between the inside and the outside, the domestic and the international, envisioned in neo-realism. On the contrary, defining the inside and the outside of the state can still be a matter of great contention. The logics animating domestic and international politics can be blurred in that sort of environment, in ways that challenge the very basis of the neo-realist approach. All of these elements resonate well in the Chinese context. The politics of Tibet or Xinjiang, or those related to Taiwan, are precisely about firming up, and then legitimizing, what is inside the state and what is out- side of it. In the case of Taiwan, the conflict thus takes place for China in a space that remains, in Ayoob's phrase cited earlier, "both internal and external."[15] All strategic decisions are therefore filtered through a logic of politics that is in fact "both internal and external." The actors involved in these decisions, the definition of the stakes engaged in possible responses to international developments – all of this connects, for example, the pur- suit of domestic legitimacy and regional strategic order as part of one single continuum. Domestic and international politics, in a sense, are one and the same. Supposing, as the neo-realists do, that there is always a radical fis- sure between the "ordering principles" guiding domestic and international politics misses that part of the story.

In turn, those who use a neo-realist language to address these issues over- look two central problems. Neo-realism leads to the idea that the balancing and counter-balancing of power in international affairs follows a reflex-like and immediate pattern: if a powerful state increases its power, others will at once want to counter-balance that rise in power because, in a *milieu* defined by anarchy, no other mechanism can guarantee continued strategic stability. The nature of the international realm compels states to act that way. What about, however, an international environment like the one just described with regard to China and Taiwan, where the specific character of the interna- tional realm is not so well separated from that of the domestic realm? Is the recourse to balance of power strategies still reflex-like and immediate, or do added considerations come into play because Taiwan remains in an hybrid space, "both internal and external" to the realm where international anarchy prevails? Any long-term observation of the strategic calculations of China when it comes to Taiwan will reveal that this is in fact the case, and that the mechanics of power balancing on that issue appear quite more complex than the neo-realist logic can allow. Opening the study of power balancing to this sort of analysis, however, runs counter to the logic of neo-realism as it now stands.

The second problem stems from the fact that, in a neo-realist worldview, the entire international realm is homogeneous. All of international politics everywhere throughout the globe, the neo-realists tell us, is animated by the same fundamental push and pull of power balancing and counter-balancing. This means that all regional politics, in any region across the world, can be understood through an analysis of this elemental dynamic. It means, as well, that regional politics are linked to global politics through this one logic. The balancing of power at a regional level will also play a role, the neo-realists claim, in the development of broader frameworks of equilibrium between larger global powers: there is always a search for balancing between the main powers of the international system, and what develops at a regional level between their respective allies and economic or political partners will feed directly in the construction of these more global power equilibria. It is on the basis of that logic that the United States can attempt, for instance, to leverage its close relations with states like Japan and South Korea in a regional setting in East Asia, against its search for a more globally defined power balance with China. All that happens at a regional level in terms of power balancing and counter-balancing, this logic holds, will echo within the broader global strategic equation opposing the United States and China.

What has been said so far shows, however, that there might be an important problem with this line of reasoning. When a state like China deals with the sort of political calculations described here with regard to an issue like Taiwan, where both the domestic and the international intermingle in ways unforeseen by neo-realism, it is neighboring states that remain the prime focus of these calculations. Defining the legitimate ambit of the state, what is inside of it and what is outside of it – all of this relates to territorial disputes, conflicting claims of sovereignty, and the like, which concern most directly the neighboring states with which these claims and disputes have to be resolved. This will influence how states in China's position define their calculations of power vis-à-vis these neighbors. The way China looks at power balancing with neighbors like Japan, for instance, or Vietnam, to say nothing of Taiwan, brings into play much more than the sort of simple, reflex-like strategic calculations underscored by the neo-realists. A complex array of historical claims about territory, nationality, and conflicting visions of legitimacy and inherited rights colors these interactions, as much as the perceptions of raw power and clout in the region. Indeed, the very definition of the power that each of these states brings to the equation cannot be understood without reference to these broader factors. This implies that the nature of power balancing in East Asia is very specifically tied to those series of factors. In turn, this means that the nature of power balancing amongst neighboring states in the region can be quite different from what is happening in other parts of the world. Also, finally, this indicates that the nature of power balancing between regional powers and extra-regional powers – in this case, between China and the United States – might work according to dynamics that are quite dissimilar from those determining regional developments, because the factors studied here will play less, or differently, in that context. The intermingling of the domestic and of the international, which is central to the power balancing between China and Taiwan, for instance, will be much less prevalent in the search for strategic balancing between China and the United States on issues that do not involve Taiwan. The balancing and counter-balancing of power at a more global level, in other words, might differ markedly from the way it operates at a more regional level. A neo-realist analysis, however, misses all of this. This type of analysis assumes, again, that a homogeneous propensity for power balancing traverses all regional and global contexts. The idea that a state like China can engage in forms of power balancing that differ in their very nature, whether they are deployed at the regional or at the global level, eludes the logic at the core of this approach. So does the idea, furthermore, that the way in which China builds its approach to power balancing at a regional level in East Asia can be specific to that region.[16]

A neo-realist analysis of the "rise of the rest" and the extent to which it entails, for instance in the case of China, a realignment of the balancing and counter-balancing of power within global international politics thus overlooks quite a lot in the issues that should matter in this type of reflection. Neo-realism assumes that it captures what is most basic and most important in international politics. This, the approach claims, consists in the efforts made by states to protect themselves by counter-balancing the power that other states could exert against them. Neo-realism ignores, though, how this basic driving force in international politics is itself fused with a series of other factors when it comes to the non-Western world: the intermingling of the domestic and the international around and within the state, the way in which this determines calculations of balance of power with other states, and the extent to which this plays differently in regional and global contexts. That is what must be understood if a proper analysis of China's rise and what it involves in terms of power balancing and counter-balancing is to be forthcoming.

As long as neo-realism remains fixed within its current assumptions, however, it will neglect these issues. It now assumes a universal distinction between the "ordering principles" underlying domestic and international politics; it also assumes a universally homogeneous propensity for power balancing, and for those reasons it cannot comprehend the intermingling of the domestic and the international, and then the manner in which this issue enters into the very construction of power balancing in a case like China. This is thus where work of the sort proposed here must be undertaken. Undoubtedly, there is such a thing in global politics as powerful states measuring their power against that of others and devising their actions in the international realm merely on that basis. The neo-realists are right to point this out. The issue, though, is that what they present as a straightforward reality – states reacting to the brute power of other states – is rather more complicated when it comes to the non-Western world. The state there often differs in its very nature from the model envisioned by the neo-realist, and this in turn affects the nature of power balancing itself. The way for neo-realism to redress that situation is to adopt, as has been proposed here, a more global, a more universal, understanding of the state. This will show the extent to which the construction of domestic and international spaces by the state, still under way in some parts of the world, impacts on the character of power balancing there. This is how neo-realism will be able to unlock the universalist conception of the state upon which it is based and to integrate in its logic all the problems outlined here. And this is how, in the end, neo-realism will be able truly to explain what is happening in a situation like the rise in power of China, and how that is likely to affect issues of global balance of power as the "rise of the rest" proceeds apace.

One final element that needs to be considered in this context is how, just as was the case with more traditional realism, all of this requires a new reading of the key neo-realist texts. Everyone who studies international politics is asked at one point or another to read Waltz's *Theory of International Politics*. Hobbes' *Leviathan* is even more of a standard in all introductory courses in political science and international studies. What do the preceding remarks tell us, however, about how we should read Hobbes and Waltz now?

The main reason why the work of Waltz and Hobbes has resonated so deeply in international studies is that it portrays itself as identifying, in the words of Waltz, "the central tendency among a confusion of tendencies, and [...] the propelling principle [among] other principles"[17] at the center of all international politics. This work depicts a basic logic for us. The state can control violence within its borders, but not outside of them. This gives the inter-state realm a very specific character, dominated by the use or threat of violence. And this, in turn, compels states to enter into patterns of power balancing and counter-balancing as the only way to manage international affairs and to prevent the recourse to violence by one state or another. This logical sequence, now the core of the neo-realist worldview, catches our attention because it aspires to bring to light the most fundamental character of international affairs – the "central tendency among a confusion of other tendencies." There might well be a wide array of other issues on the international agenda. Violence and the risk of violence, however, do remain. This forces all of us in international studies to engage with the problem. As soon as we do, Waltz and Hobbes constitute obligatory readings, because the logic of their views on the issue seems so forceful: we can disagree with it, and many in the field do, but we cannot ignore it, because it does appear to speak to crucial elements of international affairs.

The problem is that it has been difficult for both supporters and detractors of this logic to enter into this discussion without also bringing in at the same time the universalism that lies at the very core of the work of Hobbes and Waltz. Macpherson, as was said here before, calls Hobbes a "mechanical philosopher."[18] There is indeed in the work of these two thinkers the fundamental assumption that they have isolated the most basic elements, and the most basic relationships connecting these elements, in what constitutes international politics: they are now simply observing the mechanics at play in their interaction. There is nothing more basic, in their view, than violence. It corresponds to the most primordial common denominator in human relations. Violence leads unswervingly to the state, and the state leads just as directly to the sort of inter-state realm they describe to us. These are the most elemental of realities and the connections between these realities.

This is where the universalism underlying the neo-realist worldview arises. If these are primordial realities, they cannot be disassembled into more fundamental forces, which could operate differently according to context and circumstance: they are, on the contrary, always the same, and thus bound always to lead to the same consequences for international politics. Critiques of neo-realism, as has been shown here, have also often been unable to escape that universalism. They have accepted the idea that violence and the state as agent of control of violence are basic realities in international affairs, and then they have added new elements to the equation in order to present alternatives to the neo-realist position. Constructivists, for instance, very much see the control of violence by the state as a universal in international affairs, but then they add a discussion of identity and inter-subjectivity, to offer a counterpoint to neo-realism. They leave unchallenged the assumption that violence is a basic element in international affairs, which cannot be unpacked in terms of more elemental forces, which dictate how it will be organized and how it will be used.

This is, however, precisely the type of analysis that must be conducted if one is to understand the nature of violence in the non-Western world, how it is used by the state, and what specific character this gives to the international politics of that part of the world. Neo-realists, and those that critique them, miss that point. This is what creates one of the crucial problems outlined in this book. There are realities that must be taken into account if one studies violence and its impact on international life in the non-Western world. These realities, though, have not been integrated in international studies, because the language of universals that permeates the discipline has led it to overlook these issues.

How should Hobbes and Waltz be read, then, so that they can help resolve that problem? They do pose fundamental questions for all of us in international studies: what is violence? How does it relate to the nature of the state? How, finally, does that shape the features of international politics? As was said a moment ago, it is precisely because these questions appear so fundamental that their work has had such enduring appeal. What we need to do in the field, though, is to place the answers that Hobbes and Waltz give to these questions against the background of a much broader interrogation about the forces that precede the crystallization of violence, the state, and international politics, along the forms described by Hobbes and Waltz. The mistake made by the neo-realists is to believe that they have discovered, through their reading of Hobbes and Waltz, the purest distillation of the issue of violence and of its impact on international affairs. It is on that basis that they then assume they have exposed something essential in international affairs, which applies to all international environments. Critiques of neo-realism then often repeat that mistake by still accepting this understanding of violence and of the state as they develop other perspectives on international affairs.

The point made here is that, in fact, the neo-realists have a point, but that they also need to be pushed much further on it. Violence does matter, and it does shape international affairs. Neo-realism is right on that score. What is suggested here, though, is that, if violence matters, it must be studied much more closely and in much greater detail, as compared to the sort of work put forward in the neo-realist literature. The connection between the nature of violence, that of the state, and that of international affairs must be analyzed in terms of the multiple axes of development it can follow in dissimilar contexts all throughout the world. The belief that Hobbes and Waltz describe to us the one form of violence that shapes all of international politics cannot be left unquestioned in light of the issues outlined in this book. It is the sort of broader analysis proposed in these pages, instead, that must guide the consideration of the linkages between violence and international politics. This is how the neo-realist will really be able to speak to the impact of violence on the nature of international affairs throughout the world. This is also how critiques of neo-realism will have a truer sense of the nature of violence in world politics as they develop their own perspective on international affairs.

8
Reinventing Liberalism: Values and Change in the Post-Western World

Two elements have been put forward so far to underscore how international studies should proceed if it intends to give an accurate account of the way in which the "rise of the rest" is transforming global politics. The first element was the necessity of developing a more detailed understanding of the relationship between violence, agency, and rationality in situations of endemic violent conflict. The second element was the need to set in place a more nuanced analysis of the nexus connecting the nature of violence, that of the state, and that of the international realm, throughout the world.

But violence and its consequences, most obviously, are not all that should matter in this type of project. The issues put to our reflection in the field by the great Other[1] in international studies – liberalism – must also find pride of place here. The liberal language of democratization, human rights, and economic interdependence conveys problems that are extraordinarily significant at the moment in the international politics of the non-Western world. More than that, those are also very much issues that should stand at the center of any reflection on the extent to which the "rise of the rest" will force the elaboration of new understandings and new norms of global international politics. How will the West and the non-Western world discuss norms of human rights, for example, and how will they come together to shape the future of global economic interdependence – those are questions which will be key in the development and evolution of global politics in both the near and the long term. As has been shown in the preceding sections of this book, though, current liberal depictions of issues of rights and economic interdependence miss important elements when it comes to the non-Western world. As such, they must be altered in some important ways if they are to provide an adequate guide to the type of global politics likely to emerge as a result of a more forceful engagement of these issues by non-Western actors. How, then, should liberalism be changed, so as to fit better the new global politics cropping up because of the "rise of the rest"? Further to the point, how will these changes in the liberal paradigm cascade down through all of international studies, for instance amongst those whose worldview is essentially structured as a critique of liberalism, and make the field itself better suited to explain these new forms of global politics?

The first component of liberalism that must be modified is the Kantian line of reasoning, which traverses a good portion of the liberal literature. As was noted in the first part of this book, the Kantian logic rests on three central arguments. The proponents of this approach first argue that we all share, as human beings, a common human rationality, and that we can build our social interactions on the basis of that shared rationality. The need to deal with violence, these people say to the realists, does not necessarily have to be the pre-eminent factor that determines how we organize ourselves and how we deal with others. We can move beyond that. A rational search anchored in the mutual recognition of our human needs and our human identity can lead us to elaborate new social frameworks, based instead on the much higher ideals of freedom, justice, and peace.

Second, existing political arrangements rooted for instance in the need to control violence – and the state is evidently key amongst these structures – will not stop this movement toward new social forms, based on the pursuit of peace and justice. In fact, it is precisely because these political arrangements do not match our ability to express what is best and most moral in us as human beings that we are bound to change them. Their very existence and their very deficiencies demonstrate to all of us that we can do better, and that we all can come together in this project through our mutual recognition that we can indeed do better. It is thus possible to think that social arrangements founded on suspicion and the fear of violence will give way to democracy and habits of behavior where the respect of each other is the norm. These habits of democracy within states could then alter the way states behave on the outside, in their relations with each other. None of us will accept a situation where our respective state leaders engage in behavior in the international realm, violence and war for instance, which does not correspond to the values of peaceful and respectful interaction we are trying to instill in society. This is then likely to lead to the emergence, in time, of what Kant himself described as a "universal civic society."[2] Global norms of human rights and freedom will serve as the one central standard through which the actions of every individual, society, and state are to be judged by all of us. This is the "Kantian road to peace," as Michael Doyle puts it.[3] It is to this sequence that Kant's *Perpetual Peace* is devoted. It is this logic as well that inspires today the proponents of the democratic peace theory, and those who believe in the idea that the rise of a global civil society will fundamentally transform the character of international affairs.

The third argument at the core of Kantian logic, the one that ties it all together, is the claim that this logic speaks to universal realities in international affairs. We know that all human beings are rational, and can recognize this common human rationality in every other individual. We know that this gives all of us a potential for change that is always present. We can choose to follow the "Kantian road to peace" in whatever political or social circumstances we find ourselves, because movement along that road depends on a force, our rationality, which is universal and thus independent of any of those elements of circumstances and context. We know, therefore, that the Kantian logic can always prevail, in whatever part of the world we find ourselves. We can always recognize our humanity, and that of others, wherever we live around the globe. We can always decide to favor forms of politics that embody this recognition of our common humanity. This is always bound to change the character of the state we inhabit and that of its international behavior, in whatever part of the world that state is situated. The sequence linking democracy, peace, and our inclusion in a global civil society defending new and non-violent forms of international politics can thus always unfold in the way predicted by Kant and his current followers once we set it in motion, wherever we are in the world.

The literature focused on the international politics of the non-Western world brings to light, however, two problems with this series of arguments. The first problem is the same as that of all the other approaches studied here: liberalism, so to speak, starts its analysis too late. The goal of the liberal literature is to present itself as a counterpoint to the logic of realism. Liberalism takes account of the realist understandings of violence, rationality, and the state, and then pushes these elements in a direction opposite to the one taken by the realist literature. Where realism assumes that rationality always remains in tension with violence, the liberals respond that rationality can on the contrary escape and supersede the conditions created by violence in human affairs; and where the realists look at the state as the crucial force able to constrain violence and permit the advance of rationality in human affairs, the liberals reply that rationality is not dependent on the state and can by itself marginalize violence in the organization of society, both domestically and at the international level.

The problem created for the liberal literature with this way of positioning its logic as a response to realism is that it then overlooks what realism itself fails to grasp in the nature of violence, rationality, and the state in the non-Western world. The realist account of the nature of these elements neglects the series of social and political processes explaining how they take shape in that part of the world and to what extent these processes can in fact lead to results quite different from those envisaged by the realist literature. When the liberals simply take on board the understandings of violence, rationality, and the state, which are contained in realism, and then move forward with them in a new direction, they fail to see that problem. Liberals, in echo to the realists, assume the constant action of human rationality in all social contexts. They thus overlook how this sense of agency is in reality coextensive with the development of specific forms of control of violence. Liberals, drawing on realist assumptions, ascribe a certain nature to the state and proceed from that point on. Their image of how associational spaces built on rationality develop within the state and then overflow the borders of that state all rest on that prior conception of the state itself. They fail to see how the state in the non-Western world often does not correspond to those images. Spaces of violence and spaces of non-violence often coexist there within the state, and also outside of it. How the image of a peaceful and rational community encompassing the inside of the state and then over-flowing the borders of that state should be adapted to these spaces, which are at odds with the liberal logic, is not readily apparent in the liberal literature. To that extent, an analysis of the nature of violence and of that of the state – how they evolved in the non-Western world, and how the state has created hybrid spaces of violence and peace specific to that part of the world – must precede any discussion of the applicability of the liberal logic there.

The second problem with Kantian liberalism outlined earlier goes more directly to the core logic of the approach. The writings of Lee Hock Guan and Partha Chatterjee on the extent to which "entrenched primordial attachments"[4] affect the nature of "post-colonial democracies"[5] were cited in the second part of the book to describe the notions of individual self-identity that often prevail in the non-Western world. This is a world in which "primordial attachments" to ethnic and ethno-religious identities often still shape the relationship that the individual has with society and with the world at large. This makes for a situation where the individual will frequently define his self-identity in terms of his belonging to one of these ethnic or ethno-religious groups. The pursuit of one's identity, in that sense, passes through the affirmation of a broader identity, which precedes and supersedes one's own sense of the self. This makes for an image of the self that is quite different from that of the autonomous, self-referential individual, which dominates the liberal literature. The development of constitutionalism and that of a language of individual empowerment and human rights has allowed, to be sure, the recognition, in the non-Western world, of systems of rights that correspond closely to the notions of the individual defended by liberalism. The point, though, is that there is always a confrontation, a negotiation, now at play in the non-Western world, between these images of the self, which are consistent with the liberal tradition, and those rooted in more ethnic or religious communitarian identities. The point, also, is that the state most often reacts to these more communitarian identities just as much as it does to the sort of individual democratic identities described by the liberals. Constitutionalism and systems of individual rights do allow points of contact between individuals and state elites. Extra-constitutional channels still exist, however, that connect these elites to specific ethnic and ethno-religious groupings to the detriment of the language and practice of constitutionalism. Time and again, to put it differently, the state defends, in its international behavior, the interests and demands of one of these groupings, and not those of all its citizens.

This is quite different from what is imagined by the liberals. The sense of self-identity that animates individuals leads them to think that they are profoundly different from, rather than similar to, many of the individuals who surround them within their own state, or outside of it. The "primordial attachments" central to the definition of their individual self-identity still directs them to that conclusion. The behavior of the state, internally and within the international realm, follows from this sense of difference between dissimilar and unequal human identities, and indeed often reinforces it. The liberals see exactly the reverse. They underscore how individuals, when they look at themselves and others within the state or beyond its borders, are bound to mutually recognize in each other a common universal human identity. Then they show how the state will be compelled to acknowledge this expression of a universal human identity in its own citizens and in those of other states and to adopt forms of behavior on the international stage that conform to it.

The issue, of course, is that both perspectives are necessary to understand the international politics of the non-Western world. Both types of identities – the autonomous and self-referential individual described to us by the liberals and the individual defined by broader primordial communitarian attachments – now cohabit in the understandings of self-identity at the heart of debates on rights, democracy, and human identity unfolding at the moment in those parts of the world. Both types of state – the one driven by constitutionalism and rights and the one caught up in ethnic and ethno-religious identities – are piled one on the other and explain state behavior internally and internationally. It is the collisions, the tensions, and the overlaps between these forces that must be understood in order to explain how the rise of democracy and of human rights is changing the state, and then international politics, in non-Western areas.

Liberalism as it stands now, however, cannot fully engage those questions. The universalism at the center of its logic precludes that. The approach assumes at the moment that its side of the story, the self-referential individual and the state constrained in its behavior by the values of that particular individual, is the only one needed, universally, to explain the impact of these elements on international affairs. There is one form of human identity throughout the entire world, the liberals assume, not many. There is also one form of connection, the liberals continue, between that universal human identity, the state, and the nature of the international realm. They cannot integrate in their logic, then, the questions raised here about other forms of human identity and other forms of connections between the individual, the state, and international life. They cannot see, furthermore, how these other realities are in fact just as much part of the story of democratization and international change in the non-Western world. This is the crucial problem, in this sense, of liberalism at this time: its very logic does not allow it to incorporate in its analysis the questions it must take on board to explain how the issues of rights and democracy which it studies actually operate within the international politics of the non-Western world.

This is thus where work must be done. First, liberalism must move toward a broader understanding of the nature of human identity. The form of human identity that liberalism brings to our attention in the field at the moment does exist. There is such a thing as the rational self-defined individual, looking at others to find the same qualities in them, and then engaging domestic and international politics on that basis and asking that they reflect that search for the common humanity in all of us. The problem is that the universalism at the core of liberalism leads it to assume that this is all there is, all the time, in the most profound layers of human identity. This universalist conception of human identity must now give way to a broader one, which acknowledges just as much the other forms of human identity, which also sit at the core of the human experience. The "primordial attachments" that shape these other aspects of human identity must be traced to underscore their role in current debates on the issue in non-Western politics. The staging of these debates within the configuration of institutional, political, and social structures specific to the non-Western context under study must become part of the analysis. The resulting articulation of the most basic conceptions of human identity at play in that context, in tandem with those more akin to liberal worldviews, must then be put forward. This is how liberalism will have a truer sense of the dynamics of human identity at play when it comes to the non-Western world.

Second, liberalism must move toward a broader conception of the state as well. The constitutional state it assumes in its logic does exist in many parts of the non-Western world. The problem is that liberalism implicitly takes for granted that, once this constitutional state has emerged, this is all there really is to the state in those parts of the world. In fact, as was shown here, the construction of that constitutional state receptive to the values of human rights and identity embodied in liberalism does not take place in a vacuum: the ethnic and ethno-religious affiliations that preceded its formation still influence its nature and its behavior to this day. How exactly this happens must become part of the analysis proposed by liberalism. This requires liberalism, yet again, to open up its universalist assumptions and explore how different forms of state makeup, responsive to different forms of human identity, can still exist within the state, even when constitutionalism and liberal values prevail in that state. This is how, at a second level, liberalism will reach a more accurate understanding of the nature of the state in the non-Western world and will see in greater detail how the state responds to the specific mix of identities that dominates there.

And then, third, liberalism must look at the way these broader understandings of human identity and of the nature of the state can ultimately enrich its own analysis of international politics. Liberalism follows at this point a linear logic: a certain notion of human identity leads to a certain type of state, which in turn leads to a certain type of international politics. It is because of this progression that we can know that the ideals of rights and rationality enshrined in the liberal vision of human identity will eventually come to dominate international politics. What liberalism needs to define in greater details now, when it comes to non-Western international politics, is how the more fluid dynamics of identity and state behavior described here will influence the international dynamics it aims to identify and study, in ways that might well depart from the liberal logic. How will the negotiation of identity now unfolding in many parts of the non-Western world, this negotiation leading to fused amalgams of liberal and non-liberal identities, express itself at the international level? What sort of identities and rights will be defended, for instance, in the international human rights regime in which non-Western states are parties as a result of these developments? How will the "rise of the rest" give more visibility and weight to these questions and take these regimes toward avenues still unexplored by the liberal literature? How will non-Western states, caught between these debates on identity at home and global pressures on human rights and on identity that are more akin to those painted by the liberals, react in this context? How will their behavior change as the identities at home to which they react evolve and transform themselves over time? It is by dealing with these questions, instead of focusing only on the sequence now connecting the liberal visions of human identity, the state, and international affairs, that liberalism will be able to understand better the international politics of the non-Western world and how they will fit or not within the liberal vision of global politics.

This is how, then, liberalism will be able to explain how the "rise of the rest" is likely to intersect with dynamics of global democratization and global politics. Democracy and the defense of human rights are growing forces in the non-Western world. It is tempting to imagine, as the liberal now do, how these forces are bound to transform the international politics of these parts of the world. Global civil society will certainly gain, as the liberals tell us, stronger and stronger constituencies there. Non-Western states will also, in all likeliness, be compelled by these changes to involve themselves more convincingly in the global regimes intended to enshrine, both in law and in practice, values of right, rationality, and freedom in international affairs. What is crucial, though, is that a broader analysis more sensitive to the nature of identity, state behavior, and international affairs in the non-Western world is also necessary to understand how all these phenomena are likely to unfold. This is the type of analysis that can help bring to light how notions of human identity and human community are bound to order and reorder themselves in the non-Western world. This is, as well, the type of analysis that can help explain how exactly states from those parts of the world are then likely to act within the series of regimes, multilateral institutions, and broad normative frameworks studied by the liberals. Those are key questions raised by the "rise of the rest." The broadening of the liberal analysis of all these issues that is proposed here is necessary, it seems, to answer correctly those questions.

This brings the discussion back to the issue of universals in international studies. The way in which liberalism has positioned itself as a discourse on what is universal in human identity and on how this leads to a certain type of international politics has in fact precluded the approach from grasping important problems. Much broader understandings of the main notions upon which the liberal logic is articulated are required in order to comprehend and explain current changes in the non-Western world. This speaks to the need for liberalism to reengage the question of what is universal in human identity and in international politics in light of the issues studied here. This is, in the end, the challenge now posed to liberalism by the "rise of the rest." It is by addressing this challenge that liberalism will become better prepared to explain the true impact of the phenomenon on global politics.

The best way to think of a concrete case in point illustrating how this could be done is perhaps to go to the most basic assumptions that are often put up, in both the academic and the more popular media, to assess the impact of democratization in the non-Western world. Time and again, in a broad array of writings, the case is made that the push toward democracy there will be a decisive factor defining relations between the West and those parts of the world. Human rights are now the object of an ever-increasing number of international legal instruments, it is argued, and that trend is matched by the rise of a global human rights culture, which marks out very clearly how governments everywhere can and cannot treat their citizens. People throughout the entire world can use these legal norms and this global culture of rights as a means of leverage against their respective governments. Violations of human rights and basic democratic norms, for instance, are made public instantly through the internet and other electronic means, and global public pressures are then applied to the governments guilty of these offences.

This will be, the argument goes, a core feature of the post-Western world. The "rise of the rest" will be accompanied by tensions between the Western and non-Western worlds. There will be problems as power shifts and new centers of political and economic influence arise. However, the global forces of democracy and human rights will counter-balance these problems. Frameworks of rights, intertwined legal and normative regimes, and, more than anything, the human aspirations that underlie their development will shape global politics just as much as all these tensions and these problems. This will be the new global politics: divided by state and economic rivalries, but increasingly brought together by the forces unleashed by the growing democratization of the non-Western world.

The issue, though, is whether or not this type of argument corresponds to the nature of democratization in the non-Western world. Do the dynamics at play in those parts of the world really correspond to the assumptions underlying all these claims? Does the state, and then the nature of inter-state relations, actually conform to these expectations? The questions raised in this book can serve to illuminate problems overlooked in those sorts of arguments and help give a better sense of the way in which the processes of democratization now unfolding in the non-Western world will affect the nature of global politics.

Himadeep Muppidi cites in a recent text a pithy explanation of the manner in which a connection is often established between the democratization of the non-Western world and changing forms of global order. When asked by journalist Nicholas Lemann how the United States should think about a "successor idea to containment" as a guide to the construction of world order, a senior State Department official once explained that this should be

> the idea of integration. The goal of US foreign policy should be to persuade the other major powers to sign on to certain key ideas as to how the world should operate: opposition to terrorism and weapons of mass destruction, support of free trade, democracy, markets. Integration is about locking them into these policies and then building institutions that lock them in even more.[6]

The quote is from the early years of the George W. Bush administration, but it is still consistent with the orientations that guide the current foreign policy of the United States, or indeed that of the other major Western powers. Democracy is one of the "key ideas" that can define "how the world should operate." Once in place in all "major powers" throughout the world, it will "lock" these states into domestic and international policies that will force them to respect the basic values and rights entailed by democratic politics, and it will then "lock them in even more" through the web of international institutions and regimes they will then have to join as a result of the growth of democracy within their borders. This is how the major powers of the non-Western world will slowly be not so much "contained," but rather "integrated" in the new emerging global order.

This is a close reading of the liberal logic. The very "idea" of democracy is a powerful political instrument. Its growth through domestic and international politics can compel states to act in ways that conform to its ideals of rights and freedom. The very nature of international politics can then be transformed: international institutions will develop that will "lock states in even more" and force them to behave one toward the other in modes of interaction matching the fundamental norms of democracy, rights, and freedom now animating their politics at home and abroad. We know this is true universally. Notions of democracy and rights speak to the way the entire "world should operate." They are ideas that resonate everywhere, throughout all parts of the globe. And, again everywhere, we know that the states transformed by these ideas will have no choice but to be "locked in" a certain type of international behavior, no matter where they are and how they have developed previously.

It is precisely this universalism, however, that has created problems when the reality of the situation in the non-Western world has been confronted with these expectations. Two central images have been invoked to assess the possible outcomes of processes of democratization in the non-Western world. One was put forward by Francis Fukuyama in his phenomenally successful *The End of History and the Last Man*.[7] The thesis defended in the book is well known. Democracy corresponds to universal human aspirations. These aspirations might have been cut short by the introduction of unnatural systems like communism in many parts of the world. Now that these basic human aspirations that they kept suppressed for so long will be allowed to flourish. Democracy will prove, over time, to be the sole political system valid for all of humanity. The nature of global politics will then be altered according to this realization. A global consensus articulated on the need to defend basic democratic rights and freedoms will now serve as the prime driver of all international politics. While there might be difficulties and setbacks in this process because of the turbulent politics of the non-Western world, they will be resolved over time, because of the strength of the need for democracy on display in those parts of the world.

The mirror image was offered by Samuel P. Huntington, in a book which struck as deeply in the popular imagination: *The Clash of Civilizations and the Remaking of World Order*.[8] The idea here is that the pursuit of liberal democracy and human rights are not, in fact, global aspirations. Humanity is divided by deep-seated primordial identities. It is these primordial identities that will continue to underlie global politics. The difficulties encountered with the democratization agenda in the non-Western will not be resolved over time, but will instead always remain present. Global politics will not be unified by a global push toward democracy: this push toward democracy, in fact, will divide humanity even more, because of the reactions it is likely to engender in the regions of the world where other values and ideals are the norm.

What is striking about these types of arguments is the extent to which they rely on universals to build their case. Human beings always strive to attain the values and rights embodied in the liberal agenda, Fukuyama argues, because it is in their very nature to do so. The counter-argument, in that context, seems to entail a response that is just as categorical. No, Huntington replies, human beings are simply not like that. It is not part of their nature always to move in that direction, and the primordial identities that envelop their existence will continue to defeat any drive toward liberal values in the many parts of the non-Western world where these identities are antithetical to the liberal agenda.

The point, though, is that both perspectives are needed if one is to understand the nature of human identity in the non-Western world. The sculpting of human identity in those parts of the world proceeds at the moment from ideals of freedom and rights firmly inscribed in the liberal worldview, but also – just as much – from political and cultural imaginations where other forms of human identity are given pride of place. This is in fact at the moment the crucial dilemma of self-identity in a great many parts of the non-Western world: how do I define myself, as I stand at the intersection of different paths leading from several entrenched ethnic and ethno-religious affiliations and toward just as many routes to modernity and global liberal norms? To put it more starkly, what is needed in the analysis of these issues is, quite plainly, a combination of the identities painted by people like Fukuyama and Huntington. How do these two logics of identity, liberal and non-liberal, coalesce, then split in different ways, and then link up again, as the individual attempts to define her own specific identity amid all the debates on these questions unfolding at this time in the non-Western world?

The universalism that lies at the core of liberalism regarding issues of human identity still prevents the analysis from unfolding in that way. Liberalism sets up debates, such as the one exemplified by the tensions between the work of Fukuyama and Huntington, where human identity can only be defined in terms that, in fact, preclude the multi-faceted analysis of identity advocated here. It assumes that human identity is the same universally and that it should not, therefore, be submitted to a further analysis of the way it enters into diverse and fluid combinations with other types of identity in different parts of the non-Western world.

This is, then, where there must be movement on this issue of universals. It is because of the universals that fill media or policy discussions on the impact of democratization in the non-Western world that these discussions reach their current conclusions. Democracy might not exist in all the countries of the non-Western world, it is most often claimed in these discussions, but, once these countries do experience a full democratic life, each and every one of them will follow a similar path toward the respect of global norms of rights, democracy, and freedom. The air of inescapability of this argument comes from its universalist quality: democracy always ends up putting the same sort of pressure on states, and then always compels them to embrace at the global level the norms and values enshrined in the democratic agenda. It is precisely this universalist language, though, that results in the oversight of the problems studied here. Democracy is not always the same, the state does not always react to it the same way, and the international politics configured by the rise of democracy, in that context, will not always lead all states down the same path. A broader – a more truly encompassing and thus universal – understanding of the nature of human identity, of how it is evolving at the moment in the non-Western world, and of how it is spurring forward debates on the nature of democracy in those parts of the world is needed now to grasp these issues. A more global sense of the nature of the state and of how it interacts in different ways, on the basis of previous trajectories of development, with democratic pressures, is also needed in this context. Most of all, there must be a recognition that different sorts of democracies throughout the non-Western world, once they turn their attention to the international stage, will act on the basis of the democratic forces that animate them, but also in ways that reflect their specific backgrounds. The image of a universal movement toward similar norms of rights, human identity, and democracy within the liberal argument must give way to a more complex image of difference and debate on the very nature of these notions between the different sorts of democracies that are likely to populate world politics in the near future – it is through this more complex and more global understanding of the connection between democracy and international politics that the liberal argument will move closer to the reality actually unfolding around us at the moment. These are the universals that must now occupy liberal thinking.

All of this entails the need, here also, to look anew at the canon of international studies. The liberal worldview is the universalist position par excellence in international studies. Indeed, liberalism is precisely about finding out what is universal in international affairs, what unites all of us, throughout the entire world, beyond the divisions and tensions occasioned by politics, conflict, and violence. This is obviously the most noble of projects. The question at the moment, though, is whether the language of universals at the core of liberalism can still guide how we go about implementing this project in the conditions set out by current global politics. Does the liberal understanding of human identity, in other words, really fit the nature of identity in the non-Western world and the international politics that this type of identity sets in motion in those countries? Does the liberal view of the state and of inter-state relations still tie in with the new ways in which non-Western states are transforming at the moment the very nature of global politics? The point defended in these pages is that liberalism is very much in need of some reformulation if it is to provide a guide to the pursuit of its objectives of democracy, rationality, and progress in international affairs in the current context of world politics. The issue then arises: how can the liberal canon – Kant and his followers – be updated to fit current world politics and the role that the non-Western world is likely to play in it in the near future?

The most crucial claim introduced by Kant in the vernacular of international studies is the idea that we can always recognize in each other a common rationality and a common humanity. Beyond all the conflicts that separate us, we can see a shared universal quality uniting all of us. This recognition of our common humanity can lead us to sidestep the differences between us set in place by the states to which we belong, and can take us toward a new era of peace and rationality in international affairs. This is why Kant has been met with such curiosity, if not excitement, by generations of scholars and students in international studies. He provides a solution to the problem of violence posed with great acuity in the realist literature, and he offers us peace instead of the endless play of war and conflict described in that literature. More than that, he allows us to think that the solution he proposes will always work. All human beings are rational, he tells us, and hence they can always use that shared denominator to question the politics of division created by states and wars: the movement toward peace, then, is always possible. This also explains Kant's appeal in the field. There is confidence and hope in that universality: no matter how dire the circumstances of conflict and war in which we find ourselves, we know that Kant can offer a way out. Thus we have found ourselves toiling, in Kant's famous phrase quoted earlier, toward something resembling a "universal civic society"[9] – or at least the more peaceful international life he promises to us.

It is this enthusiasm for the hope brought by Kant in international studies that has sustained the enormous program of research in the discipline revolving around what Michael Doyle has termed the "Kantian road to peace."[10] This program of research has involved the development of a massive literature in two distinct areas. The notion of democratic peace has been a crucial element of this research. To what extent, Doyle and others have asked, can the recognition of the rationality and rights of individuals, entailed by the emergence of democracy within states, then render these states more peaceful in the international realm, just as Kant suggested to us centuries ago? The other element of this research program has focused more on the way in which the "empowering rights and obligations"[11] of the individual, depicted by Kant, can eventually lead to a "universal system of governance" operating above and through states and allowing the "entrenchment and enforcement of democratic public law across all peoples,"[12] as David Held puts it. Always, though, there has been a sense of universality in that entire literature, which parallels closely the one found in Kant's work. The democratic system of governance described to us by Held will be "universal." For its part, democratic peace theory "comes as close as anything," as Jack Levy puts it, "to an empirical law in international relations."[13]

The questions raised by the arguments considered in this book, though, should remain at the forefront of our reflections in the field: do these types of research agendas really still capture the nature of democracy in the non-Western world, and its likely impact on current regional and global politics? Or does the ongoing evolution of democracy in those parts of the world require instead some reappraisal of the "Kantian road to peace" and the way it can guide our thinking about issues of peace and progress in contemporary world politics? The point made in the preceding pages is that some reevaluation of the Kantian logic is indeed in order at the moment. The negotiation of liberal and non-liberal forms of identity, which is now crucial to understandings of self-identity in many parts of the non-Western world, must be integrated in that logic. The specific nature of the state in the non-Western world and how it influences the nexus connecting democracy, the state, and the inter-state realm must also become part of the Kantian logic. Can the vocabulary of rights, states, and inter-state behavior, which now frames the research agendas inspired by Kantian liberalism, accommodate, however, all these changes?

According to what has been proposed here, the answer to that question has to be that these changes will be possible only if Kantian liberalism revisits the sense of universality that stands at its very core. What Kant is often thought to bring to international studies remains, before anything else, a clear justification of why we can assume that all human beings subscribe to the same rationality. This is the force that propels the entire Kantian logic forward. All human beings live in circumstances of politics and history that underscore their differences, but it is precisely the confrontation of these differences that highlights their common search for a shared human essence. This is why we know that human beings will eventually recognize each other as fundamentally the same across state borders and political divides, and this why we also know that the legitimacy and power of the state will fade in view of the materialization of this common humanity and will allow, in time, the rise of a "universal civic society." The difficulty is that this universalist vision of human identity leads to the problem identified here with regard to the non-Western world: assuming that all human beings are the same hides from view the tension between liberal and non-liberal identities, between adhesion to a share human identity and the exaltation of difference from these liberal norms of identity – a tension that underlies debates on identity carried now in those parts of the world.

What there is also in Kant, however, is an invitation to consider precisely these types of issues. Kant tells us that liberal forms of human identity emerge through confrontation with other forms of identity. The specific circumstances and conditions through which this process occurs influence the nature and scope of its movement forward. This is the part of Kant's logic that we must read anew as we look at the politics of the non-Western world and at their impact on the evolution of global politics. What is exactly the mix of liberal and non-liberal identities that influences, at this moment and in current conditions, the conceptions of human identity, human rights, and democracy, in those parts of the world? How do these very specific configurations of identity then play within the "Kantian road to peace"? This is the aspect of Kant's work that we must now take to heart in international studies, given the particular circumstances of world politics in which the Kantian logic has to unfold at the moment. We have too readily read the further arguments of Kant on the eventual convergence of humanity toward liberal norms and on the impact of this phenomenon on international politics.

We need now, on the contrary, to focus on this one element of his work before thinking that we can go on with the implementation of his logic. This is how we can revisit the universalist language on human rationality and identity of Kantian liberalism, and open it up to a consideration of these questions that is more attuned to current global conditions.

The same could be said, too, about the conception of the state currently at play within the liberal canon. As has been said above, liberals need a much broader notion of the state if they want to capture the true nature of state institutions in the non-Western world and the way states can connect democracy at the domestic level and change at the international level. A crucial claim put forward by Kant is the idea that the state, once faced with democratic politics within its borders, will have no choice but to act internationally according to the values enshrined in that democratic politics. This is the argument that has been seized upon with such force by the proponents of the democratic peace theory and by those who see the emergence of a global civil society as leading to the development of a global system of democratic governance. More than anything else, these people are battling with the realists. The state is moved by considerations of power and violence, the realist literature suggests. Not quite, all these liberals hasten to reply on the basis of the arguments they find in Kant's writings: the state, once it becomes democratic, can move beyond these considerations and act according to the values, rights, and rationality associated with democracy. The main problem with this entire line of reasoning, as was shown here, is that the conception of the state contained in this logic draws directly from the realist understanding of the state. It presupposes, as the realists do, a stable, legitimate state, cleanly dividing the domestic and the international. The state in the non-Western world, however, is often anything but stable and legitimate, or able to delineate enduring borders between the domestic and the international realms. The image that the proponents of the "Kantian road to peace" have in mind when they think of the state does not allow them to reflect clearly, in that sense, on the realities now unfolding in the non-Western world and on the challenges these are likely to raise for the implementation of the Kantian logic in those parts of the world.

There again, though, reading Kant anew can help. Kant wants us to see that the movement forward of democracy is always a function of the concrete social forms and political institutions through which this movement proceeds. This is exactly the question raised today for liberalism by the state in the non-Western world. How will the specific trajectory of development of the state in those parts of the world impact the nature of its relationship to democracy and the way it will react to democratic forces at home when it turns its attention to international affairs? This is the one question that the proponents of the "Kantian road to peace" must still ask, in light of the actual conditions of state development that prevail at the moment in the non-Western world. The point is not, in other words, simply to work on the basis of the Kantian logic and to ask how the newly democratic states of the non-Western world will act as that logic unfolds in those parts of the world. The point, instead, is to consider the specific concrete conditions in which the Kantian logic has to develop in those parts of the world when it comes to the nature of the state there, and to see how that logic will remain affected by these conditions for the foreseeable future. This is how the contemporary followers of Kant will move away from the universalist conception of the state, which often clouds their work, and open it instead to the complexity of the state in the non-Western world and to the way this complexity should enter into their analysis. The state in the non-Western world, as was seen here, is often at once both democratic and non-democratic, reacting to democratic forces and not reacting to them. It is precisely this fluid complexity that now has to be understood by the liberals. Reading Kant in the way proposed here would open liberalism to the analysis of this complexity.

It is this reading of the liberal canon, then, that can bring about the kind of analysis suggested here: a take on democracy, its relationship to the state, and its impact on international studies that captures the nature of these phenomena in the non-Western world. Kant proposes to us, as was said before, the most noble of goals. The pursuit of peace, the search for rationality in international affairs – all of this is indeed what should guide our approach to global politics. The point for us now in the field, however, is to define how exactly that goal can be pursued thoroughly and efficiently, given the nature of democracy in the non-Western world at the moment and the way it will affect the quest for democracy and peace in global politics. Striving toward that goal, however, should not lead us to leave Kant behind. On the contrary, as has been suggested here, the very pursuit of that goal should take us back to Kant, to a new reading of his work that will show how it can still resonate within the global conditions in which we find ourselves.

The last element, finally, that must be considered in this chapter is the second component of the liberal school: the idea, advanced by Adam Smith and now by his contemporary followers, that it is trade rather than democracy that is the key element driving global politics. This is what matters in current world politics, the people close to this approach would suggest. The non-Western world has enormous areas of dire poverty, of course, but also entire zones where economic development is proceeding apace. Indeed, the so-called emerging economies – China, India, and others – are steadily increasing their economic power and completely altering in that process the very nature of the global political economy. What is crucial in all of this, these people would claim, is that this process will also lead to a recognition of shared interests and common purpose. Just as Smith predicted, economic development will lead to economic and social interdependence, which in turn will lead to political cooperation and a general lessening of geo-political tensions. Trade, as the language of the commercial peace theory would have it, will lead to peace. This is what will characterize the future of relations between the West and the "rest": a growing level of economic development in the latter, which will in turn connect it with the former in ways that will bring about a great degree of economic, and then political, convergence throughout the whole world.

Is this really, though, the way we should think about the impact of economic development in the non-Western world and its effect on global politics? The key point that needs to be underscored here is the extent to which Smith and his contemporary followers develop their line of reasoning by placing it in opposition to realism and to Kantian liberalism. This is an approach that assumes that peace, progress, and rationality are possible in international affairs, in contrast to the irrationality and constant violence that the realists assume to be the most fundamental character of international life. There is also a tension with Kantian liberalism. Kant and his followers believe that human beings, by virtue of their rationality and their identity, can transform international politics. Smith and his own followers reply instead that human rationality is not enough: a more structural, a more forceful element standing above human rationality is required to allow rationality to set in motion the changes in the nature of international affairs described by Kantian liberals. This more structural element is, obviously, the market. The market creates wealth. It does, however, much more than that. As Billet notes, for Smith and his followers, the market is "not about acquisition, but betterment."[14] The market compels me to recognize that, if I am to be free, all of us have to be free as well. If I want to gain wealth and to have the freedom to do so according to my rationality and my will, I need to create a system where I know that all individuals will have those same rights: these rights, guaranteed for everyone, will thus be guaranteed for me as well. This is what the market does – it forces me to recognize that the expression of my freedom and of my rationality passes through the development of a system that grants the same ambit of freedom and rationality to all individuals. That is why the market, in the end, makes society better, why it is not only "about acquisition." It requires us to acknowledge, almost in each of our daily actions, the freedom and the rationality animating all human beings: it demands of us, in that sense, that we build our interactions one with the other on the most important values and rights possible.

This is why, also, the market can change international politics. As it expands through national borders and links ever increasing areas of the human community, the market brings to light the search for individual freedom and rationality that moves each individual in that human community. It shows to all of us that we are all the same, demanding the expression of our freedom and our individual rationality, and it also shows to all of us that we require, in that sense, the development of the very market dynamics that make the expression of these rights possible. The market, then, becomes more important than the state. The state is profoundly artificial. It creates social affiliations, and thus conflicts, which can always be manipulated according to the politics and geo-strategic machinations of the day. The market, on the contrary, brings to the fore a much deeper and innate yearning for freedom and rationality, which is inscribed in all human beings and connects all of us at a much more profound and permanent level. This is how, over time, the market can come to change the nature of international affairs: it demonstrates to all of us to that the best way to create conditions where our rights and freedoms will be respected, whether nationally or globally, is to favor market forces over allegiance to the state and to build models of politics that encourage economic interdependence over national sovereignty and power. This will move us away from a state-centered world of conflict and war and toward one of interdependence and greater freedom and peace.

If the liberalism of Smith and his followers departs from the "Kantian road to peace" with this emphasis on the market as an agent of change in international affairs, it remains tied to the entire liberal approach, though, with the profound sense of universality that underlies its logic. All of us throughout the world desire the same freedom and the same rights, Smith and his contemporary followers claim. In all societies and in all circumstances, the market can always provide a better outlet for this quest for freedom than the state will ever be able to offer. We know, then, that in all parts of the world where market forces are allowed to grow, they will displace the state as the center of gravity of social and political allegiance: people will prefer the freedom and growth provided by the market over the conflicts and war engineered by the state. We also know, then, that the logic of the commercial peace will prevail everywhere market forces can flourish.

It is with this image in mind that today's followers of Adam Smith tell us that the expansion of market dynamics in the non-Western world will eventually lead to some form of global convergence and political accommodation. The issues raised by the literature focused on the dynamics of economic development in the non-Western world call attention, however, to the problems entailed by such an image. Basically two sets of concerns arise. The first problem is the one faced by all the other approaches described here. To the extent that it positions itself as a critique of other existing approaches, the liberalism of Smith and his followers locks itself in the broad worldview adopted by these approaches, and it overlooks what they themselves miss when it comes to the reality of international life in the non-Western world. As an example, realism assumes that the state controls violence within its borders. When they describe the way in which the market can challenge the power of the state, Smith and his followers react to this realist understanding of the state by imagining a pacified social space and then focussing on the economic relations governed by the rules of commerce and capitalism that can operate within that pacified space. The presence of violence within some non-Western states, however, may mean that it is force and intimidation as much as the rules of capitalism that determine how wealth moves around and how the market operates in those states. How this changes completely the workings of the market and how it interrelates with the state is not something that can be easily reconciled with the liberal logic. And yet this is a gap that must be bridged if liberalism is to address some of the actual conditions of economic development found in the non-Western world.

The second problem is that, even if the elements of individual rationality, market forces, and state structures composing the logic of the commercial peace are indeed all present, their nature in the non-Western world is such that this logic cannot operate in the manner envisaged by Smith and his followers. The market, first of all, cannot be understood without reference to a "postulate of external dominance," as Stephan Haggard put it here earlier, in the discussion of the Dependency School of development.[15] In other words, whether or not one subscribes to the arguments of the Dependency School, it has to be recognized that the nature of economic development in the non-Western world today needs to be seen against the background of the historical and social trajectories that have marked those parts of the world. Market dynamics there have unfolded in the context of centuries of colonialism and post-colonialism. The market in the non-Western world, in that sense, functions through "external dominance": its rules and its mechanisms are largely set from the outside, by actors who remain beyond its reach. Again, one does not have to get too close to the Dependency School to admit that this complicates Smith's image of the market as the expression of uncontrolled and self-defined rationalities and wills.

The problems concerning the state and human rationality brought to light here go even more directly to the core of the commercial peace. The evolution of market dynamics in the non-Western world must be explained in terms of the interrelationship between these dynamics and the state itself. It is the state that orchestrated the export-driven strategies that drove capitalist development in many parts of the non-Western world. Often, it is also actors very close to the state that control economic development and benefit from it – the profound role of the military in China's economic expansion, for example, comes immediately to mind. This creates a situation quite different from what Smith and his followers have in mind. They envision the market as a space separate from the state, a space from where it is possible to question the very legitimacy and power of the state as the instrument through which society should be organized and regulated. In all these situations where the market and the state are intertwined in the way just described, however, capitalist development does not take away from the power and legitimacy of the state, in fact it adds to them. Mention was made, for instance, of the extent to which the legitimacy of many states in East Asia has been buttressed, more than anything else, by their ability to deliver an economic over any other sort of political or social agenda. There is an issue, also, with the nature of human rationality. Contemporary followers of Smith assume that the market liberates and energizes a core human rationality, a central freedom of the will, which lies in every human being. What was shown here, though, is that issues of individual self-identity are often quite a bit more complex in the non-Western world and bring to the fore identities that often stand completely at odds with liberal visions of the individual.

This makes for a situation that is rather different from the one associated with the image of the commercial peace. The commercial peace assumes the presence of an individual who, when freed by the market, espouses liberal values, and then uses these values to challenge the power of the state both domestically and internationally. The reality in the non-Western world, though, might well be that this individual takes up non-liberal values when given greater freedom and power by the market. This individual, also, might remain a strong supporter of the power of the state rather than someone who wants to weaken the legitimacy of state institutions, since it is precisely through the power and organizational capacity of the state that he can enrich himself. These are the realities that will connect the individual, the market, and the behavior of the state, domestically and internationally, in the non-Western world.

This goes directly to the ability of the commercial peace thesis to explain how market dynamics are likely to influence the international politics of the non-Western world and, by extension, the global trends linking those parts of the world with the rest of the planet. The issue, though, is that the image driving the logic of the commercial peace at the moment does not allow for the consideration of all these problems. There is a universalism at the core of this image that seals it off from a thorough engagement of these questions. For Smith and his followers, the individual, the market, and then the influence of the market on domestic and international politics can only be one and the same, all the time and everywhere. In response, then, the self-enclosed universals that compose this image must be opened up to the realities studied here. This matters in terms of the approach itself, but also, and much more importantly, because this line of reasoning is so influential within the workings of the global economic architecture.

In this sense, there must be, in the first instance, a much broader vision of worldwide capitalist development brought into liberalism. The literature studied here underscored how there is no such a thing as capitalist development *per se*. Instead, there are different types of capitalism spread throughout the world, which have to be understood in their diversity and their interrelationship. The case that arises from a study of international life in the non-Western world, though, goes much further. Liberalism also needs a much broader understanding of the nature of the state throughout the world. How the state controls violence, how that shapes its nature, how other factors also define the nature of the state and then that of its interaction with the market – all of this must be part of the equation. The diversity of human identity throughout the world, and how it influences the rights and values that the individual will want to defend once he feels empowered to do so by his growing wealth, must also become part of the analysis.

The best way to have a concrete example in mind for all these issues is perhaps to think of the pronouncements, whether in the media or within policy circles, which hold that growing trade with China, accompanied by market liberalization in the country, will eventually lead to some form of *rapprochement* between the West and the Chinese. This is, evidently, one of the fundamental questions linked to the "rise of the rest." The line of reasoning at the core of the notion of the commercial peace underlies many of these pronouncements. Dennis A. Rondinelli, for instance, sums up the argument and underscores how it assumes that the development of market mechanisms in a country like China compels it to a "strategy [...] of adaptation to changing global forces and innovation to take advantage of and leverage new opportunities," and that this, in turn, will force change both within the government, the private sector, and society at large.[16] There is, in that sort of argument, exactly the logic defended by Smith and his followers. The market changes both society and the state, it opens them up to many more "global forces" and norms, and indeed, it requires of them that they "adapt" to these forces and norms. There is also, in that line of thinking, the emphasis on the market brought by Smith within the liberal view. The promotion of freedom and rationality by the West is not enough to transform the rest of the world: it is the market that forces states and societies in those parts of the world to adapt to the global dynamics of change. Finally, there is also, in that argument, the universalism of Smith and his followers. Societies and states throughout Asia might have eminently specific cultural or political traditions: market liberalization, however, will push all of them, including China, in the same direction and compel them to adapt to global capitalism and to the set of norms it embodies.

A look at the reality of the situation in China, however, immediately brings to the fore the type of problems raised here with regard to such a model of reasoning. The work of Gilpin and others was cited earlier, for instance to underscore how capitalism in a country like China does not demonstrate the growth of a unified global capitalist system so much as the emergence of "conflict among rival models of capitalism."[17] Capitalism in the non-Western world cannot be detached from the broader historical and social trajectories that shaped its rise and evolution. How exactly that plays out in the current process of market enlargement in China, how that shapes the forms of capitalism found there, and how that produces conflict with, rather than integration into, the global capitalist system – all these are questions that must be raised now to understand truly ongoing developments in the Chinese economy and their impact on the global economy. The problem is that the logic of the commercial peace, with its vision of a universally similar capitalism, does not easily allow for the consideration of such questions.

Also, interactions between capitalist markets and the state in China remain quite different from what can be assumed from the logic of the commercial peace. The logic of the commercial peace leads one to imagine an economic space outside the state, from where it is possible to question the legitimacy of state institutions and to build new social constituencies, independent of state power. The reality in China does not fit easily within this image. As was just said, it is often actors close to the state, like the military, rather than actors outside the state and opposed to its power that benefit the most from market liberalization in the country. The concrete example of these issues that comes up immediately in the literature, however, is the role played by the state in China in the creation of zones of economic development. Xiangmin Chen, for instance, talks about the way the state has been able to "bend borders" at the periphery of China to fashion "transborder economic regions" – the most famous of these transborder economic zones being, perhaps, the Greater Tumen Subregion.[18] These transborder zones are witnesses to strong economic growth and infrastructure expansion. More than that, they operate according to rules of economic and political governance, which are quite specific to each of them. This is the point. The state either engineers the development of these special zones or at least allows it to happen. To that extent, then, the growth of market dynamics in China does not happen in spaces situated outside the state. On the contrary, the spaces where market dynamics are most prevalent are precisely these spaces created by the state, these spaces where the state remains exceedingly present. A view of China based on the notion of the commercial peace, with its emphasis on market spaces detached from the state, misses that part of the story.

The notion of human identity at play within the logic of the commercial peace, finally, does not serve well those who use that logic to survey current developments in China. The logic of the commercial peace assumes that an unproblematized and clear human identity is freed by the market. This fundamental sense of what it is to be a human being becomes, then, the criterion through which pressure is applied on the state to ensure that its behavior, both domestically and internationally, respects the basic rights and freedoms associated with that core human identity. Notions of self-identity in China, however, are considered at the moment from the angle of much broader – and often still unanswered – questions about what it means to be Chinese, how that differs from being Western, and how that connects to elemental debates about notions of human rights, human freedom, and the like. Exactly the sort of tensions between liberal and non-liberal identities that were described here as central components of the notions of human identity now unfolding in the non-Western world, in other words, are at the center of all these debates in China. It is this more fluid and ambiguous conception of self-identity that enters into different forms of interface with the market and the state through the process of market liberalization. An approach based on the logic of the commercial peace, where a constant human identity always leads to the same type of pressure on the state once it is liberated by the market, also misses that other part of the story.

Using the logic of the commercial peace, in that sense, to look at all these issues, leads to many oversights. The nature of the market, of the state, and of human identity, and then the nature of the interrelationships between these different elements, is not quite what it is assumed to be according to that logic. The issue, though, is that the commercial peace as it is formulated at the moment cannot easily address this problem. It is universals that drive the entire line of reasoning upon which the problem is based: the market always frees the same essential and universal quality in human beings, its proponents argue, and this always leads in turn to similar transformations in the nature of domestic and international politics. This language of universals stands in the way of the consideration of the forms of identity, market dynamics, and state development, which is necessary in order to comprehend fully a situation like the one in China at the moment. It is at this level, then, that work must be done now.

Such a reengagement of the logic of the commercial peace requires a new reading of the foundational texts of Smith and his followers, upon which this entire logic is based. This is similar to what was said about the other approaches defining international studies at the moment. It is the constant reference to such foundational texts in the classroom and in the literature that has maintained in the field the habits of thought that make it now difficult to see the problems underscored here regarding the nature of international affairs in the non-Western world and the impact of those parts of the world on global politics: if the changes proposed in these pages are to be forthcoming, these texts must be read, used, and taught differently.

The one key pillar that supports the whole intellectual edifice built in the writings of Smith and his contemporary followers is the idea that the market performs a function that no other social institution can carry out: it allows us to express freely our will and our rationality. The market is the "impartial spectator" described by Smith.[19] It forces all of us, automatically and "impartially," to recognize the greater wealth and freedom that will accrue to everyone if each of us plays by its rules. The market, then, creates freedom for all of us. This is how it undermines the legitimacy of the state: it shows that state institutions repress that freedom, which human beings should in fact seek elsewhere, in economic rather than in political communities. This is also how the market can then change the very nature of international politics. It displaces the state as the central mode of social organization, and it substitutes at the same time the dynamics of mutual interdependence and sociability, upon which it relies, to the dynamics of conflict and violence associated with a more state-centered international life.

From the perspective of the argument defended in these pages, however, this emphasis on the market comes at a cost. Smith takes on board existing conceptions of the individuals and the state, and then adds his understanding of the market to the mix, in order to show how it is market dynamics that can truly deliver the promises of freedom and rationality, which are linked instead to human identity or to state development in the writings of many of his contemporaries. He does not, in other words, query the nature of human identity or state development: he merely moves forward with these notions, in a logic that now connects them to his vision of the market. This leads him to a self-enclosed constellation of assumptions and mutually reinforcing premises that, in his view, has universal value. Indeed, within his logic, he can imagine that what he says will always be true, regardless of circumstances or geography. This is, however, where there is a cost to his logic. This language of universals does not allow him to deal with the sort of problems described here with regard to the non-Western world. These problems stand outside a logic that assumes, on the contrary, that no situation or problem can stand beyond its purview. It cannot, as long as it remains unchanged, resolve this contradiction.

Those who follow Smith today end up in the same intellectual impasse. They connect his assumptions about the nature of human rationality, the emancipatory power of the market, and the implications of these elements for international politics exactly as he does, and they arrive at a sense of universality similar to the one that underlies Smith's work. When Keohane and Nye talk about the influence of market forces on international politics, they feel confident that the arguments they put forward pertain to all of "world politics."[20] When Haas identifies "human needs and desires" that can be addressed by economic integration, he assumes that they will give impetus to universal pressures, which in turn will lead to the construction of a "true world community."[21] It is, however, this universalist dimension, at the heart of all these arguments, that prevents them from attaining the level of detail necessary to describe properly how the dynamics they describe will pan out in the non-Western world.

What is needed in this literature, then, is a much greater sensitivity to the different ways in which the elements brought together by the logic of the commercial peace have evolved around the world. How does the organization of violence affect the nature of the state in the non-Western world? How does the state influence specific dimensions of human identity? How has the market evolved in those parts of the world? All these questions must be taken into account in order to understand properly how connections between human identity, market dynamics, and state behavior operate in the non-Western world. This is a line of inquiry that can make apparent where precisely, in the non-Western world, the connections between these different elements operate in the manner envisaged by the logic of the commercial peace, where they do not, and where tensions with global norms of development and governance are thus likely to occur.

Contemporary students of Smith have to read his work today while keeping in mind this broader analytical agenda. The connections he establishes between human identity, the market, and the state must be seen as one possible manifestation of these connections. He certainly puts forward an instructive argument regarding a certain view of the important dynamics unfolding at the moment both in the non-Western world and, more generally, in global politics itself. The question that must be asked when reading him, though, is how exactly this specific configuration of human identity, market forces, and state behavior he describes to us has been able to emerge. What are its preconditions in terms of the elements studied here – the control of violence by the state, for example? And then, obviously, where do these preconditions exist today, and where are they absent? This is how the entire *problématique* that Smith puts to us will connect to the growth of liberal capitalism in the non-Western world and to its impact on global politics. And this is how, in the end, the assumption of universality at the core of this approach will open itself up to the consideration of the issues raised here.

9
The Way Forward: Searching for New Universals in Global Politics

Specialists in international studies must thus focus their attention on at least four specific elements of analysis if they want to understand better the new global politics emerging as a result of the "rise of the rest." The first of these elements concerns the nature of violence. Those who work in international studies quite often assume, as a matter of course, that violence follows from the mere exercise of rationality and agency: one uses violence in a rational manner, in order to attain political objectives that would not be reached otherwise. This is the heritage of realism and its take on violence. What has been shown here, however, is that this understanding of violence, agency, and rationality stands in tension with a series of social and political developments: one must then also look at these developments in order to understand fully how violence operates, but also how the concepts used to analyze its sources and its effects are themselves put together. International studies as a discipline must question the accounts it gives of violence in the non-Western world in those terms. This is important in the study of the zones of violence that exist in the non-Western world and of the likely local, regional, and global responses to these situations. This is important, also, in terms of the discipline itself. International studies has often evolved as a series of new responses to realist tenets. In that sense, opening realist tenets to a form of analysis more congruent with the realities of the non-Western world will also create new lines of inquiry within these other approaches and would make them more likely to capture the nature of international life in those parts of the world.

The second element that must be integrated in international studies if the discipline is to explain fully the new global politics created by the "rise of the rest" is a broader understanding of the state. International studies as a discipline has evolved on the basis of a fundamental premise: there is a difference of kind between domestic politics, where politics, law, and morality can unfold, and international politics, where they cannot. This is also part of the realist heritage in the discipline. This has served, moreover, as the point of departure for the approaches in international studies that criticize existing

193

notions of state power and state sovereignty and propose movements of different sorts toward new forms of international politics. The analysis of the state in the non-Western world and of its engagements in the dynamics of global change must proceed, though, from a different point of departure. The way in which the state was developed in those parts of the world is crucial in that regard. The state in the non-Western world was most often created from the outside, in ways that, to this day, lead to sustained conflicts and tensions within its borders. There can be deep ethnic or religious cleavages, for example, which challenge in a palpable and continued fashion the idea that the state is able to establish its control and legitimacy over the territory it encompasses. There are often regional dimensions to these tensions as well, and to the efforts to address them. In that context, thinking in terms of a dichotomy where there is a pacified space of legitimacy and order within the state and another type of political space, outside the state, where other rules of politics prevail fails to capture the reality at hand. Here, on the contrary, the inside and the outside of the state are intermingled. If international studies as a discipline is to give a correct account of the trajectories of development that non-Western states carry with them and of the role they are likely to play as they start occupying a larger place in global politics, these issues must become part of the analysis. This is needed in the consideration of the "rise of the rest" and of its impact on global affairs. This is essential, also, within international studies itself, as the discipline pushes forward a series of debates on the nature of the state and on the future of notions like that of state power and state sovereignty.

The third and fourth elements have to do with the two central forces which are often seen as transforming at the moment both the non-Western world and the nature of its role in global affairs: democratization and unprecedented levels of economic development. Time and again, discussions about democratization in the non-Western world borrow from Kantian liberalism. As people steadily gain freedoms and push forward the development of democratic institutions, the argument goes, they are bound to demand that their state act accordingly and respect all their newly acquired rights. This will compel the state to change its behavior internally, toward its citizens, and externally as well, by participating more directly within the series of multilateral frameworks and regimes set in place to protect these freedoms and rights. Norms of human rights, democracy, and freedom will thus become much more significant components of international behavior throughout the entire world in that context. What must be acknowledged in counterpoint, though, is the difficulty of superimposing that logic on the current development of democracy in the non-Western world. Evidently there is an evolving sense of democracy and constitutionalism, which can be witnessed in many parts of the non-Western world where it did not exist before. The key point, however, is that the discourse and practice of democracy often fail to displace completely, in these areas, the other types of social affiliations, rooted for example in ethno-religious identities, which act at cross-purpose with the logic of democratic politics as imagined by Kant and his contemporary followers. What emerges in such a context is not so much the series of changes envisioned in Kantian liberalism, as a situation where democratic and non-democratic forms of social affiliations cohabit in a fluid and ever changing manner. This is the negotiation of liberal and non-liberal identities, which is such a central component of democratic politics in many parts of the non-Western world. More importantly, the state reacts as much to pressures coming from non-democratic modes of affiliation as it does to pressures emanating from more democratic ones. The way it acts on the outside, in its relations with other states and with multilateral institutions, will then reflect that situation. If international studies is to give an account of the impact of democratization on the international behavior of non-Western states, it must therefore learn to capture the sheer complexity and fluidity of all these processes. This entails challenging liberal understandings of the nature of human identity and of the relationship between the individual, the state, and the character of international politics. Here, too, this matters at two levels. The consideration of the dynamics set in motion by the "rise of the rest" requires this type of analysis. This is also important for international studies as a discipline. Debates about human identity within the field remain, more often than not, responses to liberal views on this issue. Opening liberalism to a greater understanding of the nature of human identity throughout the world will thus influence as well, in that sense, the scope of analysis of the approaches that position themselves as responses to Kantian liberalism.

Economic development in the non-Western world is the fourth element that must be considered carefully in order to bring to light the full dimensions of the global politics set in motion at the moment by the "rise of the rest." Increasing levels of economic development in the non-Western world are often seen as an unstoppable force for change, in a logic inspired this time by market liberalism. An upsurge in economic growth, it is argued, creates new middle classes, which are more likely to challenge the power of the state. This has immediate consequences for the nature of international politics. These new wealthy classes will want trade facilitation to dominate the international agenda, not inter-state tensions, because this suits their interests much more closely. Development and the growth of wealth, in that optic, will lead to economic interdependence and political convergence at the global level. Economic growth in the non-Western world, though, cannot be disconnected from the trajectories of social, political, and economic development that have given rise to it. This means that the forms of capitalism taking shape there will reflect these broader conditions. Also, the social demands that are given impetus by newly enriched classes might be rooted in notions of individual and social identities that are quite a bit more complex than the unproblematized identity envisaged by market liberals. Just as much, the relationship between the state and the economy could develop in such a way that economic growth would not challenge the power of the state, but rather add new dimensions to it. This points to the emergence of forms of global capitalism and global political economy that could differ in some significant degree from the liberal models that often guide the study of the emerging markets. International studies must capture the complex tensions involved in all these issues. This is important in the consideration of the "rise of the rest," and also in the series of debates that traverse the discipline at the moment regarding the nature of economic development and its impact on current global politics.

It is also crucial for international studies to look inward, within its own logic, if it is to approach all these issues in the way proposed here. Arguing that a broader understanding of the nature of the state throughout the non-Western world, for instance, should be incorporated within international studies does not suffice to ensure that the discipline will proceed forward on that basis. There is a logic of universals at its core, which prevents a movement in that direction and, indeed, makes that sort of analysis appear nonsensical. This speaks to the issue of how it is possible for international studies to incorporate the series of issues brought forward here with regard to the non-Western world and its impact on current global politics. The case that has been made in this book is that international studies must reengage, in context, the issue of universals. A fundamental component of that case, though, is that this should not lead to the end of the search for universals in the discipline, but rather to the reinvention of that search.

Some of the recent advances in international studies revolving around the constructivist and post-Marxist literature have yet to be examined, though, in this last part of the book. The issues brought forward up to this point – violence, the nature of the state, the power of democratization and of economic development – are matters typically associated with realist and liberal analyses of international affairs. The constructivist and post-Marxist literature goes in another direction. Its aim is not so much to consider the nature of global politics itself, as it is articulated through the series of problems studied here so far. Its objective, instead, is to look at international studies itself, in order to see how the discipline must amend its logic and its claims before it can gain a better grasp of all those problems. How that project, as formulated in this literature, can also help fashion an enhanced understanding of the global politics of the post-Western world must still be considered here.

Beyond that, however, lies an even more important issue. The constructivist and post-Marxist literature is about the future of international studies. Fundamentally, this literature proposes a critique of past approaches in the study of international affairs, and then invites all of us in the field to move beyond these traditional approaches and to give a new direction to the entire discipline. The question that this raises for the argument defended here, most evidently, is whether or not this new direction does take us toward a better understanding of the post-Western world. The argument about to be defended here is that this literature has in fact managed to open up a crucial debate in international studies about the likely future of the discipline. This debate, however, must be reoriented in some very significant ways if the future evolution of international studies is to bring it in line with the post-Western world it now has to explain. Determining how we develop the discipline from this point on is crucial, in other words, but ongoing reflections on this issue within the discipline still need to enter a new path if they are to usher in a better understanding of the new global politics emerging around us. Marking out this new path is a vital challenge for international studies at the moment. Indeed, this is the last element that must be in place if the discipline is to engage fully the international politics of the non-Western world.

According to what has been argued here so far, the constructivist and post-Marxist literature is correct in one regard and wrong in two other regards. The one thing it does well is to open up the question of universals in international studies. It starts with a simple postulate: the world in which we live, and the knowledge we have of that world, are socially constructed. The world, to put it differently, is never a given entity existing by itself. The choices we make and the actions we take all participate in its evolution: they give it, in the end, a character that reflects each of these choices and actions. The same is true of the knowledge we have of our world. Knowledge can never be a neutral and objective assessment of the reality that surrounds us. It remains mired at all times in the specific perspectives and agendas we bring to our attempt to know the world and, to that extent, it can vary profoundly if those broader agendas and perspectives themselves change.

It is from that angle that this literature then considers the more mainstream realist and liberal approaches in international studies. This brings it in direct opposition to the logic of universals, which underlies these more mainstream approaches. The realists will argue, for instance, that the behavior of states can be reduced to universal forces and problems, which explain the conduct of all states throughout the entire world. Proponents of this literature will reply, in contrast, that these claims to a knowledge of universal realities are always dependent on a specific prior set of perspectives and research agendas. What is said about universals – the universal aspects of state behavior, for instance – is thus no more than the expression of a certain vision of the world, one anchored in a particular set of intellectual preferences and inclinations. According to this literature, this is in fact what all of us in international studies must understand more than anything else. The field has always worked on the basis of universal claims about international affairs. We need to substitute to this language of universals a language of particulars. We need, in essence, to recognize the specific standpoints from which we have worked, and to acknowledge the extent to which it is the particular nature of these intellectual standpoints that has led us to believe that we could somehow uncover universal components of international affairs. This is the agenda of research that must shape the future evolution of the discipline.

A part of this argument parallels the logic of inquiry which has guided this book. Just as the constructivist and post-Marxist literature would have it, the point has been made here that the universals that have figured so prominently in the development of international studies must be thoroughly scrutinized. They rest on a series of prior assumptions, which limit their scope and push the discipline toward faulty or inadequate visions of global international politics. There is great value, moreover, in leading international studies toward this type of self-examination at this point in time. Non-Western approaches to international affairs are now influencing global politics to an ever-growing degree. International studies must know if it has the language, concepts, and worldviews that will allow it to explain this new world. This, then, requires the discipline to engage in precisely the exercise of introspection and reexamination of basic claims proposed by the constructivist and post-Marxist literature.

If this constitutes one way in which this literature is right according to what has been argued here, it is still wrong, however, in two other ways. The first mistake made by this literature is to position itself as a critique of mainstream international studies and, in so doing, to overlook many of the issues and questions about the non-Western world that are also overlooked by more mainstream approaches. This is what is demonstrated by a more thorough engagement with the literature focused on international life in those parts of the world. Constructivism borrows from post-modernism to argue that rationality allows us to reconstruct our world in a way that is not envisaged by mainstream international studies. The notion of rationality that is taken as the point of departure of that claim, however, remains the one found in mainstream international studies, mainly in the realist approach. This means that it adopts an understanding of the concept that assumes, just as is the case with realism, that rationality is always able to transform the political environment we share as human beings. Realism, though, does not take into account that the relationship between violence, agency, and rationality in the non-Western world is such that rationality cannot always act as an instrument of change in politics. Realism overlooks this problem, and constructivism, because it positions itself as a movement forward from realism, also fails to take that issue into account within its own logic.

The same can be said of the other elements that enter into the composition of the constructivist logic. Constructivism takes from Habermasian critical theory the idea that the conduct of international politics can underscore our shared human rationality. This can lead to a questioning of the politics of difference and hostility, which often underlie international affairs; and, in turn, this can bring about the elaboration of forms of international politics that are more clearly articulated on the pursuit of cooperation and unity. This sense of the nature of human rationality and human identity follows from an engagement with the liberal understanding of these notions. The liberal view on human rationality and human identity does not take into account, however, the extent to which the dynamics of identity formation in the non-Western world often generate there, at the moment, also a belief that we do not, as human beings, share a common worldwide identity. Furthermore, it is frequently the tensions between these liberal and non-liberal identities that shape, more than anything else, both domestic and international politics. Liberalism fails to integrate this problem within its logic, and constructivism, because it builds on that logic, also overlooks the issue.

When the constructivists, finally, get to their claims about the state and the way it can change its behavior in the international arena, it is a profoundly realist understanding of the state that they adopt. Just as realists would do, they see the state as a coherent and legitimate entity, in control of violence within its border and able to use the means of violence at its disposal as an instrument of power in the inter-state realm. This understanding of the state misses a lot, though, when it comes to the nature of the state in the non-Western world. The state in those parts of the world is often still in development. It remains illegitimate in the eyes of many segments of its own population. It is an assemblage of competing centers of power, which often prevent it from acting in foreign affairs as a unified and coherent structure. Perhaps most importantly, how it uses violence, and where it uses it, is quite different from what the realist model of the state would entail – for instance in its recourse to violence as an instrument of power within its own borders. All of this affects the nature of the state and the ways in which it acts on the international stage – ways unforeseen by the realists. The constructivists, since they keep the realist understanding of the state as the opening position in their own logic, also overlook these problems.

This is, in essence, then, the issue with the constructivist view of international politics. It positions itself as a reply to existing approaches in international studies. It explores some of the driving concepts in these approaches and it attempts to reorient them in a new direction. As it does all of this, however, it still remains within the confines of concepts and approaches that overlook many aspects of the international politics of a large part of the world. Constructivism moves forward from existing concepts and approaches, and it fails to question whether or not the analytical path that is opened in this manner does yield the best insights possible on the nature of contemporary global politics. As long as it remains in this position, though, it will neglect some of the most important problems through which the non-Western world is now shaping global politics around us.

The issue is the same for the other approaches in international studies aiming to critique mainstream thinking in the field, which have been regrouped here under the rubric of post-Marxism. The approaches share with constructivism the idea that the nature of international politics is extremely fluid and can always be traced back to shifting historical and social developments. Global politics is, in this sense, socially constructed. It can be reconstructed, then, in ways that will allow for a greater degree of fairness and peace in world affairs. Mainstream approaches overlook the extent to which international politics is embedded in deeper and ever changing historical and social configurations, and they thus fail to recognize the extent to which substantial alterations are possible in the very nature of global politics.

For the post-Marxist approach, though, it is the material world that determines the interplay of forces shaping the nature and evolution of global politics. Capitalist production, in this light, is a form of economic development, but it also entails a series of inequities between rich and poor that severely limit what the latter group can achieve, both socially and politically. Wallerstein, for example, shows how the "capitalist world-economy"[1] has created an integrated social, economic, and political global polity. The globalized capitalism that goes across this global polity serves the interests of a rich core of countries much more than those of the poorer periphery. The states in these less favored peripheral zones, moreover, do not have enough influence in global economic and political structures of governance to change their situation. Robert Cox and others also invite us to see how global politics is about "world orders"[2] that have many interrelated material and ideational dimensions. Global capitalism does shape world politics. It favors some and puts others in situations of dire poverty and powerlessness. The resulting global configurations of power, however, cannot be understood without reference to the broader frameworks of ideas, values, and institutions, which guide the conduct of international politics. These ideas, values, and institutions support and legitimize the global economic order: the latter would not exist without them.

This is the key argument in this approach. All of us working in international studies must recognize that our explanations of global politics need to open with an examination of global economics. This is where the forces defining the existing global order take shape. We need to acknowledge how these forces play themselves out differently in various parts of the world and how, in particular, the evolution of the non-Western world will be profoundly weighed down by the resulting configurations of global power. We also need to see, finally, how the legitimacy and sustainability of that global order are tied to the broader ideas, values, and institutions that give world politics its current character. Changes in the nature of world politics are possible, then, but only to the extent that all these elements themselves can change.

The idea, defended in this approach, that we should all be sensitive to the specificity of international life in the non-Western world and to the way it fits within global politics certainly corresponds to the argument put forward in this book. The issue, though, is how we get at those issues. The post-Marxists claim that the categories they use – the nature of capitalism, that of the state, and the like – allow us to unpack the different dynamics that participate in the constitution of international politics in the non-Western world and elsewhere. These categories are often problematic, though, when it comes to describing the international life of the non-Western world. For example, they imply that the problem of violence has been resolved. Capitalism as a category depicts economic flows based on the evolution of elements like production, trade, and finance. In the non-Western world, however, it can sometimes be that raw violence, much more than any of those elements, governs the different ways in which wealth is acquired and distributed. The post-Marxists, in other words, argue that capitalism and the other institutional and ideational forces it entails shape the international politics of the non-Western world. What must be brought into this analysis, though, is the extent to which the organization of violence still precedes and shapes the organization of all these elements in many parts of the world. The categories of analysis put forward by the post-Marxist approach will speak to the realities of the non-Western world only if this is done.

In this sense, the post-Marxist approach, just like constructivism, starts too late. It looks at capitalism and at the way the latter shapes the material world, and it moves forward from that point on. It should start earlier, with the way violence itself shapes the material world and with the ensuing organization of politics and economics. This would draw attention to factors in the evolution in the non-Western world, for instance in the nature of wealth acquisition, which are bound to be overlooked otherwise. The issue goes back, then, to the point just brought up with regard to the constructivist approach. Post-Marxists position their work as a critique of the more mainstream approaches in international studies. It is in reaction to the understandings of economics, politics, and so on found in those approaches that they develop their examination of world politics. In doing so, however, they overlook many of the issues – like the impact of violence on the nature of non-Western international politics – that are also overlooked in those mainstream approaches. This is a crucial problem when it comes to the ability of the post-Marxist approach to capture the character of the international politics of the non-Western world in its accounts of global politics.

This is, then, a first problem. Recent advances in constructivism and post-Marxism have evolved as critiques of mainstream approaches in international studies. Those mainstream approaches have misunderstood international politics, this more recent literature has claimed, because they have worked on the basis of a faulty logic. They have imagined grand narratives of power and violence in the case of the realists, and of progress and morality in world affairs in the case of the liberals. This is a wrong way to proceed, because these grand narratives are always historically and socially situated. They are simply the most visible manifestations of prior conceptual and moral commitments, which are themselves embedded in specific historical and social circumstances. They describe, moreover, realities that are ever changing. What we need to do in international studies, then, is to unravel these prior assumptions and to understand how they figure in our conceptions of international politics. This is how we will understand better the nature of international studies itself. This is also how we will get to the more profound nature of international affairs. We will finally get to see the extent to which, in reality, international politics is always constructed and reconstructed by the interplay of varied and fluid forces. This is the way forward for the discipline.

The case made here, however, shows the flaws in this line of argument. What is presented by this more recent literature as the way forward for international studies ends up, in fact, compounding the problems the discipline has always had when it comes to the non-Western world. Mainstream realist and liberal approaches overlook a lot of the fundamental constituents of international life in those parts of the world. When critiques of these approaches use them as the opening position of their argument, they, too, overlook these fundamental elements. They certainly force a debate within the discipline. What they also do, though – and exactly for the same reason – is to push aside the question of what is missing in the discipline in the first instance when it comes to certain parts of the world. This means that, in the end, these more recently developed approaches are just as likely to overlook some of the most important questions raised by the new global politics emerging around us as the other approaches, which they criticize.

The second problem with these more recent advances in international studies is, in a sense, much more profound. It has to do with the very project they put at the heart of the discipline. The entire constructivist and post-Marxist literature is based on the idea that international studies will move forward if it rejects the language of universals, which has framed its development from the start, and if it substitutes, for that language of universals, a new language of particulars. All of us interested in global politics, it is suggested by these approaches, should accept that we cannot capture the complexity of international affairs through references to universal laws and tenets of international life. Thinking in such universal terms obscures more than it reveals. It conceals the layers of assumptions that precede and shape the formulation of these universals. It also presents in static and global terms international realities that remain fluid and tied to specific contexts and circumstances.

The argument presented in this book, however, points in the exactly opposite direction. International studies should not reject its language of universals, it should instead reinvent it. The discipline should definitely engage in a reexamination of the assumption that it can speak at the moment to all of international politics. In fact, as was noted here a moment ago, this is where the argument put forward in this book intersects with a part of the logic of constructivism and post-Marxism. The current language of universals at the core of international studies is in reality limited in its reach and in its ability to speak to the full complexity of current global politics. This needs to be recognized in the discipline. The point that follows from this argument, though, is not that the discipline should constantly be focused on the specificities of contexts and circumstances that underlie global politics. The point is, instead, that the discipline needs to work on the basis of better universals: it must adopt a better language of concepts and approaches, which will allow it to capture what is indeed universal, what is indeed truly global, in current global politics.

There is a "necessity of universalism,"[3] to quote again the phrase used by Neil Lazarus, which must structure the way international studies approaches the analysis of global politics. A large component of the task at hand in this book was to tease out the full implications of this point for international studies as a field of study. International studies has relied on a self-referential language of universals. The understanding of the state that has driven most debates and advances in the discipline, for instance, has been assumed to apply to all states throughout the world. It has been shown here, though, that this language of universals could not capture many of the realities that shape the international politics of the non-Western world and its impact on global politics. To do that, a new approach to the question of universals in global affairs is needed. This is really what has been demonstrated here: it is indeed possible to take the language of universals at the core of international studies and to make it more dynamic and more sensitive to all these realities, which it fails to capture at the moment. This is the project that should occupy the discipline at the moment.

The project that has driven many of the recent advances in international studies, though, has been the reverse one. This has brought about a fundamental quandary. The particular is always a function of the universal: what is said about the specifics of a given situation can only be a reflection of prior categories, which supersede the character of this particular situation. Recent approaches in international studies have searched for what is particular and different in each context of international politics. The key issue, though, is that they have failed to acknowledge how this language of the particular they aimed to develop always remained a function of the universals to which they were reacting. In this, they have hidden as much as they have revealed about the non-Western world. They have set in motion a critique of the universals underlying international studies: they have also overlooked, however, what was also overlooked in the categories of thought established by these universals. They have led, in other words, to a vitally important departure for international studies: this new axis of reflection, though, has pushed the discipline further away from many of the issues defining the international politics of the non-Western world, rather than closer to them. The only way out of this trap is to engage in a reflection about both the universal and the particular. The broad categories that frame the study of different forms of international politics around the world must themselves be opened up, and the process through which they are built must be a predominant object of study in international studies. This is how what is truly specific about the non-Western world will be captured by the discipline.

This brings the argument, then, back to the idea defended here. The project driving international studies at the moment should be, more than anything else, a renewed and open-ended exploration of the universals that traverse global politics. This is what will reveal what has been missed by the discipline when it comes to the non-Western world. And this is how, in the end, the discipline will develop a language allowing it to describe accurately the changes now being imposed on global politics by those parts of the world.

This is a first reason that militates in favor of the project defended in this book. The arguments presented here also point to a second reason. This one is quite pragmatic. If there is one point that has been made clear by the arguments introduced in this book, it is that the issue of universals will be a crucially important political issue in world affairs in the near future. In fact, to put it even more starkly, global politics will revolve to a considerable extent around the need to define new universals. This is what the rise of the non-Western world is bringing about. New actors, new perspectives, and new agendas are being added to the structures and values upon which global politics has traditionally relied. What is bound to follow is a profound debate on the nature of the new bonds and shared agendas that will shape global politics in the future. In that sense, this will be a debate about nothing less than the new universals that should drive global affairs.

International studies can make a significant contribution to that process by bringing both expertise and sustained reflection to bear on that global discussion. To do so, however, it must enter into precisely the sort of investigation of universals in contemporary global politics that has been proposed here. The "necessity of universalism," to put it differently, is not only a conceptual consideration: it is also, as was said earlier, a political one. Searching for universals allows us to move beyond a discourse of difference and to open up a discussion about the best ways of developing a shared political and social agenda. This is where we are now in global politics, as the calls for greater voice and stronger representation coming out of the non-Western world force a new debate on the values, agendas, and institutions that will move global politics forward in the near future. International studies must position itself in a way that will allow it to confront that challenge. This is also, then, why the project proposed in this book is important at this point. Conversely, the search for the particular, which has animated international studies for a while, is more difficult to justify now, in the current global context. A constant search for the particular, an unending fascination with the specificities of individual circumstances, does not permit the emergence of a common agenda, which can allow us to move forward politically and socially at a global level. This is a project that has generated a formidable critique of international studies. The nature of current global politics, however, now forces a new agenda on the discipline.

Once all of this has been said, then, what is the significance of the recent advances in the constructivist and post-Marxist literature, as international studies attempts to explain the new global politics caused by the "rise of the rest"? This is a literature that marks an important reflective moment in the discipline. It forces, as Mark Neufeld puts it, a "theoretical reflection on the process of theorizing itself."[4] Clearly, this is needed in the context of current global politics. Realist and liberal approaches are based on an interlocking web of ontological, epistemological, and normative assumptions, which leads them to assume that they speak to all of international politics throughout the world. It is only if this web of assumptions is opened up to scrutiny, however, that these approaches will attain a truly global scope, one that may allow them to give a more correct account of developments in the non-Western world and of their impact on world politics. The more recent literature in international studies invites the discipline to precisely that type of scrutiny and, to that extent, it serves a most worthwhile objective, in view of ongoing trends in world affairs.

As was just explained, problems arise, though, with the direction taken by this literature as it enters into that reexamination of international studies. This is a literature that reacts to existing categories of thought and debate in international studies: it thus overlooks what international studies itself overlooks when it comes to the non-Western world. This is certainly an issue with the research agenda raised by constructivism. Constructivists point out that the categories of state identity and rationality, which have underlain the development of international studies, are considerably more malleable than the discipline has depicted them in the past. States can change the way they look at other states, and this, in turn, will change the very nature of international politics. Anarchy remains "what states make of it," and states can thus give to the international realm a new character, defined less by anarchy and conflict and much more by a rational search for progress and cooperation in world affairs. The research agenda that should occupy the discipline, in that context, is clear. It should be about the need to identify the exact dynamics through which states build the common norms and common identities that can thrust international politics toward greater cooperation and rationality. This research agenda should be, in a word, about how states become socialized one to the other as they enter into a common search for better forms of international politics.

Building in this way a research agenda on these categories of state behavior, rationality, and identity creates considerable problems, however, with regard to the non-Western world, since these categories fail to capture important aspects of international life in those parts of the world. The constructivist logic assumes the presence of an underlying shared identity, which can be drawn upon in order to guide the process of international cooperation and give it substance and meaning. What there is in the non-Western world now, though, is a volatile and uneven negotiation between liberal forms of identity, which go directly to this constructivist sense of shared identity across the international spectrum, and other forms of non-liberal identities, which negate, by their very logic, this assumption of shared identity and rationality. It is these non-liberal identities, as much as liberal ones, that non-Western states often bring to their interaction with other states. How this fits within the constructivist logic is unclear at the moment, because of the categories upon which this logic is based. The same is true with regard to the nature of the state. Constructivism assumes an internally coherent state, which can change its international behavior as it becomes socialized in the common values and rationality that the approach studies. The non-Western state, however, is often fragmented and illegitimate to such a degree that it cannot enter into the process of socialization depicted by constructivism. Some parts of the state do become socialized to international norms. Other parts, though, are completely detached from that process, and then undermine its evolution from the inside of the state apparatus. There again, the categories used by constructivism fail to capture that issue.

What does this say about the contribution of constructivism to the study of current global politics? The "rise of the rest" involves a process where non-Western states are being asked to become socialized into established global norms and institutions. It is, however, the non-liberal identities just mentioned that these states will bring to that process, as much as the liberal ones envisaged by the constructivists. It is also a fragmented and still developing state that the non-Western world will take into that process, much more than the fully developed state imagined by constructivism. If it wants to speak to current global dynamics, then, the approach must enlarge its categories so that they include all these issues. Constructivism must not simply react to the categories of mainstream international studies. It cannot adopt the understanding of the state that is at play in realism, or the notions of rationality and identity that have developed mainly in the liberal literature. This is what has led the approach to overlook many of the developments now unfolding in the non-Western world. Constructivism needs instead to work from the sort of much more global approach that has been explored here. This is what will bring to light the specificity of the state-building process in the non-Western world and its impact on the way in which non-Western states will become socialized in global norms in the near future. This is also what will underscore the confrontation of liberal and non-liberal identities shaping non-Western international politics at the moment, and its effects on the processes of global socialization studied by the approach. It is in that context, then, that constructivism will speak to the most defining issues of global politics at the moment.

China can be used one last time to provide a concrete example of these issues. A key question driving the current research agenda on China in international studies is whether or not the country will behave as a "responsible power." Will China's rising influence in global affairs be accompanied by a fuller embrace of global norms and legal standards? Will the country's military might be employed in a manner responsive to global needs, for instance through an increased participation in international peace operations? Will China, at another level, use its growing economic pre-eminence to prop up the global economic architecture and sustain it over the long term?[5] This is a research agenda to which constructivism can contribute a lot. The approach can certainly underscore, for instance, the way in which China's understanding of its role as a responsible power will evolve, in part as a function of the processes of socialization constructivists aim to bring to light. The issue goes further, in this sense, than the questions of use of power and adherence to norms studied by the realists and the liberals: it has to do, beyond all of this, with the extent to which China will internalize the global norms defining the character of current global politics, and then the extent to which it will allow them to shape its very identity and the manner in which it relates to other states.

This is, however, where the problems pointed out here with regard to constructivism emerge. To give one example, constructivism assumes the presence of a coherent and fully developed state, which enters into processes of socialization influencing its identity and worldview. In a case like China's, though, issues surrounding the legitimacy of many segments of the state are still objects of harsh internal debates. It is these internal debates and tensions, furthermore, that determine how the state will act on the international stage. Constructivism, in that sense, assumes too much too quickly. The approach presupposes a fully formed state, which interacts with the outside world and becomes socialized to it in that process. In a case like China's, however, different groups within the state might well be socialized to international norms: other groups, though, will perhaps be totally opposed to these norms and, moreover, have the power to steer the state away from them. This is the dynamic that must be understood if the interaction between China and the rest of the world is to be understood properly. Constructivism, though, works from an understanding of the state drawn from realism, as was shown here, which does not allow it to capture those deeper dynamics and their impact on the issues it studies.

These problems with constructivism have been studied in greater detail earlier in this book, for example with reference to the work of Alastair Iain Johnston on the pertinence of a constructivist approach in the study of China's international stance.[6] The point that needs to be made here, though, is that these problems are now forcing constructivism to incorporate in its logic the sort of broader perspective advocated here. By positioning itself as a reaction to mainstream realism and liberalism, the approach has locked itself in conceptual categories that serve it badly at the moment when it considers the international politics of the non-Western world. Constructivism, in this sense, will address current global politics if it looks beyond these categories and questions the extent to which they speak to the international life of the non-Western world. It is by entering into this exercise – asking, for instance, if its understanding of the state matches the case at hand – that the approach will be most useful in explaining phenomena like the impact of China's rise on current global international politics.

This leads to a broader comment on constructivism itself. It has been said here that the main authors who have formed the canon of the discipline, writers like Machiavelli, Morgenthau, and Kant, must be read anew in the context of ongoing changes in the global international environment. The same is undoubtedly true of very current authors like Wendt and the constructivists. They have launched a remarkably important research agenda for international studies in recent years. Understanding that the dynamics of state identity are more supple than mainstream international studies allows, and that this has an impact on processes of socialization and mutual understanding in world affairs, is key to a better understanding of global politics at the moment. The issue that matters now, though, is that the states that are going to be called upon to be socialized in global norms as a result of the "rise of the rest" are non-Western states. These states will bring with them an element of specificity in terms of their character and of the values and identities they will bring to bear on processes of global socialization, which must be brought into the constructivist analysis if it is to fit the conditions now in play in world politics.

But how, then, should someone like Wendt be read now in order for the reader to get at these issues? The force of Wendt's argument rests on the compelling interplay of reflections he has brought to bear on international studies. He argues that there is such a thing as the "essential state," or the "state-as-such,"[7] and the image goes to realities that are well accepted in the field. There is such a thing, all students of international affairs would agree, as a centralized "institutional–legal order, focused around the state, which determines the legitimate rules through which 'conflict is handled and society is ruled.' "[8] Wendt then puts this understanding of the state in tension with the social construction of identity and rationality, which has been an unavoidable point of debate in international studies in recent years because of the influence of post-modernism and critical theory on the field. This leads him to his *via media*: the state has a reality all its own, but this reality exists through a negotiation of identities at the inter-state level that has been overlooked by many in international studies. The argument has had an enormous appeal in the discipline because, as was said before, it has raised the possibility of a movement beyond the debates between realists, liberals, and proponents of post-modernism and critical theory, which have weighed down the field for a while.

The question that arises in light of the argument advanced in this book, however, is quite straightforward: what is missed by this line of inquiry with regard to the non-Western world and its impact on global international politics? And, from what has been argued here so far, the answer is apparent. The image of the "essential state" capable of controlling conflict and violence and of overseeing society overlooks the extent to which the state in the non-Western world often still falls short of these objectives. Conversely, the social construction of rationality and identity envisaged by the constructivist fails to capture, as was shown here, many of the dynamics that enter into the construction of identity in those parts of the world. All these overlooked factors, however, must be incorporated in the constructivist logic if the latter is to provide a point of entry into the study of current global politics.

This means, then, that Wendt must be read now in terms of both what he says and what he overlooks. His argument has an important place in international studies. The "essential state" he describes does get constructed and reconstructed through the processes of identity formation he describes. However, what is left out – the specific aspects of state and identity formation that the non-Western world brings into the equation – must be used as a counterpoint to his argument. How is the non-Western state, for example, still not in line with Wendt's "essential state"? Does the negotiation of liberal and non-liberal identities, at play in many parts of the non-Western world, add new complexities to the processes of identity formation and socialization he describes? It is this reading of Wendt's work that will push the constructivist research agenda in the direction it must take now. It will place issues of state identity and socialization firmly at the center of ongoing research in international studies. It will also, however, highlight the specific effect of the non-Western world on these issues at the moment and the way this problem needs to be integrated in the constructivist worldview.

The same set of remarks can equally be made with regard to post-Marxism. The approach provides at the moment, in the eyes of its proponent, a crucial counter-argument to constructivism, as international studies starts to consider with greater attention the rise of the non-Western world. The material organization of the world – and chiefly, in this regard, the nature of world capitalism – shapes and limits the changes that can occur at the more institutional and ideational levels studied by the constructivists. This is overlooked in constructivism, the post-Marxists claim; and yet this is central to any study of the non-Western world now. The non-Western world is precisely that part of the world whose evolution today is influenced and limited in the most direct way by the character of global capitalism. The "rise of the rest" does point to a rising economic dynamism in many parts, for instance in the Asia Pacific region. This phenomenon cannot be understood, however, without reference to the broader forces at play in global capitalism. It is these forces and, to use Cox's phrase, the institutional and ideational "world order"[9] they entail that will provide the framework of limits and opportunities that will, in the end, determine how the increasing power of the non-Western world will play itself out. This shows that a post-Marxist perspective is crucial at the moment.

A post-Marxist analysis might add another piece to the puzzle of how to consider the "rise of the rest," but the approach is not, however, without its own problems. For instance, it studies the organization of production through capitalism, and it then moves forward, to the implications of that process for the other institutional and ideational forces shaping at the moment the international politics of a given segment of the global political economy. In the non-Western world, however, it can still be the case that it is the organization of violence that precedes and shapes the organization of production. A post-Marxist perspective does not enter into the analysis of these questions because it proceeds on the basis of categories – capitalism, the state, and the like – which themselves do not recognize the place of violence in the non-Western world. This is the problem with constructivism: the approach critiques mainstream international studies and, for that reason, fails to see many of the problems that more mainstream approaches overlook. This is also the problem with post-Marxism. It reacts to the categories and postulates of realism and liberalism. For that reason, though, it fails to integrate in its analysis issues, like the specific place and role of violence in non-Western international politics, which are crucial to the non-Western world and yet absent in important ways from the realist and liberal worldview.

The solution, then, is the same for post-Marxism as it was for constructivism. The approach must move beyond a critique of mainstream international studies. It must look at the categories that informed its logic as it positioned itself as a critique of mainstream approaches, and acknowledge in its analysis the extent to which these categories are themselves being challenged by developments unfolding at the moment in the non-Western world. For example, post-Marxism must look at the categories of capitalism, state development, and the like, whose interaction it studies, and it must consider the way in which these realities are often still being shaped by prior configurations of violence and conflict in the non-Western world. It is by taking this additional step that post-Marxism will capture the full measure of the phenomena it aims to explain. The approach will show, as it claims to do, that the capitalist "world order" will determine the evolution of the non-Western world even as those parts of the world see its influence on world affairs increasing. It will also show, however, how the forms of violence, conflict, and conflict resolution prevalent in the non-Western world enter into this whole equation.

This would certainly open a most useful research agenda for international studies as it considers the "rise of the rest." One concrete example that can be mentioned in this regard is the so-called security–development nexus. Development and security in the non-Western world have often been considered in the past as two rather separate issues. Development had to do, essentially, with the economics of industrialization and related issues. Security, for its part, was a more political question, related to issues of conflict, war, and terrorism. What is widely acknowledged now, on the contrary, is that development and security are intertwined: economic progress is necessary to political legitimacy and stability and, conversely, legitimacy and stability in politics allow greater economic development. Furthermore, the need to understand this interrelationship between security and development in the non-Western world has been a key point of focus in global policy circles since the terrorist attacks of 9/11. As Mark Duffield noted a few years ago in his study of what he called the "merging of security and development,"

> the threat of an excluded South fomenting international stability through conflict, criminal activity and terrorism is now part of a new security framework. Within this framework, underdevelopment has become dangerous.[10]

Zones of underdevelopment are now seen as "dangerous" in global policy circles because they can generate interrelated patterns of widespread "conflict, criminal activity, and terrorism." Underdevelopment in the non-Western world, to say things more starkly, can lead to terrorism in the Western world. The search for security, then, must remain tied, in this "new security framework," to efforts to promote development throughout the non-Western world.

A post-Marxist perspective could be very instructive as thinking on this "new security framework," which links security and development, proceeds further. Such a perspective can underscore, from the very start of the analysis, the limits and patterns that global capitalism imposes on development in the non-Western world. It can show that the worldviews prevalent in international financial institutions influence the nature of development in those parts of the world in ways that are not always beneficial and productive. Or it can illustrate, for example, how the different forms of state–market interactions that exist in the non-Western world create further obstacles to economic development there.

To get at the full complexity of these issues, though, post-Marxism must integrate in its analysis a concern with violence. It must study how patterns of widespread criminality and lawlessness, conflict, terrorism, and sheer brutality still shape the organization of economic development in many areas of the non-Western world. It must look at the interrelationship between these phenomena and broader patterns of political and economic development in those parts of the world. It must also look, in counterpoint, at the way processes of conflict resolution influence development. For instance, international peace operations in the non-Western world now always combine efforts to end violent conflict with more extensive attempts to rebuild the entire economic and institutional architecture of the country where they are taking place. How do processes of peace-building, market-building, and state-building, in that context, influence one another? How should that inform the study of the market dynamics likely to emerge in the long term in the zones of the non-Western world that have experienced these international peace interventions? Finally, what is the place of all these issues in the "world orders" studied by the post-Marxists – how does the security world order exemplified by current international peace operations intersect with the capitalist world order post-Marxists study? Those are the questions that a post-Marxist approach must incorporate in its analysis. Indeed the work of Duffield, and also the research done by people like Roland Paris and Oliver Ramsbotham, demonstrate that raising these types of questions in the study of international peace operations can yield fascinating results.[11]

This all means, then, that post-Marxism must enter into the sort of exercise proposed here. It must look beyond the categories of state, capitalism, and the like, which have framed its logic of inquiry. It must see how there are realities in the non-Western world, such as the role of violence in the organization of economics and politics, which are not fully captured by these categories. And it must develop a new research agenda, which will correspond to this broader vision of the "world orders" that determine at the moment the evolution of the non-Western world.

This has implications for the way in which the work of Robert Cox and others who pursue a post-Marxist research agenda should be read today. Cox has introduced in international studies a research agenda that is crucially important. Thinking in terms of "world orders" in the manner he outlines provides, as was explained here, a significant counterpoint to the current influence of constructivism in the discipline. It also presents international studies with compelling questions about the character of global capitalism and its impact on global international politics. The issue at the moment, though, is how this approach should be put to use as international studies considers the implications of the "rise of the rest." This leads to some tensions in post-Marxism. The story of global capitalism, for example, has been the story of the exploitation of the non-Western world by Western capitalist forces. The "rise of the rest" is changing that. There are non-Western forms of capitalism, emanating for instance from China, that are now shaping the nature of global capitalism. Post-Marxism can usefully point out that these phenomena will unfold within the series of patterns and constraints it brings to light. The fact remains, though, that a possible post-Western "world order," a potential post-Western form of global politics, is something new for the approach. The argument that has been put forward here, in that context, is that post-Marxism will not be able to consider the full effect of this new "world order" unless it looks again at its own basic logic of inquiry, in view of current developments in the non-Western world. This will show how issues such as violence must be given a more prominent place in a post-Marxist analysis of world politics. This means, then, that the work of Cox must be read exactly like the work of Wendt: as a key point of entry in the description of world politics, but also as an invitation to ask what is still overlooked in that description in terms of the international politics of the non-Western world at the moment. It is this reading of Cox's work that will then set in motion the research agenda that post-Marxism needs to develop now in light of the changing place of the non-Western world in global politics.

This brings the discussion to the last element that should be a part of the reinvention of international studies proposed in this book. International studies as a discipline has always been concerned with the issue of "what next?" This has taken the field through a series of debates that have most recently culminated in what has been described here as a contest between a language of the universal and a language of the particular.[12] Indeed, this is the most central question that has divided the discipline over the past few years: should we look for what is universal to international affairs throughout the world, or should we instead accept that this is a wrong formulation of the problem, and look instead to the much more limited reality of international affairs in this or that particular context? And the movement, over the past few years, has been toward a deeper consideration of the latter option. This is really what the more recent advances in the field, studied here in relation to constructivism and post-Marxism, have been about. These are approaches which claim that the language of universals, which has defined international studies in the past, must now give way to a language of particulars. The idea that there can be categories of thought that describe universal realities must be abandoned. On the contrary, it must be acknowledged that reality is ever changing. The categories and methods we adopt in international studies must operate from that basis, and recognize that all of international politics is much more fluid and malleable than approaches like realism and liberalism have claimed. In the end, what is really proposed here, though, is that the discipline must now take yet another step forward. This is ultimately what the discussions of universals proposed here entails. The more recent project defended in international studies – how to move away from universals, and more toward a study of the particular – must now itself give way to a search for new universals. This is where the future of the discipline lies now.

If nothing else, the cost of the recent debates about this entire issue of the universal and the particular has been prohibitive for international studies. The very nature of this debate, in the terms in which it has been posed, has prevented its resolution. It this sense, it has effectively immobilized the discipline by forcing it into an endless back and forth from which it could not extricate itself. The language of universals, at a first level, has prevented proponents of realism and proponents of liberalism, the two key approaches that have acted as bookends in the evolution of international studies, from coming to terms in a meaningful way. If a set of postulates captures the very character of international politics all the time and everywhere, then other explanations are, by definition, false. To that extent, one can only choose one side or the other: either the realists, or instead the liberals, are correct. It is certainly possible to call for explanations of international politics that draw on diverse aspects of these different approaches. One can try, for instance, to find some middle ground between realist and liberal perspectives on the best remedies to international violence. This immediately brings into play, however, more profound worldviews, which remain distant and thus force a choice one way or the other.

At a second level, there has also been an intractable debate between proponents of a language of universals and proponents of a language of the particular. If all international politics is such that it should always be explained through a language of particulars, then both realists and liberals are, by definition, wrong, and their critics are right. Here again, the terms of the debate are such that one has to choose a camp or the other: either a language of the universal is still correct, as it has always been in international studies, or it is instead a language of the particular that is correct and should now underlie the development of the discipline. A reconciliation between the two is impossible; and this, in turn, has also mired the discipline into an endless back and forth.

At a third level, finally, the cost of these understandings of the universal and of the particular in international studies has been to keep the literature that focuses on the non-Western world at the margins of core debates within the discipline. The more traditional approaches, which rest on an unquestioned language of universals, have not seen any value in engaging questions that, according to their core logic, they had no reason to consider. The more recent literature, which has attempted to critique this language of universals and to substitute for it a language of particulars, has remained caught in a self-enclosed debate with these more traditional approaches and, for this reason, it has overlooked what these approaches also overlook when it comes to the non-Western world. Part of its logic, then, has entailed a return to an assumption of universal scope: the insights and the critiques put forward here, this literature has claimed, can be assumed to apply to all of international politics throughout the world. To that extent, the literature focused on the non-Western world has also failed to find in this more recent literature a point of entry into the most important debates that have occupied international studies as a discipline over the past few years. Many of the elements associated with international life in the non-Western world have been overlooked in this more recent literature. Its very logic – the idea that debates with more traditional approaches were bound to have worldwide ramifications – has also prevented it from engaging fully the issues and debates set forth in the literature focused on the non-Western world. In this context also, then, people have talked past one another, instead of allowing more meaningful exchanges.

It is the intractable nature of all these debates that has paralyzed international studies. In the logic of each of these literatures, of each of these approaches, reconciliation is impossible. An endless back and forth, then, is the only remaining option. And yet, as has been explained here, a tighter integration of all these approaches is precisely what is needed now in order to understand the nature of international politics in the non-Western world and its rising influence on global politics worldwide.

This is where the next step forward proposed here for international studies comes in the discussion. The discipline must not attempt to resolve all these debates between those different approaches, but rather, as was suggested in the introduction, it must go beyond them. At their core, these different approaches are divided by irreconcilable views on what is universal and what is particular in international affairs. An essential component of the argument presented here shows, though, that it is possible to go beyond these tensions between the universal and the particular and, in fact, to bring the two together. Bringing together the universal and the particular in this way allows for a closer integration of approaches which have remained distant up to this point because of their logic and which can now complement each other in a common analytical framework. This is, then, the next step forward for international studies. For a long time, the discipline was about the search for universals in international politics. More recently, it has been about a movement in the opposite direction, toward a search for the particular in international affairs. Now international studies must go beyond those debates. It is possible to do so, as was shown here. Indeed, this is precisely what is required by the nature of current global politics and by the need to draw upon sets of literature that have so far remained distant one from the other.

In that context, the question of "what next" for international studies becomes clearer. The increasing importance of the non-Western world in the evolution of global politics requires, as has been demonstrated here, that international studies reconsider a number of elements. The nature of violence in those parts of the world must be understood in greater detail. The character of the state must also be the focus of deeper analysis. The nature of democratization, the nature of economic development must be reconsidered as well. To that list can be added the two issues studied in this last chapter. The way in which international studies has looked in recent years at the processes of socialization through which the non-Western world is likely to be integrated in the global political and diplomatic architecture must be reexamined. The connection between global capitalism and the organization of conflict and conflict resolution in the non-Western world must also be the object of deeper analysis. Those are all issues that will be central in determining the impact of the non-Western world on global politics. Engaging all these questions, though, means a step forward for the discipline, one that entails a reexamination of its basic language about what is universal and what is particular in international affairs. This is the last element in the reinvention of international studies proposed in this book. Indeed, according to what has been said here, the extent to which all of us in international studies take part in this exercise will also be the extent to which we are able to understand the new world now taking shape around us.

Conclusion

It is Western powers that have traditionally shaped and controlled the entire economic and diplomatic architecture set in place to regulate world affairs. It is these same powers that have been rich, powerful, and able to set the tone and agenda of global politics. All of this, however, is changing. The rising economic, strategic, and political clout of many non-Western states is giving them a degree of control over the evolution of world politics that, historically, they have never had. This marks a fundamental shift in world affairs. In counterpoint, all of us working in international studies need to position ourselves intellectually in a way that allows us to see what is happening around us and to clarify the consequences of this shift in power on the nature of global affairs.

Indeed, the extent to which this represents the starting point of any reflection about the nature of current global politics and the ongoing evolution of international studies as a discipline needs to be underscored. The end of the Cold War marked a fundamental transformation of the international system. The rise of the so-called unipolar moment, where the United States towered above all other actors in global politics, also changed the nature of international affairs. We are now past this moment, however, and we are witnessing instead the "rise of the rest." This is a new moment in international politics. This points then, as was suggested at the beginning of this book, to the question of our times for international studies: how can we capture, in our explanations of global politics, the changes brought about in the very nature of world affairs by the "rise of the rest"?

This is a new question for the discipline. Attempting to answer it, though, immediately brings forward an apparent contradiction. The world is becoming less Western-centric. International studies has remained, throughout its evolution, Western-centric. Can the discipline, then, understand and explain current changes in global politics? Or does its very nature, on the contrary, prevent it from fully understanding the series of changes it must now address?

These issues bring into play another question – this time a very old one. Specialists of international affairs have always recognized, and often lamented, that international studies as a discipline has remained through-out its whole development an eminently Western affair. The issue, however, has been to know what to do about this problem. What has been shown here is that it is crucial for international studies as a discipline to ask, in that context, *why* it has remained Western-centric for so long.

This is where the importance of the language of universalism, which has been central to all components of international studies, gains its full significance. What has also been shown here, however, is the depth of the problem that this situation poses for international studies, as the discipline now looks at the non-Western world and considers questions that have often lain beyond its familiar purview. It would be tempting to see the issue as one of hubris, which could then be remedied through an appeal to broader modesty in international studies. The discipline, it could be claimed, has not fully understood the international politics of the non-Western world because, quite simply, it did not need to do so. The action was elsewhere, in the global politics created by the power and supremacy of the Western world, and those working in international studies knew they could explain that well enough. Now that the non-Western world contributes to an unprecedented degree to the power dynamics and institutional developments underlying the evolution of global politics, international studies simply has to bring to the discipline a greater awareness of the non-Western experience of international politics and of how it will affect global affairs. This is only a matter of bringing more attention to parts of the world that have perhaps not figured as prominently as they should have in the development of the discipline.

The problem, however, is not one of hubris, it is one of logic. There is, in all the approaches that comprise international studies, an interlocking series of postulates and logical sequences that support the assumption that international studies already captures the universal forces animating all of international politics throughout the world. This quite literally blocks any attempt to look at the issues that must be studied at the moment if the "rise of the rest" and its impact on global politics are to be fully understood. How is it possible to integrate what is specific about the international politics of the non-Western world in a discipline which, according to its most fundamental tenets, assumes that there cannot be such a thing? If international studies captures universal trends and forces in international politics, how can specific forms of international affairs still lie beyond its scope and now require greater study?

To understand fully the non-Western world and its growing impact on global politics, then, international studies itself has to change. This is what was demonstrated in this book. A number of key elements certainly have to become part of the research agenda driving the discipline. The nature of the state in the non-Western world, the nature of the market, and other such realities all have to be studied in more detail in order to produce a better account of the way in which the non-Western world will influence global politics.

Beyond all of that, though, international studies itself must still reexamine its basic logic. The sense of universalism that courses through the entire evolution of international studies has given an inward-looking character to the discipline. The assumption that international studies speaks to universal realities has left the discipline trapped, in essence, in its current conventions and debates. This is why it has not been able to look beyond itself, so to say, and toward the non-Western world. The assumption of universal validity at the heart of international studies has also divided the discipline against itself. It has created an all-consuming debate between proponents of a language of universals in the discipline and proponents of a language of particulars that, in truth, can never be resolved. This debate, just as importantly, has obscured as much as it has revealed about the international politics of the non-Western world and the ongoing "rise of the rest" in global politics.

The point now is to move beyond these debates. More than anything else, this is what the current moment in global politics requires of international studies. What is also crucial, though, is determining how exactly it is possible to do this. In this context, the discipline should still aim to speak a language of universals – but one that, along the lines of what has been suggested here, is much more dynamic, in counterpoint to all the changes transforming at the moment the very character of world affairs. This is how international studies could start to resolve many of the debates in which it has been caught in recent years. This is how, also, international studies should now move forward, in parallel with the current movement of global politics.

The last element that needs to be emphasized here is how high the stakes are in all of this. Global politics will be shaped to an ever-increasing degree by the non-Western world from this point on. Democratization, conflict resolution, development, or international stability will all move forward within processes and agendas designed to a growing degree by non-Western actors. The most basic issues of peace, democracy, or security in international affairs will remain tied to this phenomenon. By any measure, this points to extraordinarily important stakes.

The added issue, though, is that international studies itself will play a role in these new global politics. It has been said here that the discipline speaks a certain language, related mainly to the understandings of the universal and of the particular, which structure the different insights it has put forward over the course of its development. This language, though, underlies debates and insights which go far beyond the limits of the discipline itself. People working for instance in policy circles, in the media, or within advocacy groups all draw from the language, debates, and prescriptions of international studies to articulate their own positions. To that extent, international studies will help build the world it studies. It will provide the images with which we will envision our world and it will ask the questions with which we will debate its future.

This gives a measure of the stakes facing the discipline itself at the moment. Developing a better understanding of international life in the non-Western world, making this type of work a core axis of analysis in international studies, going beyond the sort of language and debates that have impeded these projects before – all of this is about more than international studies. The choices made within the discipline and the movement forward they could allow might well have parallels, in the end, within global politics itself. It is to this intriguing and important moment in international studies that this book hoped to contribute in some modest way.

Notes

Introduction: Understanding the Post-Western World

1. Stanley Hoffmann, "An American Social Science: International Relations," *Dædalus* 106, 3 (Summer 1977), 41–60. The text cited here is from James Der Derian, ed., *International Relations Theory. Critical Investigations* (New York: New York University Press, 1995), 212–241. The passage in on page 222 of this book.
2. See for instance Ole Waever, "The Sociology of a Not so International Discipline: American and European Developments in International Relations," *International Organization* 52 (Autumn 1998), 687–723.
3. Fareed Zakaria, "The Rise of the Rest," *Newsweek* (May 12, 2008).
4. Ibid.
5. Ibid.
6. Ibid.
7. Parag Khanna, *The Second World. Empires and Influence in the New Global Order* (New York: Random House, 2008), xii.
8. Fareed Zakaria, *The Post-American World* (New York: Norton & Company, 2008).
9. Jessica C. E. Gienow-Hecht, ed., *Decentering America* (New York: Berghahn Books, 2007).
10. David Rothkopf, *Running the World. The Inside Story of the National Security Council and the Architects of American Power* (New York: Public Affairs, 2005).
11. One can consult, for example, Giorgio Shani, "Toward a Post-Western IR: The *Umma, Khalsa Panth*, and Critical International Relations Theory," *International Studies Review* 10, 4 (December 2008), 722–734.
12. Samuel Huntington, *The Clash of Civilizations and the Remaking of World Order* (New York: Touchtone, 1998).
13. Another concept in vogue to describe rising centers of power is the "BRICs" – Brazil, Russia, India, and China. This brings a large part of the discussion back to India and China. It will also be interesting to see, in the medium and longer term, how Russia will want to be Asian as much as it is European.
14. Arlene B. Tickner and Ole Waever, eds, *International Relations Scholarship around the World (Worlding beyond the West)* (London: Routledge, 2009).
15. Amitav Acharya and Barry Buzan, eds, *Non-Western International Relations Theory. Perspectives on and beyond Asia* (London: Routledge, 2009).
16. Alexander Wendt, *Social Theory of International Politics* (Cambridge: Cambridge University Press, 1999), 38.
17. In echo to Wittgenstein's famous aphorism to the effect that we can never solve a problem, we can only move beyond it.
18. See, among many examples, Andrew Linklater, "The Question of the Next Stage in International Relations Theory: A Critical–Theoretical Point of View," *Millennium* 21, 1 (1992), 77–98.

1 Competing Universals: Realism

1. The phrase "competing universals," which gives this chapter and the next their titles, is in echo to the notion of "competing universalities" put forward by Judith Butler. See Judith Butler, "Competing Universalities," in Judith Butler, Ernesto Laclau, and Slavoj Žižek, eds, *Contingency, Hegemony, Universality. Contemporary Dialogues on the Left* (London and New York: Verso, 2000), 136–181.
2. R. B. J. Walker, *Inside/Outside: International Relations as Political Theory* (Cambridge: Cambridge University Press, 1993), 24.
3. Niccolò Machiavelli, *The Prince* (Edited by Quentin Skinner and Russell Price) (Cambridge: Cambridge University Press, 1985), 61.
4. Michael W. Doyle, *Ways of War and Peace* (New York and London: W. W. Norton & Company, 1997), 101.
5. Sheldon Wolin, *Politics and Vision* (Boston: Little, Brown, 1960), 200–202.
6. Niccolò Machiavelli, *The Discourses* (Translated by Leslie Walker, Edited by Bernard Crick) (Harmondsworth: Penguin, 1970), Book III, chapter XXXXIII, 517.
7. David Boucher, *Political Theories of International Relations* (Oxford: Oxford University Press, 1998), 141.
8. Hans J. Morgenthau, *Politics Among Nations. The Struggle for Power and Peace*, 3rd ed. (New York: Knopf, 1963).
9. Ibid., 33.
10. Ibid., 9.
11. Ibid., 28–29.
12. Statements like "all politics is a struggle for power" abound. See for instance ibid., 27.
13. Ibid., 3.
14. Ibid., 4.
15. Ibid.,10.
16. E. H. Carr, *The Twenty Years' Crisis 1919–1939* (London: Macmillan,1983).
17. Ibid., 10.
18. Ibid.
19. Ibid., 232.
20. Ibid., 10.
21. Ibid., 5.
22. Ibid., 21.
23. Ibid., 63–64. Carr quotes chapters XV and XXIII in *The Prince*.
24. C. B. Macpherson, "Introduction," in Thomas Hobbes, ed., *Leviathan* (London: Penguin Books 1968), 52. All subsequent references are to this edition.
25. Hobbes, *Leviathan*, chapter XIII, 186.
26. Macpherson, "Introduction," 24. Macpherson describes in this passage the influence of Hobbes on "English political thought" and notes, for instance, that the writings of Locke follow from the assumptions put forward in *Leviathan*.
27. Hobbes, *Leviathan*, chapter XIV, 189–190.
28. Gregory S. Kavka, *Hobbesian Moral and Political Theory* (Princeton: Princeton University Press, 1986), 88.
29. On this theme, see for instance J. W. N. Watkins, *Hobbes's System of Ideas*, 2nd ed. (London: Hutchinson and Company, 1973); and Marjorie Greene, "Hobbes and the Modern Mind," in M. Greene, ed., *Anatomy of Knowledge* (London: Routledge, 1969), 3–23.
30. Hobbes, *Leviathan*, chapter V, 115.

31. Macpherson, "Introduction," 21.
32. Kenneth N. Waltz, *Theory of International Politics* (Reading, Massachusetts: Addison-Wesley, 1979).
33. Ibid., 10.
34. Ibid., 90.
35. Ibid., 88.
36. Ibid., 103–104.
37. Ibid., 66.
38. Ibid., 116.
39. Ibid.
40. Ibid., chapter 4, passim.
41. Ibid., 66.
42. Ibid., 186. Waltz also makes reference here to Robert J. Art and Kenneth N. Waltz, eds, *The Use of Force* (Boston: Little, Brown, 1971).
43. Ibid., 88.
44. Ibid., chapter 6, passim.
45. Ibid., 205.
46. See for instance Mohammed Ayoob, *The Third World Security Predicament. State Making, Regional Conflict, and the International System* (Boulder: Lynne Rienner Publishers, 1995).

2   Competing Universals: Liberalism

1. Tim Dunne, "Liberalism," in John Baylis and Steve Smith, eds, *The Globalization of World Politics. An Introduction to International Relations* (Oxford: Oxford University Press, 2001), 163.
2. John Locke, *The Two Treaties of Government* [1689?] (Edited with an Introduction and Notes by Peter Laslett) (Cambridge: Cambridge University Press, 1960), *The Second Treatise*, paragraph 19, p. 280 in this edition. Emphasis in the original.
3. Ibid., paragraph 16, p. 278. Emphasis in the original.
4. Ibid., paragraph 21, p. 282. Emphasis in the original.
5. The second edition of *The Critique of Pure Reason*, where Kant responds to the reviews addressed to the first version of the text, is the best known one. It was published in 1787. *The Critique of Practical Reason* was also published in 1787, and grew out of the revisions added to the *Critique of Pure Reason*. *Idea for a Universal History from a Cosmopolitan Point of View* was published in 1784, while *Perpetual Peace: A Philosophical Sketch* came out in 1795. The best compendium of all these texts is Lewis White Beck, ed., *Kant: Selections* (New York and London: Scribner/Macmillan, 1988). The subsequent excerpts from Kant's texts are taken from this volume.
6. See for instance the argument defended in Lewis White Beck, *A Commentary on Kant's Critique of Practical Reason* (Indianapolis: Library of Liberal Arts, 1960). Kant opens up the second edition of the *Critique of Pure Reason* with a "Preface and Introduction" which itself starts with some thoughts on "The Copernican Revolution in Metaphysics." See Kant, *Critique of Pure Reason*, in Beck, *Kant: Selections*, 95.
7. Ibid., 98–99
8. Ibid., 273.
9. Ibid., 418.
10. Ibid., 419.

11. Kant, *Perpetual Peace: A Philosophical Sketch*, in Beck, ed., 430–457.
12. Ibid., 434.
13. Ibid.
14. Wade L. Huntley, "Kant's Third Image: Systemic Sources of the Liberal Peace," *International Studies Quarterly* 40 (1996), 51.
15. Kant, *Perpetual Peace: A Philosophical Sketch*, in Beck, ed., 440.
16. Kant, *Foundation of the Metaphysics of Morals*, in Beck, ed., 271.
17. On the importance of this question in Kantian studies, see for instance Steven B. Smith, "Defending Hegel from Kant," in Howard Lloyd Williams, ed., *Essays on Kant's Political Philosophy* (Chicago: University of Chicago Press, 1992), 280–286.
18. Kant, "On the Common Saying: 'This May be True in Theory, but It Does Not Apply in Practice,'" in Hans Heiss, ed., *Kant: Political Writings* (Cambridge: Cambridge University Press, 1970), 90.
19. Ibid.
20. David Boucher, *Political Theories of International Relations* (Oxford: Oxford University Press, 1998), 272.
21. Erik Gartzke, "Preferences and the Democratic Peace," *International Studies Quarterly* 44, 2 (June 2000), 192.
22. Jack Levy, "Domestic Politics and War," *Journal of Interdisciplinary History* 18, 4 (Spring 1988), 653. See also Jack Levy, "The Democratic Peace Hypothesis: From Description to Explanation," *Mershon International Studies Review* 38 (1994), 352.
23. See Melvin Small and David Singer, "The War-Proneness of Democratic Regimes," *Jerusalem Journal of International Relations* 1 (1976), 50–69.
24. See R. J. Rummel, "Libertarianism and International Violence," *Journal of Conflict Resolution* 27 (1983), 27–71. See also R. J. Rummel, "Democracies Are Less Warlike than Other Regimes," *European Journal of International Relations* 1 (1995), 457–479.
25. Erik Gartzke, for example, notes that "Oneal and Russett – together and with other co-authors – provide what is widely regarded as the leading quantitative research program in support of the democratic peace thesis." Erik Gartzke, "Preferences and the Democratic Peace," *International Studies Quarterly* 44, 2 (June 2000), 192. On Oneal and Russett, see J. R. Oneal and B. Russett, "The Classical Liberals Were Right: Democracy, Interdependence, and Conflict, 1950–1985," *International Studies Quarterly* 41, 2 (1997), 267–293; J. R. Oneal and B. Russett, "Is the Liberal Peace Just an Artifact of Cold War Interests? Assessing Recent Critiques," *International Interactions* 25, 3 (1999), 213–241.
26. Michael Doyle, "Kant, Liberal Legacies, and Foreign Affairs, Part 1," *Philosophy and Public Affairs* 12, 3 (Summer 1983), 205–254; Michael Doyle, "Kant, Liberal Legacies, and Foreign Affairs, Part 2," *Philosophy and Public Affairs* 12, 4 (Fall 1983), 323–353.
27. See for instance Michael W. Doyle, *Ways of War and Peace. Realism, Liberalism, and Socialism* (New York and London: W.W. Norton & Company, 1997), 279.
28. Ibid., 282.
29. Ibid., 282, 283.
30. Bruce Russett, *Grasping the Democratic Peace. Principles for a Post-Cold War World* (Princeton: Princeton University Press, 1993), 4.
31. See for instance Michael Doyle, "A Liberal View: Preserving and Expanding the Liberal Pacific Union," in T. V. Paul and John Hall, eds, *International Order and the Future of World Politics* (Oxford: Oxford University Press, 1999), 41–66.
32. See for instance David Held, "Democracy, the Nation-State and the Global System," in David Held, ed., *Political Theory Today* (Cambridge: Polity Press, 1991), and David Held, "Democracy: From City–States to a Cosmopolitan Order?,"

Political Studies (September 1992). The quote is from David Held, *Democracy and the Global Order. From the Modern State to Cosmopolitan Governance* (Stanford: Stanford University Press, 1995), 227.

33. Ibid., 232.
34. Ibid., 233.
35. Ibid.
36. Ibid., xi.
37. See for instance Richard Falk, "Global Civil Society and the Democratic Prospect," in Barry Holden, ed., *Global Democracy. Key Debates* (London and New York: Routledge, 2000), 162–179, and Richard Falk, "Global Civil Society: Perspectives, Initiatives, and Movements," *Oxford Development Studies* 26 (1998), 99–110. More broadly, see Richard Falk, *On Humane Governance: Towards a New Global Politics* (Cambridge: Polity Press, 1995).
38. Richard Falk, "Global Civil Society and the Democratic Prospect," in Barry Holden, ed., *Global Democracy. Key Debates* (London and New York: Routledge, 2000), 165.
39. Ibid., 171.
40. On the way in which Smith's work resonates through later developments in liberal economics and their relation to the American capitalist spirit, see for instance E. Roll, "The Wealth of Nations 1776–1976," *Lloyds Bank Review* 119 (January 1976), 12–22 and T. W. Hutchison, "Adam Smith and *The Wealth of Nations*," *Journal of Law and Economics* 19, 3 (October 1976), 507–528.
41. Adam Smith, "The Theory of Moral Sentiments", in *The Works of Adam Smith*, Volume 1 (Otto Zeiler, 1963). See part III, passim.
42. Glenn R. Morrow, *The Ethical and Economic Theories of Adam Smith* (New York: Longmans, Green, and Co. 1923), 31.
43. Adam Smith, "The Theory of Moral Sentiments", in *The Works of Adam Smith*, part III, chapter II.
44. C. R. Fay, "Adam Smith and the Dynamic State," *Economic Journal* 40 (March 1930), 28.
45. L. Billet, "The Just Economy: The Moral Basis of the *Wealth of Nations*," *Review of Social Economy* 34 (December 1976), 303. Also see, for example, A. L. Macfie, "Adam Smith's *Moral Sentiments* as Foundation for his *Wealth of Nations*," *Oxford Economic Papers* 11 (October 1959), 209–228.
46. Adam Smith, *An Inquiry into the Nature and Causes of the Wealth of Nations* (Edited and with an Introduction, Notes, Marginal Summary and Index by Edwin Cannan) (Chicago: University of Chicago Press, 1976), Book IV, chapter II.
47. Ibid., part III, chapter IV.
48. David Mitrany, *A Working Peace System* (Chicaco: Quadrangle Books, 1966).
49. Ibid., 72.
50. Ibid., 63.
51. Ernst B. Haas, *Beyond the Nation-State. Functionalism and International Organization* (Stanford: Stanford University Press, 1964).
52. Ibid., 6.
53. Robert O. Keohane and Joseph S. Nye, *Power and Interdependence. World Politics in Transition* (Boston: Little, Brown and Company, 1977).
54. Ibid., 5.
55. Ibid., 23.
56. Ibid., 24–25.
57. Ibid., 25.
58. Ibid.

59. Robert O. Keohane, *After Hegemony. Cooperation and Discord in the World Political Economy* (Princeton: Princeton University Press, 1984).
60. Richard Rosecrance, *The Rise of the Trading State. Commerce and Conquest in the Modern World* (New York: Basic Books, 1986).
61. Ibid., ix.
62. See E. D. Mansfield and J. C. Pevehouse, "Trade Blocs, Trade Flows, and International Conflict," *International Organization* 54 (2000), 775–808 and E. D. Mansfield, J. C. Pevehouse, and D. H. Bearce, "Preferential Trading Arrangements and Military Disputes," *Security Studies* 9 (1999–2000), 92–118.
63. See Bruce Russett and John R. Oneal, *Triangulating Peace: Democracy, Interdependence, and International Organizations* (New York: W. W. Norton, 2001); John R. Oneal, Bruce Russett, and Michael L. Berbaum, "*Causes* of Peace: Democracy, Interdependence, and International Organizations, 1885–1992," *International Studies Quarterly* 47 (2003), 371–393.
64. Richard Rosecrance, *The Rise of the Trading State*, 40–41.
65. Erik Gartzke and Quang Li, "War, Peace, and the Invisible Hand: Positive Political Externalities of Economic Globalization," *International Studies Quarterly* 47 (2003), 563.
66. Michael Mousseau, "The Nexus of Market Society, Liberal Preferences, and Democratic Peace: Interdisciplinary Theory and Evidence," *International Studies Quarterly* 47, 4 (December 2003), 489.
67. David Mitrany, *A Working Peace System*, 18. Emphasis added.
68. Ibid. Emphasis in the original.
69. Robert O. Keohane and Joseph S. Nye, *Power and Interdependence*, 5. Emphasis added.
70. Ibid., 21–22.

3 Situating the Particular: After Constructivism

1. The best introduction in English to Foucault is Paul Rabinow, ed., *The Foucault Reader* (New York: Pantheon Books, 1984). Also see, from the works of Foucault himself, Michel Foucault, *The Order of Things* (London: Tavistock, 1970).
2. The best introduction in English to Derrida's work might be Jacques Derrida, *Writing and Difference* (Translated by Alan Bass) (Chicago: University of Chicago Press, 1978). Also see Jacques Derrida, *Of Grammatology* (Translated by Gayatri Chakravorty Spivak) (Baltimore: Johns Hopkins University Press, 1976).
3. See, as an example: Richard K. Ashley, "Untying the Sovereign State: A Double Reading of the Anarchy Problematique," *Millennium* 17, 2 (1988), 227–262.
4. See for instance David Campbell, *Writing Security: United States Foreign Policy and the Politics of Identity* (Manchester: Manchester University Press, 1992).
5. R. B. J. Walker, *Inside/Outside: International Relations as Political Theory* (Cambridge: Cambridge University Press, 1993).
6. Ibid., ix.
7. On this theme, see for instance Jürgen Habermas, "An Alternative Way out of the Philosophy of the Subject: Communicative versus Subject-Centered Reason," in *The Philosophical Discourse of Modernity: Twelve Lectures* (Translated by Frederick Lawrence) (Boston: MIT Press, 1987).
8. Andrew Linklater, *Men and Citizens in the Theory of International Relations* (London: Macmillan, 1982).

9. Andrew Linklater, *Beyond Realism and Marxism: Critical Theory and International Relations* (London: Macmillan, 1990).

10. Andrew Linklater, *The Transformation of Political Community: Ethical Foundations of the Post-Westphalian Era* (Cambridge: Polity Press, 1998).

11. On the link between forms of rationality and the nature of international politics, see in particular Linklater, *Beyond Realism and Marxism*. On the nature of the emancipation project proposed by Linklater, see Linklater, *The Transformation of Political Community*, and Linklater, *Men and Citizens in the Theory of International Relations*.

12. Alexander Wendt, *Social Theory of International Politics* (Cambridge: Cambridge University Press, 1999), 38.

13. Maja Zehfuss, *Constructivism in International Relations: The Politics of Reality* (Cambridge: Cambridge University Press, 2002).

14. Bill McSweeney, *Security, Identity, and Interests: A Sociology of International Relations* (Cambridge: Cambridge University Press, 1999).

15. See, amongst others, Stefano Guzzini and Anna Leander, eds, *Constructivism and International Relations* (London: Routledge, 2006). Another important study on the place of constructivism in the evolution of international studies is K. M. Fierke and Knud Erik Jørgensen, *Constructing International Relations – The Next Generation* (Armonk, New York: M. E. Sharpe, 2001).

16. Alexander Wendt, *Social Theory of International Politics* (Cambridge: Cambridge University Press, 1999).

17. Ibid., 201.

18. Ibid, 202. Wendt quotes from Roger Benjamin and Raymond Duvall, "The Capitalist State in Context," in Roger Benjamin, ed., *The Democratic State* (Lawrence, Kansas: University of Kansas Press, 1985), 25–26.

19. Ibid., 92.

20. Ibid., 1.

21. Ibid., 20.

22. Ibid.

23. Alexander Wendt, "Anarchy Is What States Make of It: The Social Construction of Power Politics," *International Organization* 46, 2 (1992), 391–425.

24. See Immanuel Wallerstein, *The Capitalist World-Economy*, (Cambridge: Cambridge University Press, 1979). The most elaborate expression of Wallertein's views is found in the different volumes of *The Modern World-System*. See Immanuel Wallerstein, *The Modern World-System*, Vol. 1: *Capitalist Agriculture and the Origins of the European World-Economy in the Sixteenth Century*; Vol. 2: *Mercantilism and the Consolidation of the European World-Economy, 1600–1750; The Second Era of Great Expansion of the Capitalist World-Economy* (San Diego: Academic Press, 1974, 1980, 1989).

25. Wallerstein, *The Capitalist World-Economy*, 6.

26. The clearest expression of the dependency theory is perhaps found in Fernando Henrique Cardoso and Enzo Faletto, *Dependency and Development in Latin America* (Translated by Marjory Mattingly Urquidi) (Berkeley: University of California Press, 1979). Also see Andres Gunder Frank, *Dependent Accumulation and Underdevelopment* (New York: Monthly Review Press, 1979).

27. Cardoso and Faletto, *Dependency and Development in Latin America*, 160.

28. On these themes of space and time in Wallerstein's work, see for instance Stephen Hobden and Richard Wyn Jones, "Marxist Theories of International Relations," in John Baylis and Steve Smith, eds, *The Globalization of World Politics*.

An Introduction to International Relations (Oxford: Oxford University Press, 2001), 206–210.

29. Karl Marx, "The German Ideology," in Lloyd D. Easton and Kurt H. Guddat, eds, *Writings of the Young Marx on Philosophy and Society* (New York: Doubleday, 1967), 409. Emphasis in the original.

30. Marx and Engels, "The Communist Manifesto," in D. McLennan, ed., *Karl Marx. Selected Writings* (Oxford: Oxford University Press, 1977), 224–225. This quotation taken from Andrew Linklater, "Marxism," in Scott Burchill and Andrew Linklater, eds, with Richard Devetak, Matthew Paterson, and Jacquie True, *Theories of International Relations* (New York: St. Martin's Press, 1996), 123.

31. The terms is used, for instance, by Linklater in his study of Marxism. See Linklater, "Marxism," 132.

32. See, for example: Theda Skocpol, *States and Social Revolutions* (Cambridge: Cambridge University Press, 1979).

33. See, amongst others, Stephen Gill, ed., *Gramsci, Historical Materialism and International Relations* (Cambridge: Cambridge University Press, 1993); or, more recently, Stephen Gill, *Power and Resistance in the New World Order*, 2nd ed. (London: Palgrave Macmillan, 2008).

34. On the Gramscian approach, see Alison J. Ayers, *Gramsci, Political Economy, and International Relations Theory. Modern Princes and Naked Emperors* (London: Palgrave Macmillan, 2008).

35. Robert W. Cox, *Production, Power, and World Order. Social Forces in the Making of History* (New York: Columbia Press, 1987).

36. Ibid., ix.

37. Ibid., 1.

38. Ibid.

39. Antonio Gramsci, *Selection from the Prison Notebooks* (Edited and translated by Quintin Hoare and Geoffrey Nowell Smith) (New York: International Publishers, 1971).

40. Ibid., 134.

41. Ibid.

42. Ibid., 138.

43. See Timothy J. Sinclair's comments on the concepts in his "Beyond International Relations Theory: Robert W. Cox and Approaches to World Order," in Robert W. Cox with Timothy J. Sinclair, eds, *Approaches to World Order* (Cambridge: Cambridge University Press, 1996), 11. For Cox's use of the phrase, see Robert Cox, "Social Forces, States, and World Orders: Beyond International Relations Theory," *Millennium* 10, 2 (Summer 1981).

44. Cox, "Social Forces, States, and World Orders: Beyond International Relations Theory." The text quoted here is published in Robert O. Keohane, ed., *Neorealism and/its Critics* (New York: Columbia University Press, 1986), 207. Emphasis in the original.

45. Ibid., 214. Cox is drawing here from the work of the eighteenth-century thinker Giambattista Vico, another major influence on him.

4   Violence, Rationality, and the State

1. Pinar Bilgin, "Thinking Past 'Western' IR?," *Third World Quarterly* 29, 1 (2008), 6.

2. H. K. Bhabha, *The Location of Culture* (London: Routledge, 1994). The text is quoted on page 6 of Bilgin, "Thinking Past 'Western' IR?"

3. Mohammed Ayoob, *The Third World Security Predicament. State Making, Regional Conflict, and the International System* (Boulder, Colorado: Lynne Rienner Publishers, 1995), 47.
4. Robert H. Jackson, *Quasi-States. Sovereignty, International Relations and the Third World* (Cambridge: Cambridge University Press, 1990).
5. See, among others, Charles Tilly, *Coercion, Capital, and European States, A.D. 990–1990* (Oxford: Basil Blackwell, 1990).
6. R. B. J. Walker, *Inside/Outside: International Relations as Political Theory* (Cambridge: Cambridge University Press, 1993).
7. Sheldon Wolin, "Violence and the Western Political Tradition," *American Journal of Orthopsychiatry* 33 (1963), 20.
8. Sheldon Wolin, *Politics and Vision* (Boston: Little, Brown, 1960), 200.
9. Stephanie G. Neuman, ed., *International Relations Theory and the Third World* (New York: St. Martin's Press, 1998).
10. Ibid., 3. Neuman quotes from Kenneth N. Waltz, *Theory of International Politics* (Reading, Massachusetts: Addison-Wesley, 1979), 61.
11. Neuman, *International Relations Theory and the Third World*, 3. Neuman quotes from J. David Singer, "The Global System and its Subsystems: A Developmental View," in James Rosenau, ed., *Linkage Politics: Essays on the Convergence of National and International Systems* (New York: Free Press, 1969), 30.
12. Mohammed Ayoob, *The Third World Security Predicament*, 85.
13. Ibid., 15.
14. Ibid., 9.
15. Kenneth N. Waltz, *Theory of International Politics* (Reading, Massachusetts: Addison-Wesley, 1979), 88.
16. Thomas Hobbes, *Leviathan* (London: Penguin Books, 1968), chapter XIV, 189–190.
17. Ibid., chapter XVII, 227.
18. Kenneth N. Waltz, *Theory of International Politics*, 9.
19. Ibid., 103–104. Italics in the original.
20. Ibid.
21. Ibid., 90.
22. C. B. Macpherson, "Introduction," in Thomas Hobbes, ed., *Leviathan* (London: Penguin Books, 1968), 21.
23. Kenneth Waltz, *Theory of International Politics*, 66.
24. Muthiah Alagappa, "Asian Practice of Security. Key Features and Explanations," in Muthiah Alagappa, ed., *Asian Security Practice. Material and Ideational Influences* (Stanford: Stanford University Press, 1998), 660.
25. Ibid., 661, 663.
26. This is a statement in Indonesian State Law quoted by Muthiah Alagappa in *Comprehensive Security: Interpretations in ASEAN Countries*. Research Paper and Policy Studies, no 26, Institute of East Asian Studies, University of California at Berkeley. It is taken here from David Capie and Paul Evans, *The Asia–Pacific Security Lexicon* (Singapore: Institute of Southeast Asian Studies, 2002), 66. Emphasis added.
27. Noordin Sopiee, "Malaysia's Doctrine of Comprehensive Security," *Journal of Asiatic Studies* 27 (1993), 2, 262. Cited by: David Capie and Paul Evans, *The Asia–Pacific Security Lexicon*, 69.

5 Politics, Economics, and Self-Identity

1. Tim Dunne, "Liberalism," in John Baylis and Steve Smith, eds, *The Globalization of World Politics. An Introduction to International Relations* (Oxford: Oxford University Press, 2001), 163.

2. Lee Hock Guan, "Introduction," in Lee Hock Guan, ed., *Civil Society in Southeast Asia* (Singapore: Institute of Southeast Asian Studies, 2004), 11.

3. Partha Chatterjee, "On Civil and Political Society in Post-Colonial Democracies," in Sudipta Kaviraj and Sunil Kilnani, eds, *Civil Society: History and Possibilities* (Cambridge: Cambridge University Press, 2001).

4. Ernest Gellner, "The Importance of Being Modular," in J. A. Hall, ed., *Civil Society: Theory, History, Comparison* (Cambridge: Polity Press, 1995), cited in Lee Hock Guan, "Introduction," 18.

5. Chua Beng Huat, "The Relative Autonomies of the State and Civil Societies," in Gillian Koh and Ooi Giok Ling, eds, *State–Society Relations* (New York: Oxford University Press, 2000).

6. Nancy Fraser, "Transnationalizing the Public Sphere," in Max Pensky, ed., *Globalizing Critical Theory* (New York: Rowan & Littlefield, 2005), 37.

7. Immanuel Kant, *Critique of Pure Reason*, in Lewis White Beck, ed., *Kant: Selections* (New York and London: Scribner/Macmillan, 1988), 98–99.

8. Ibid., 318.

9. Kant, *Idea for a Universal History from a Cosmopolitan Point of View*, in Beck, ed., *Kant: Selections*, 419.

10. Ibid., 422.

11. Michael W. Doyle, *Ways of War and Peace. Realism, Liberalism, and Socialism* (New York and London: W. W. Norton & Company, 1997), 279.

12. Ibid., 282.

13. Ibid.

14. Michael Doyle "A Liberal View: Preserving and Expanding the Liberal Pacific Union," in T. V. Paul and John Hall, eds, *International Order and the Future of World Politics* (Oxford: Oxford University Press, 1999), 41–66.

15. David Held, *Democracy and the Global Order: From the Modern State to Cosmopolitan Governance* (Stanford: Stanford University Press, 1995), xi.

16. Ibid., 232.

17. Richard Falk, "Global Civil Society and the Democratic Prospect," in Barry Holden, ed., *Global Democracy: Key Debates* (London and New York: Routledge, 2000), 165, 171.

18. Kant, *Idea for a Universal History from a Cosmopolitan Point of View*, in Beck, ed., *Kant: Selections*, 415.

19. Kant, *Critique of Pure Reason*, in Beck, ed., *Kant: Selections*, 98.

20. On the notion of cooperative security in Asia, see David B. Dewitt, "Common, Comprehensive, and Cooperative Security," *Pacific Review* 7, no. 1 (1994). On the discourse and practice of track-two diplomacy in general, see Louise Diamond and John McDonald, *Multi-Track Diplomacy: A Systems Approach to Peace* (West Harford: Kumarian Press, 1996).

21. See for instance Paul M. Evans, "Building Security: The Council for Security Cooperation in the Asia Pacific (CSCAP)," *Pacific Review* 7, no. 2 (1994), 125–139.

22. On the broad dynamics which led to the development of the notion of human security, see "Redefining Security: The Human Dimension," *Current History* (May 1995), 229–236. On the Canadian involvement in the development and promotion of the concept, see Lloyd Axworthy, "Canada and Human Security: The Need for Leadership," *International Journal* 52, no. 2 (Spring 1997), 183–196. Axworthy was Canada's Foreign Minister.

23. See for instance Pranee Thiparat, ed., *The Quest for Human Security: The Next Phase of ASEAN?* (Bangkok: Institute of Security and International Studies, 2001).

(ASEAN stands for Association of Southeast Asian Nations.) Also see my "Human Security in Vietnam, Laos, and Cambodia," *Contemporary Southeast Asia* 24, no. 3 (December 2002), 509–527.

24. On this, see my "Civil Society and Regional Security: Tensions and Potentials in Post-Crisis Southeast Asia," *Contemporary Southeast Asia* 22, no. 3 (December 2000), 550–569.

25. Rizal Sukma, "Human Security and Political Stability: Should There Be a Tension?" in Pranee Thiparat, ed., *The Quest for Human Security*, 65.

26. Mely Caballero-Anthony, "Human Security and Comprehensive Security in ASEAN," in Pranee Thiparat, ed., *The Quest for Human Security*, 35.

27. On the formation of liberal identity in Southeast Asia, see also my "Civil Society and Regional Security: Tensions and Potentials in Post-Crisis Southeast Asia."

28. Adam Smith, *The Theory of Moral Sentiments*, in *The Works of Adam Smith*, vol. 1 (Otto Zeiler: 1963), part III, chapter I.

29. Fernando Henrique Cardoso and Enzo Faletto, *Dependency and Development in Latin America* (Berkeley: University of California Press, 1973).

30. Peter Evans, *Dependent Development* (Princeton: Princeton University Press, 1979). See also Peter Evans and Michael Timerlake, "Dependence, Inequality, and Growth in Less Developed Countries," *American Sociological Review* 45 (1980), 531–552.

31. Stephan Haggard, *Pathways from the Periphery: The Politics of Growth in the Newly Industrializing Countries* (Ithaca: Cornell University Press, 1990), 16.

32. Haggard's main work, in this perspective, remains *Pathways from the Periphery*, though a series of other writings are of quite some importance. See for instance Stephan Haggard, "The Newly Industrializing Countries in the International System," *World Politics* 38 (1986), 343–370.

33. Frederic C. Deyo, ed., *The Political Economy of the New Asian Industrialism* (Ithaca: Cornell University Press, 1987).

34. Frederic C. Deyo, *Dependent Development and Industrial Order: An Asian Case Study* (New York: Praeger, 1981).

35. Richard E. Barrett and Soomi Chin, "Export-Oriented Industrializing States in the Capitalist World System: Similarities and Differences," in Deyo, ed., *The Political Economy of the New Asian Industrialism*, 31.

36. Bruce Cumings, "The Origins and Development of the Northeast Asian Political Economy: Industrial Sectors, Product Cycles, and Political Consequences," in Deyo, ed., *The Political Economy of the New Asian Industrialism*, 45.

37. The main reference here should be: Chalmers Johnson, *MITI and the Japanese Miracle* (Stanford: Stanford University Press, 1982).

38. This calls into play the literature on the "bureaucratic–authoritarian state," developed with a focus on Latin America, in parallel with similar studies devoted to Asia. The classic author here is Guillermo A. O'Donnell. See for instance his *Modernization and Bureaucratic-Authoritanianism in South American Politics* (Berkeley: University of California at Berkeley, 1973).

39. The literature on these questions is enormous. Useful starting points might be Bela Belassa, *The Newly Industrializing Countries in the World Economy* (New York: Pergamon, 1981), and David Yoffie, *Power and Protectionism: Strategies of the Newly Industrializing Countries* (New York: Columbia University Press, 1983).

40. Adam Smith, *The Theory of Moral Sentiments*, in *The Works of Adam Smith*, vol. 1 (Otto Zeiler: 1963), part III.

41. Ibid., Book IV, chapter II.

42. Ernst B. Haas, *Beyond the Nation-State. Functionalism and International Organization* (Stanford: Stanford University Press, 1964), 6.
43. Ibid.
44. David Mitrany, *A Working Peace System* (Chicago: Quadrangle Books, 1966), 63.
45. Robert O. Keohane and Joseph S. Nye, *Power and Interdependence. World Politics in Transition* (Boston: Little, Brown, and Company, 1977), 24.
46. David Mitrany, *A Working Peace System*, 63.
47. Adam Smith, *An Inquiry into the Nature and Causes of the Wealth of Nations*, part III, chapter IV.
48. Ernst B. Haas, *Beyond the Nation-State. Functionalism and International Organization*, 6.
49. Ibid.

6   The Construction of Difference in International Affairs

1. Henry R. Nau, "Identity and the Balance of Power in Asia," in G. John Ikenberry and Michael Mastanduno, eds, *International Relations Theory and the Asia-Pacific* (New York: Columbia University Press, 2003).
2. Ibid., 225.
3. Edward W. Said, *Orientalism* (New York: Random House, 1978).
4. Ibid., 3.
5. Gyan Prakash, *After Colonialism. Imperial Histories and Postcolonial Displacement* (Princeton: Princeton University Press, 1995).
6. Dipesh Chakrabarty, *Provincializing Europe. Postcolonial Thought and Historical Difference* (Princeton: Princeton University Press, 2000).
7. See for example Gayatri Chakravorty Spivak, *Toward a History of the Vanishing Present* (Cambridge, Massachusetts: Harvard University Press, 1999).
8. Gayatri Chakravorty Spivak, "Can the Subaltern Speak?," in Bill Ashcroft, Gareth Griffiths and Helen Tiffin, eds, *Toward a History of the Vanishing Present*, quoted in *The Post-Colonial Studies Reader*, 2nd ed. (London and New York: Routledge, 2006), 32.
9. Ngugi Wa Thiong'o, *Decolonizing the Mind. The Politics of Language in African Literature* (Portsmouth: Heinemann, 1986).
10. Trinh T. Minh-ha, *When the Moon Waxes Red. Representation, Gender, and Cultural Politics* (New York and London: Routledge, 1991).
11. Kwame Anthony Appiah, "The Illusions of Race," in Emmanuel Eze, ed., *African Philosophy: An Anthology* (Oxford: Blackwell, 1998).
12. See Pal Ahluwalia, *Politics and Post-Colonial Theory: African Inflections* (New York: Routledge, 2001).
13. On the extent to which this literature has been sidestepped in the literature in international studies, see the special issue of *Alternatives* devoted to race and international studies – *Alternatives* 26, 4 (October/December 2001). In particular, see Sankaran Krishna, "Race, Amnesia, and the Education of International Relations," in that special issue.
14. Alastair Iain Johnston, "Socialization in International Institutions. The ASEAN Way and International Relations Theory," in G. John Ikenberry and Michael Mastanduno, eds, *International Relations Theory and the Asia-Pacific*, 113.
15. Amitav Acharya, *Constructing a Security Community in Southeast Asia. ASEAN and Problem of Regional Order* (London and New York: Routledge, 2001). ASEAN stands for "the Association of Southeast Asian Nations."

16. Ibid., 4.
17. Ibid.
18. Ibid.
19. Ibid.
20. Amitav Acharya, *The Quest for Identity. International Relations of Southeast Asia* (Oxford and New York: Oxford University Press, 1997), 1. To "imagine" a region is a reference to Benedict Anderson: "If the nation-state can be an 'imagined community,' to use Benedict Anderson's classic formulation, why not regions?" (p. 2 of the book).
21. Mely Caballero-Anthony, *Regional Security in Southeast Asia. Beyond the ASEAN Way* (Singapore: Institute of Southeast Asian Studies, 2005), 7.
22. Ibid., 4.
23. See my "Civil Society and Regional Security: Tensions and Potentials in Post-Crisis Southeast Asia," *Contemporary Southeast Asia* 22, 3 (December 2000), 550–569.
24. Vedi R. Hadiz, ed., *Empire and Neoliberalism in Asia* (London and New York: Routledge, 2006).
25. Vedi R. Hadiz, "Introduction," in Vedi R. Hadiz, ed., *Empire and Neollberalism in Asia*, 1.
26. Ibid., 3.
27. Ibid., 16. See Garry Rodan and Kevin Hewison, "Neoliberal Globalization, Conflict, and Security. New Life for Authoritarianism in Asia?," in Vedi R. Hadiz, ed., *Empire and Neoliberalism in Asia*, 105–122.

7 Reinventing Realism: Power and Violence in the Post-Western World

1. His *Hegemony and Socialist Strategy* (written with Chantal Mouffe) is now something of a classic: Ernesto Laclau and Chantal Mouffe, *Hegemony and Socialist Strategy: Towards a Radical Democratic Politics* (London: Verso, 1989, 3rd reprint). Also see Ernesto Laclau, *New Reflections on the Revolution of Our Time* (London: Verso, 1990). For a fascinating debate on Laclau's views on universality, see Judith Butler, Ernesto Laclau, and Slavoj Žižek, *Contingency, Hegemony, Universality: Contemporary Dialogues on the Left* (London: Verso, 2000).
2. Laclau talks about how the universal is that which "overflows its particularity": Ernesto Laclau, *Emancipations* (London: Verso, 1996), 22.
3. See Neil Lazarus, "The Necessity of Universalism," *Differences: A Journal of Feminist Cultural Studies* 7, 1 (1995), 15–47.
4. For further elaboration on all these points, see Simon Critchley and Oliver Marchart, eds, *Laclau: A Critical Reader* (London and New York: Routledge, 2004).
5. Sheldon Wolin, "Violence and the Western Political Tradition," *American Journal of Orthopsychiatry* 33 (1963), 20.
6. See, among many other works, Caroline Hughes, "Surveillance and Resistance in the Cambodian Elections: The Prisoner's Dilemma?" *Southeast Asian Affairs* (1999), 92–108.
7. See my *Peace, Power, and Resistance in Cambodia. Global Governance and the Failure of International Conflict Resolution* (London and New York: Macmillan and St. Martin's Press, 2000).
8. Amongst many examples, see Steven Simon, "The Price of the Surge. How U.S. Strategy is Hastening Iraq's Demise," *Foreign Affairs* (May/June 2008), 57–76.

9. Niccolo Machiavelli, *The Prince* (Edited by Quentin Skinner and Russell Price) (Cambridge: Cambridge University Press, 1985), 61.
10. Hans J. Morgenthau, *Politics Among Nations: The Struggle for Power and Peace*, 3rd ed. (New York: Knopf, 1963), 33.
11. Kenneth N. Waltz, *Theory of International Politics* (Reading, Massachusetts: Addison-Wesley, 1979), 88.
12. G. John Ikenberry, ed., *America Unrivaled: The Future of the Balance of Power* (Ithaca and London: Cornell University Press, 2002).
13. G. John Ikenberry, "Introduction," in G. John Ikenberry, ed., *America Unrivaled: The Future of the Balance of Power*, 3.
14. Robert H. Jackson, *Quasi-States: Sovereignty, International Relations, and the Third World* (Cambridge: Cambridge University Press, 1990), 1.
15. Mohammed Ayoob, *The Third World Security Predicament: State Making, Regional Conflict, and the International System* (Boulder, Colorado: Lynne Rienner Publishers, 1995), 9.
16. On these two issues – the extent to which the recourse to balancing strategies is somewhat automatic for states, and differences in balancing strategies in regional and global contexts – Ikenberry's edited collection certainly remains a good primer. See in particular William C. Wohlforth, "US Strategy in a Unipolar World," 98–120 and Michael Mastanduno, "Incomplete Hegemony and Security Order in the Asia-Pacific," 181–211 both in G. John Ikenberry, ed., *America Unrivaled. The Future of the Balance of Power.*
17. Kenneth N.Waltz, *Theory of International Politics* (Reading, Massachusetts: Addison-Wesley, 1979), 10.
18. C. B. Macpherson, "Introduction," in Thomas Hobbes, ed., *Leviathan* (London: Penguin Books, 1968), 21.

8 Reinventing Liberalism: Values and Change in the Post-Western World

1. Liberalism was described earlier as the great Other in international studies, in opposition to realism, through a reference to Tim Dunne's description of the liberal worldview as the "historical alternative" in the evolution of the field. See Tim Dunne, "Liberalism," in John Baylis and Steve Smith, eds, *The Globalization of World Politics. An Introduction to International Relations* (Oxford: Oxford University Press, 2001), 163.
2. Immanuel Kant, *Critique of Pure Reason*, in Lewis White Beck, ed., *Kant: Selections* (New York and London: Scribner/Macmillan, 1988), 418.
3. Michael W. Doyle, *Ways of War and Peace. Realism, Liberalism, and Socialism* (New York and London: W.W. Norton & Company, 1997), 279.
4. Lee Hock Guan, "Introduction," in Lee Hock Guan, ed., *Civil Society in Southeast Asia* (Singapore: Institute of Southeast Asian Studies, 2004), 11.
5. Parta Chatterjee, "On Civil and Political Society in Post-Colonial Democracies," in Sudipta Kaviraj and Sunil Kilnani, eds, *Civil Society: History and Possibilities* (Cambridge: Cambridge University Press, 2001).
6. Himadeep Muppidi, "Colonial and Post-Colonial Global Governance," in Michael Barnett and Raymond Duvall, eds, *Power in Global Governance* (Cambridge: Cambridge University Press, 2005), 279. Nicholas Lemann is the Washington correspondent of *The New Yorker*. He was quoting Richard Haas, then a State

Department official in the George W. Bush administration. The passage is from Nicholas Lemann, "The Next World Order," *The New Yorker*, April 1, 2002, 46.

7. Francis Fukuyama, *The End of History and the Last Man* (New York: Avon Books, 1992).

8. Samuel P. Huntington, *The Clash of Civilizations and the Remaking of World Order* (New York: Simon and Schuster, 1996). An interesting counterpoint is Fareed Zakaria, *The Future of Freedom: Illiberal Democracy at Home and Abroad* (New York: W.W. Norton, 2003).

9. Immanuel Kant, *Critique of Pure Reason*, in Lewis White Beck, ed., *Kant Selections* (New York and London: Scribner/Macmillan, 1988), 418.

10. Michael W. Doyle, *Ways of War and Peace. Realism, Liberalism, and Socialism* (New York and London: W. W. Norton & Company, 1997), 279.

11. David Held, *Democracy and the Global Order. From the Modern State to Cosmopolitan Governance* (Stanford: Stanford University Press, 1995), xi.

12. Ibid., 233.

13. Jack Levy, "Domestic Politics and War," *Journal of Interdisciplinary History* 18, 4 (Spring 1988), 653. See also Jack Levy, "The Democratic Peace Hypothesis: From Description to Explanation," *Mershon International Studies Review* 38 (1994), 352.

14. Leonard Billet, "The Just Economy: The Moral Basis of the *Wealth of Nations*," *Review of Social Economy* 34 (December 1976), 303.

15. Stephen Haggard, *Pathways from the Periphery. The Politics of Growth in the Newly Industrializing Countries* (Ithaca: Cornell University Press, 1990), 16.

16. Dennis A. Rondinelli, "Globalization and the Asian Economic Response," in Dennis A. Rondinelli and John M. Heffron, eds, *Globalization and Change in Asia* (Boulder, CO: Lynne Rienner, 2007), 39. Rondinelli himself, though, underscores the points made here and shows the extent to which the nature of market liberalization in the Asia Pacific is specific to that region.

17. On this phrase, see Robert Gilpin, "Sources of American–Japanese Conflict," in G. John Ikenberry and Michael Mastanduno, eds, *International Relations Theory and the Asia Pacific* (New York: Columbia University Press, 2003), 298.

18. Xiangming Chen, *As Borders Bend. Transnational Spaces on the Pacific Rim* (New York: Rowman & Littlefield Publishers, 2005).

19. Adam Smith, *The Theory of Moral Sentiments*, in *The Works of Adam Smith* (Otto Zeiler, 1963), Part III, Chapter II.

20. Robert O. Keohane and Joseph S. Nye, *Power and Interdependence. World Politics in Transition* (Boston: Little, Brown and Company, 1977), 5.

21. Ernst B. Haas, *Beyond the Nation-State. Functionalism and International Organization* (Stanford: Stanford University Press, 1964), 6.

9 The Way Forward: Searching for New Universals in Global Politics

1. Immanuel Wallerstein, *The Capitalist World-Economy* (Cambridge: Cambridge University Press, 1979).

2. Robert W. Cox, *Production, Power, and World Order. Social Forces in the Making of History* (New York: Columbia Press, 1987).

3. Neil Lazarus, "The Necessity of Universalism," *Differences* 7, 1 (1995), 15–47.

4. See Mark Neufeld, *The Restructuring of International Relations Theory* (Cambridge: Cambridge University Press, 1995). The remark, and Neufeld's fuller comments on it, are found in the section "Defining Theoretical Reflexivity."

5. See for instance the sections on China as a responsible power in Susan Shirk, *China: Fragile Superpower* (New York: Oxford University Press, 2007).
6. The text cited earlier was Alastair Iain Johnston, "Socialization in International Institutions. The ASEAN Way and International Relations Theory," in G. John Ikenberry and Michael Mastanduno, eds, *International Relations Theory and the Asia Pacific* (New York: Columbia University Press, 2003).
7. Alexander Wendt, *Social Theory of International Politics* (Cambridge: Cambridge University Press, 1999), 201.
8. Ibid., 202. Wendt quotes Roger Benjamin and Raymond Duvall, "The Capitalist State in Context," in Roger Benjamin, ed., *The Democratic State* (Lawrence, Kansas: University of Kansas Press, 1985), 25–26.
9. Robert W. Cox, *Production, Power, and World Order. Social Forces in the Making of History.*
10. Mark Duffield, *Global Governance and the New Wars* (London: Zed Books, 2000).
11. Ibid. Roland Paris, "International Peacebuilding and the 'Mission Civilisatrice,'" *Review of International Studies* 28 (2002), 637–656. Oliver Ramsbotham, "Reflections on UN Post-Settlement Peacebuilding," *International Peacekeeping* 7 (Spring 2000), 169–189. See also my *Peace, Power, and Resistance in Cambodia. Global Governance and the Failure of International Conflict Resolution* (London and New York: Macmillan, 2000).
12. On these issues, see Andrew Linklater, "The Question of the Next Stage in International Relations Theory: A Critical–Theoretical Point of View," *Millennium* 21, 1 (1992), 77–98; Michael Banks, "The Inter-Paradigm Debate," in Margo Light and A. J. R. Groom, eds, *International Relations: A Handbook of Current Theory* (London: Frances Pinter, 1985), 7–26.

Bibliography

Acharya, Amitav. *The Quest for Identity: International Relations of Southeast Asia*. Oxford and New York: Oxford University Press, 1997.

Acharya, Amitav. *Constructing a Security Community in Southeast Asia: ASEAN and the Problem of Regional Order*. London and New York: Routledge, 2001.

Acharya, Amitav, and Barry Buzan, eds. *Non-Western International Relations Theory: Perspectives on and Beyond Asia*. London: Routledge, 2009.

Ahluwalia, Pal. *Politics and Post-Colonial Theory: African Inflections*. New York: Routledge, 2001.

Ahmad, Aijaz. "Between Orientalism and Historicism: Anthropological Knowledge of India." *Studies in History* 7, 1 (1991), 135–163.

Alagappa, Muthiah. "Asian Practice of Security: Key Features and Explanations." In *Asian Security Practice: Material and Ideational Influences*. Muthiah Alagappa, ed. Stanford: Stanford University Press, 1998.

Anderson, Benedict. *Imagined Communities*. Revised edition. London and New York: Verso, 1991.

Appadurai, Arjun. *Modernity at Large: Cultural Dimensions of Globalization*. Minneapolis: University of Minnesota Press, 1996.

Appiah, Kwame Anthony. "The Illusions of Race." In *African Philosophy: An Anthology*. Emmanuel Eze, ed. Oxford: Blackwell, 1998.

Art, Robert J., and Kenneth N. Waltz, eds. *The Use of Force*. Boston: Little, Brown, 1971.

Ashcroft, Bill, Gareth Griffiths, and Helen Tiffin, eds. *The Post-Colonial Studies Reader*. Second edition. London and New York: Routledge, 2006.

Ashley, Richard K. "Untying the Sovereign State: A Double Reading of the Anarchy Problematique." *Millennium* 17, 2 (1988), 227–262.

Axworthy, Lloyd. "Canada and Human Security: The Need for Leadership." *International Journal* 52, 2 (Spring 1997), 183–196.

Ayers, Alison J., ed. *Gramsci, Political Economy, and International Relations Theory: Modern Princes and Naked Emperors*. London: Palgrave Macmillan, 2008.

Ayoob, Mohammed. *The Third World Security Predicament: State Making, Regional Conflict, and the International System*. Boulder: Lynne Rienner Publishers, 1995.

Balibar, Étienne, and Immanuel Wallerstein. *Race, Nation, Class: Ambiguous Identities*. London and New York: Verso, 1991.

Banks, Michael. "The Inter-Paradigm Debate." In *International Relations: A Handbook of Current Theory*. Margot Light, and A. J. R. Groom, eds. London: Frances Pinter, 1985, 7–26.

Barnett, Michael, and Raymond Duvall, eds. *Power in Global Governance*. Cambridge: Cambridge University Press, 2005.

Bartelson, J. "The Trial of Judgment: A Note on Kant and the Paradoxes of Internationalism." *International Studies Quarterly* 39, 2 (June 1995), 255–279.

Beck, Lewis White. *A Commentary on Kant's Critique of Practical Reason*. Indianapolis: Library of Liberal Arts, 1960.

Belassa, Bela. *The Newly Industrializing Countries in the World Economy*. New York: Pergamon, 1981.

Benjamin, Roger, and Raymond Duvall. "The Capitalist State in Context." In *The Democratic State*. Roger Benjamin, ed. Lawrence, Kansas: University of Kansas Press, 1985.

Berlin, Isaiah. "The Originality of Machiavelli." In *Against the Current*. Isaiah Berlin, ed. New York: Penguin, 1980.

Bilgin, Pinar. "Thinking Past 'Western' IR." *Third World Quarterly* 29, 1 (2008), 5–23.

Billet, L. "The Just Economy: The Moral Basis of the Wealth of Nations." *Review of Social Economy* 34, 3 (December 1976), 295–315.

Bleiker, Roland. "Retracting and Redrawing the Boundaries of Events: Postmodern Inferences with International Theory." *Alternatives* 22, 1 (January–March 1997), 57–85.

Boucher, David. *Political Theories of International Relations*. Oxford, New York: Oxford University Press, 1998.

Bourdieu, Pierre. *Outline of a Theory of Practice*. Translated by Richard Nice. Cambridge: Cambridge University Press, 1977.

Brown, Chris. *International Relations Theory: New Normative Approaches*. London: Harvester Wheatsheaf, 1992.

Bull, Hedley. "Hobbes and the International Anarchy." *Social Research* 48, 4 (Winter 1981), 717–738.

Burchill, Scott. "Realism and Neo-realism." In *Theories of International Relations*. Scott Burchill et al., eds. New York: Palgrave Macmillan, 2001.

Butler, Judith, Ernesto Laclau, and Slavoj Žižek. *Contingency, Hegemony, Universality. Contemporary Dialogues on the Left*. London: Verso, 2000.

Caballero-Anthony, Mely. "Human Security and Comprehensive Security in ASEAN." In *The Quest for Human Security: The Next Phase of ASEAN?*. Pranee Thiparat, ed. Bangkok: Institute of Security and International Studies, 2001.

Caballero-Anthony, Mely. *Regional Security in Southeast Asia: Beyond the ASEAN Way*. Singapore: Institute of Southeast Asian Studies, 2005.

Campbell, David. *Writing Security: United States Foreign Policy and the Politics of Identity*. Manchester: Manchester University Press, 1992.

Cantalupo, Charles. *A Literary "Leviathan." Thomas Hobbes's Masterpiece of Language*. Lewisburg: Bucknell University Press, 1991.

Capie, David, and Paul Evans. *The Asia-Pacific Security Lexicon*. Singapore: Institute of Southeast Asian Studies, 2002.

Cardoso, Fernando Henrique, and Enzo Faletto. *Dependency and Development in Latin America*. Berkeley: University of California Press, 1973.

Carr, E. H. *The Twenty Years' Crisis 1919–1939*. London: Macmillan, 1983.

Chakrabarty, Dipesh. *Provincializing Europe: Postcolonial Thought and Historical Difference*. Princeton: Princeton University Press, 2000.

Chan, Stephen, Peter Mandaville, and Roland Bleiker, eds. *The Zen of International Relations: IR Theory from East to West*. London: Palgrave Macmillan, 2001.

Chatterjee, Partha. *Nationalist Thought in the Colonial World: A Derivative Discourse?* London: Zed Books, 1986.

Chatterjee, Partha. *The Nation and Its Fragments: Colonial and Postcolonial Histories*. Princeton: Princeton University Press, 1993.

Chatterjee, Shibashis. "The State in International Relations Reconsidered." *International Studies* 35, 3 (July–September 1998), 269–293.

Chaturvedi, Vinayak. *Mapping Subaltern Studies and the Postcolonial*. London and New York: Verso, 2000.

Chen, Xiangming. *As Borders Bend: Transnational Spaces on the Pacific Rim*. New York: Rowman & Littlefield, 2005.

Christiansen, Thomas. "European and Regional Integration." In *The Globalization of World Politics*. John Baylis, and Steve Smith, eds. Oxford: Oxford University Press, 2001.

Critchley, Simon, and Oliver Marchart, eds. *Laclau: A Critical Reader*. London and New York: Routlegde, 2004.

Clark, I. "Beyond the Great Divide: Globalization and the Theory of International Relations." *Review of International Studies* 24, 4 (October 1998), 479–498.

Collins, Alan. *Security and Southeast Asia: Domestic, Regional and Global Issues*. Boulder: Lynne Rienner Publishers, 2003.

Cooke, Paul D. *Hobbes and Christianity*. London: Rowan & Littlefield Publishers, 1996.

Cox, Michael, Tim Dunne, and Ken Booth, eds. *Empires, Systems and States: Great Transformations in International Politics*. Cambridge: Cambridge University Press, 2001.

Cox, Robert W. "Social Forces, States, and World Orders: Beyond International Relations Theory." *Millennium* 10, 2 (Summer 1981), 126–155.

Cox, Robert W. "Gramsci, Hegemony, and International Relations: An Essay in Method." *Millennium* 12, 2 (Summer 1983), 162–175.

Cox, Robert W. *Production, Power, and World Order: Social Forces in the Making of History*. New York: Columbia Press, 1987.

Cox, Robert W. "Towards a Post-Hegemonic Conceptualization of World Order." In *Governance Without Government: Order and Change in World Politics*. James N. Rosenau, and Ernst-Otto Czempiel, eds. Cambridge: Cambridge University Press, 1992.

Cox, Robert W. *Political Economy of a Plural World*. London: Routledge, 2002.

Cox, Robert W., and Timothy Sinclair. *Approaches to World Order*. Cambridge: Cambridge University Press, 1996.

Cumings, Bruce. "The Origins and Development of the Northeast Asian Political Economy: Industrial Sectors, Product Cycles, and Political Consequences." In *The Political Economy of the New Asian Industrialism*. Frederic C. Deyo, ed. Ithaca: Cornell University Press, 1987.

Derrida, Jacques. *Of Grammatology*. Translated by Gayatri Chakravorty Spivak. Baltimore: John Hopkins University Press, 1976.

Derrida, Jacques. *Writing and Difference*. Translated by Alan Bass. Chicago: University of Chicago Press, 1978.

Dewitt, David B. "Common, Comprehensive, and Cooperative Security." *Pacific Review* 7, 1 (1994), 1–15.

Deyo, Frederic C. *Dependent Development and Industrial Order: An Asian Case Study*. New York: Praeger, 1981.

Deyo, Frederic C., ed. *The Political Economy of the New Asian Industrialism*. Ithaca: Cornell University Press, 1987.

Diamond, Louise, and John McDonald. *Multi-Track Diplomacy: A Systems Approach to Peace*. West Harford: Kumarian Press, 1996.

Doyle, Michael W. "Kant, Liberal Legacies, and Foreign Affairs, Part 1." *Philosophy and Public Affairs* 12, 3 (Summer 1983), 205–235.

Doyle Michael W. "Kant, Liberal Legacies, and Foreign Affairs, Part 2." *Philosophy and Public Affairs* 12, 4 (Fall 1983), 323–353.

Doyle, Michael W. *UN Peacekeeping in Cambodia*. Boulder: Lynne Rienner, 1995.

Doyle, Michael W. *Ways of War and Peace*. New York and London: W. W. Norton & Company, 1997.

Doyle, Michael W. "A Liberal View: Preserving and Expanding the Liberal Pacific Union." In *International Order and the Future of World Politics*. T. V. Paul, and John Hall, eds. Oxford: Oxford University Press, 1999.

Duffield, Mark. *Global Governance and the New Wars*. London: Zed Books, 2000.

Dunn, Kevin C., and Timothy M. Shaw, eds. *Africa's Challenge to International Relations Theory*. London: Palgrave Macmillan, 2001.

Dunne, Tim. "Liberalism." In *The Globalization of World Politics, An Introduction to International Relations*. John Baylis, and Steve Smith, eds. Oxford: Oxford University Press, 2001.

Elman, Miriam Fendius. "The Never-Ending Story: Democracy and Peace." *International Studies Review* 3 (1999), 87–103.

Evans, Paul M. "Building Security: The Council for Security Cooperation in the Asia Pacific (CSCAP)." *Pacific Review* 7, 2 (1994), 125–139.

Evans, Peter. *Dependent Development*. Princeton: Princeton University Press, 1979.

Evans, Peter, and Michael Timerlake. "Dependence, Inequality, and Growth in Less Developed Countries." *American Sociological Review* 45 (1980), 531–552.

Etzioni, Amitai. *From Empire to Community: A New Approach to International Relations*. London: Palgrave Macmillan, 2004.

Falk, Richard. *On Humane Governance: Towards a New Global Politics*. Cambridge: Polity Press, 1995.

Falk, Richard. "Global Civil Society: Perspectives, Initiatives, and Movements." *Oxford Development Studies* 26 (1998), 99–110.

Falk, Richard. "Global Civil Society and the Democratic Prospect." In *Global Democracy: Key Debates*. Barry Holden, ed. London and New York: Routledge, 2000.

Fay, C. R. "Adam Smith and the Dynamic State." *Economic Journal* 40 (March 1930), 25–34.

Fierke, K. M., and Knud Erik Jørgensen. *Constructing International Relations – The Next Generation*. Armonk, New York: M. E. Sharpe, 2001.

Foucault, Michel. *The Order of Things*. London: Tavistock, 1970.

Frank, Andres Gunder. *Dependent Accumulation and Underdevelopment*. New York: Monthly Review Press, 1979.

Fraser, Nancy. "Transnationalizing the Public Sphere." In *Globalizing Critical Theory*. Max Pensky, ed. New York: Rowan & Littlefield, 2005.

Fukuyama, Francis. *The End of History and the Last Man*. New York: Free Press, 1992.

Gandhi, Leela. *Postcolonial Theory: A Critical Introduction*. New York: Columbia University Press, 1998.

Gartzke, Erik. "Preferences and the Democratic Peace." *International Studies Quarterly* 44, 2 (June 2000), 191–212.

Gartzke, Erik, and Quang Li. "War, Peace, and the Invisible Hand: Positive Political Externalities of Economic Globalization." *International Studies Quarterly* 47 (2003), 561–586.

Gellner, Ernest. "The Importance of Being Modular." In *Civil Society: Theory, History, Comparison*. J. A. Hall, ed. Cambridge: Polity Press, 1995.

Giddens, Anthony. *A Contemporary Critique of Historical Materialism*, vol. 2: *The Nation-State and Violence*. Berkeley: University of California Press, 1987.

Gienow-Hecht, Jessica C. E., ed. *Decentering America*. New York: Berghahn Books, 2007.

Gilbert, Mark. *Surpassing Realism. The Politics of European Integration since 1945*. New York: Rowman & Littlefield, 2003.

Gill, Stephen, ed. *Gramsci, Historical Materialism and International Relations.* Cambridge: Cambridge University Press, 1993.

Gill, Stephen. *Power and Resistance in the New World Order.* Second edition. London: Palgrave Macmillan, 2008.

Gramsci, Antonio. *Selection from the Prison Notebooks.* Edited and translated by Quintin Hoare, and Geoffrey Nowell Smith. New York: International Publishers, 1971.

Greene, Marjorie. "Hobbes and the Modern Mind." In *Anatomy of Knowledge.* M. Greene, ed. London: Routledge, 1969.

Guan, Lee Hock. *Civil Society in Southeast Asia.* Singapore: Southeast Asian Studies, 2004.

Guzzini, Stefano, and Anna Leander, eds. *Constructivism and International Relations: Alexander Wendt and his Critics.* London: Routledge, 2006.

Haas, Ernst B. *Beyond the Nation-State: Functionalism and International Organization.* Stanford: Stanford University Press, 1964.

Habermas, Jürgen. *Knowledge and Human Interests.* Boston: Beacon Press, 1972.

Habermas, Jürgen. "An Alternative Way Out of the Philosophy of the Subject: Communicative versus Subject-Centered Reason." In *The Philosophical Discourse of Modernity: Twelve Lectures.* Translated by Frederick Lawrence. Boston: MIT Press, 1987.

Hadiz, Vedi R., ed. *Empire and Neoliberalism in Asia.* London and New York: Routledge, 2006.

Haggard, Stephan. "The Newly Industrializing Countries in the International System." *World Politics* 38 (1986), 343–370.

Haggard, Stephan. *Pathways from the Periphery: The Politics of Growth in the Newly Industrializing Countries.* Ithaca: Cornell University Press, 1990.

Hardt, Michael, and Antonio Negri. *Empire.* Cambridge, MA: Harvard University Press, 2000.

Held, David. "Democracy, the Nation-State and the Global System." In *Political Theory Today.* David Held, ed. Cambridge: Polity Press, 1991.

Held, David. "Democracy: From City–States to a Cosmopolitan Order?" *Political Studies* 40 (September 1992), 10–39.

Held, David. *Democracy and the Global Order: From the Modern State to Cosmopolitan Governance.* Stanford: Stanford University Press, 1995.

Hobbes, Thomas. *Leviathan.* London: Penguin Books, 1968.

Hobden, Stephen, and Richard Wyn Jones. "Marxist Theories of International Relations." In *The Globalization of World Politics: An Introduction to International Relations.* John Baylis, and Steve Smith, eds. Oxford: Oxford University Press, 2001.

Hoffman, Stanley. "An American Social Science: International Relations." *Dædalus* 106 (1977), 41–60.

Holsti, Kalevi J. *The State, War, and the State of War.* Cambridge: Cambridge University Press, 1996.

Horkheimer, Max. "Traditional and Critical Theory." In *Critical Theory: The Essential Readings.* Ingram, David, and Julia Simon-Ingram, eds. New York: Paragon House, 1992.

Huat, Chua Beng. "The Relative Autonomies of the State and Civil Societies." In *State–Society Relations.* Gillian Koh, and Ooi Giok Ling, eds. New York: Oxford University Press, 2000.

Hughes, Caroline. "Surveillance and Resistance in the Cambodian Elections: The Prisoner's Dilemma?" *Southeast Asian Affairs* 25 (1999), 92–108.

Huntington, Samuel. *The Clash of Civilizations and the Remaking of World Order.* New York: Touchtone, 1998.

Huntley, Wade L. "Kant's Third Image: Systemic Sources of the Liberal Peace." *International Studies Quarterly* 40 (1996), 45–76.

Hurrell, Andrew. *On Global Order. Power, Values, and the Constitution of International Society.* Oxford: Oxford University Press, 2007.

Hutchison, T. W. "Adam Smith and *The Wealth of Nations.*" *Journal of Law and Economics* 19, 3 (October 1976), 507–528.

Ikenberry, G. John, ed. *America Unrivaled: The Future of the Balance of Power.* Ithaca and London: Cornell University Press, 2002.

Ikenberry, G. John, and Michael Mastanduno, eds. *International Relations Theory and the Asia Pacific.* New York: Columbia University Press, 2003.

Inayatullah, Naeem, and David L. Blaney. *International Relations and the Problem of Difference.* New York and London: Routledge, 2004.

Ingram, David, and Julia Simon-Ingram, eds. *Critical Theory: The Essential Readings.* New York: Paragon House, 1992.

Jackson, Robert H. *Quasi-States: Sovereignty, International Relations and the Third World.* Cambridge: Cambridge University Press, 1990.

Job, Brian L. ed. *The Insecurity Dilemma: National Security of Third World States.* Boulder, CO: Lynne Rienner, 1992.

Johnson, Chalmers. *MITI and the Japanese Miracle.* Stanford: Stanford University Press, 1982.

Johnston, Alastair Iain. "Socialization in International Institutions: The ASEAN Way and International Relations Theory." In *International Relations Theory and the Asia-Pacific.* G. John Ikenberry, and Michael Mastanduno, eds. New York: Columbia University Press, 2003.

Kant, Immanuel. *Political Writings.* Hans Reiss, ed. Cambridge: Cambridge University Press, 1970.

Kant, Immanuel. *Kant: Selections.* Lewis White Beck, ed. New York and London: Scribner/Macmillan, 1988.

Katzenstein, Peter, ed. *The Culture of National Security.* New York: Columbia University Press, 1996.

Kavka, Gregory S. *Hobbesian Moral and Political Theory.* Princeton: Princeton University Press, 1986.

Keohane, Robert O. *After Hegemony, Cooperation and Discord in the World Political Economy.* Princeton: Princeton University Press, 1984.

Keohane, Robert. O, ed. *Neorealism and Its Critics.* New York: Columbia University Press, 1986.

Keohane, Robert O., and Joseph Nye. *Power and Interdependence: World Politics in Transition.* Boston: Little, Brown and Company, 1977.

Khanna, Parag. *The Second World: Empires and Influence in the New Global Order.* New York: Random House, 2008.

Krishna, Sankaran. "Race, Amnesia, and the Education of International Relations." *Alternatives* 26, 4 (October/December 2001), 401–423.

Laclau, Ernesto. *New Reflections on the Revolution of Our Time.* London: Verso, 1990.

Laclau, Ernesto. *Emancipations.* London: Verso, 1996.

Laclau, Ernesto, and Chantal Mouffe. *Hegemony and Socialist Strategy: Towards a Radical Democratic Politics.* London: Verso, 1989.

Larrain, Jorge. *Ideology and Cultural Identity: Modernity and the Third World Presence.* Cambridge: Polity Press, 1994.

Lazarus, Neil. "The Necessity of Universalism." *Differences: A Journal of Feminist Cultural Studies* 7, 1 (1995), 15–47.

Lazarus, Neil. *Nationalism and Cultural Practice in the Postcolonial World.* Cambridge: Cambridge University Press, 1999.

Legro, Jeffrey W., and Andrew Moravcsik. "Is Anybody Still a Realist?" *International Security* 24, 2 (Fall 1999), 5–55.

Lenin, V. I. *Imperialism, the Highest Stage of Capitalism: A Popular Outline.* Thirteenth edition. Moscow: Progress Publishers, 1966.

Levy, Jack. "Domestic Politics and War." *Journal of Interdisciplinary History* 18, 4 (Spring 1988), 653–673.

Levy, Jack. "The Democratic Peace Hypothesis: From Description to Explanation." *Mershon International Studies Review* 38 (1994), 352–354.

Linklater, Andrew. *Men and Citizens in the Theory of International Relations.* London: Macmillan, 1982.

Linklater, Andrew. "The Question of the Next Stage in International Relations Theory: A Critical–Theoretical Point of View." *Millennium* 21, 1 (1992), 77–98.

Linklater, Andrew. "Marxism." In *Theories of International Relations.* Scott Burchill, Andrew Linklater, Richard Devetak, Matthew Paterson, and Jacquie True, eds. New York: St. Martin's Press, 1996.

Linklater, Andrew. *The Transformation of Political Community: Ethical Foundations of the Post-Westphalian Era.* Cambridge: Polity Press, 1998.

Lizée, Pierre P. "Civil Society and Regional Security: Tensions and Potentials in Post-Crisis Southeast Asia." *Contemporary Southeast Asia* 22, 3 (December 2000), 550–569.

Lizée, Pierre P. *Peace, Power, and Resistance in Cambodia: Global Governance and the Failure of International Conflict Resolution.* London and New York: Macmillan and St. Martin's Press, 2000.

Locke, John. *The Two Treaties of Government (1689).* Peter Laslett, ed. Cambridge: Cambridge University Press, 1960.

Macfie, A. L. "Adam Smith's *Moral Sentiments* as Foundation for his *Wealth of Nations.*" *Oxford Economic Papers* 11 (October 1959), 209–228.

Machiavelli, Niccolò. *The Prince.* Quentin Skinner, and Russell Price, eds. Cambridge: Cambridge University Press, 1985.

Machiavelli, Niccolò. *The Discourses.* Edited and translated by Leslie Walker. Bernard Crick. Harmondsworth: Penguin, 1970.

Macpherson, C. B. "Introduction." In *Leviathan.* Thomas Hobbes, ed. London: Penguin Books, 1968.

Mahbubani, Kishore. *Beyond the Age of Innocence: Rebuilding Trust between America and the World.* New York: Public Affairs, 2005.

Makinda, S. M. "International Security and Eclecticism in International Relations Theory." *Cooperation and Conflict* 35, 2 (June 2000), 205–216.

Mansfield, E. D., and J. C. Pevehouse. "Trade Blocs, Trade Flows, and International Conflict." *International Organization* 54 (2000), 775–808.

Mansfield, E. D., J. C. Pevehouse, and D. H. Bearce. "Preferential Trading Arrangements and Military Disputes." *Security Studies* 9 (1999–2000), 92–118.

Marx, Karl. "Contribution to the Critique of Political Economy." In *Writings of the Young Marx on Philosophy and Society.* Karl Marx. Lloyd D. Easton, and Kurt H. Guddat, eds. New York: Doubleday, 1967.

Marx, Karl, and Frederick Engels. "The Communist Manifesto." In *Karl Marx: Selected Writings.* D. McLennan, ed. Oxford: Oxford University Press, 1977.

Mbembe, Achille. *On the Postcolony.* Berkeley: University of California Press, 2001.

McSweeney, Bill. *Security, Identity, and Interests: A Sociology of International Relations.* Cambridge: Cambridge University Press, 1999.

Minh-ha, Trinh T. *When the Moon Waxes Red: Representation, Gender, and Cultural Politics.* New York and London: Routledge, 1991.

Mittelman, James H. "Coxian Historicism as an Alternative Perspective in International Studies." *Alternatives* 23, 1 (January–March 1998), 63–92.

Mitrany, David. *A Working Peace System.* Chicago: Quadrangle Books, 1966.

Morgenthau, Hans J. "Introduction." In *A Working Peace System.* David Mitrany, ed. Chicago: Quadrangle Books, 1966.

Morgenthau, Hans J. *Politics among Nations: The Struggle for Power and Peace.* Third edition. New York: Knopf, 1963.

Morrow, Glenn R. *The Ethical and Economic Theories of Adam Smith.* New York: Longmans, Green, and Co., 1923.

Mousseau, Michael. "The Nexus of Market Society, Liberal Preferences, and Democratic Peace: Interdisciplinary Theory and Evidence." *International Studies Quarterly* 47, 4 (December 2003), 483–510.

Neufeld, Mark. *The Restructuring of International Relations Theory.* Cambridge: Cambridge University Press, 1995.

Neuman, Stephanie G., ed. *International Relations and the Third World.* New York: St. Martin's Press, 1998.

O'Donnell, Guillermo. *Modernization and Bureaucratic-Authoritarianism in South American Politics.* Berkeley: University of California Press, 1973.

O'Neal, R. John, and Bruce Russett. "The Classical Liberals Were Right: Democracy, Interdependence, and Conflict, 1950–1985." *International Studies Quarterly* 41, 2 (1997), 267–293.

O'Neal, R. John, and Bruce Russett. "Is the Liberal Peace Just an Artifact of Cold War Interests? Assessing Recent Critiques." *International Interactions* 25, 3 (1999), 213–241.

O'Neal, R. John, Bruce Russett, and Michael L. Berbaum. "Causes of Peace: Democracy, Interdependence, and International Organizations, 1885–1992." *International Studies Quarterly* 47 (2003), 371–393.

Osiander, Andreas. "Rereading Early Twentieth-Century IR Theory: Idealism Revisited." *International Studies Quarterly* 42, 3 (September 1998), 409–432.

Paris, Roland. "International Peacebuilding and the 'Mission Civilisatrice.'" *Review of International Studies* 28 (2002), 637–656.

Pehnt, W. "Modernity: An Unfinished Project." In *Critical Theory: The Essential Readings.* David Ingram, and Julia Simon-Ingram, eds. New York: Paragon House, 1992.

Pensky, Max, ed. *Globalizing Critical Theory.* New York: Rowman & Littlefield, 2005.

Poggi, Gianfranco. *The State: Its Nature, Development, and Prospects.* Stanford: Stanford University Press, 1990.

Prakash, Gyan. *After Colonialism: Imperial Histories and Post-Colonial Displacement.* Princeton: Princeton University Press, 1995.

Rabinow, Paul, ed. *The Foucault Reader.* New York: Pantheon Books, 1984.

Ramsbotham, Oliver. "Reflections on UN Post-Settlement Peacebuilding." *International Peacekeeping* 7 (Spring 2000), 169–189.

Richards, Gareth Api. "Challenging Asia–Europe Relations from Below? Civil Society and the Politics of Inclusion and Opposition." *Journal of the Asia Pacific Economy* 4, 1 (1999), 146–170.

Rodan, Garry, and Kevin Hewison. "Neoliberal Globalization, Conflict, and Security. New Life for Authoritarianism in Asia?" In *Empire and Neoliberalism in Asia*. Vedi R. Hadiz, ed. London and New York: Routledge, 2006.

Roll, E. "The Wealth of Nations 1776–1976." *Lloyds Bank Review* 119 (January 1976), 12–22.

Rondinelli, Dennis A., and John M. Heffron, eds. *Globalization and Change in Asia*. Boulder, CO: Lynne Rienner, 2007.

Rosamond, B. *Theories of European Integration*. Basingstoke: Macmillan, 2000.

Rosecrance, Richard. *The Rise of the Trading State: Commerce and Conquest in the Modern World*. New York: Basic Books, 1986.

Rothkopf, David. *Running the World: The Inside Story of the National Security Council and the Architects of American Power*. New York: Public Affairs, 2005.

Rousseau, Jean-Jacques. *The Social Contract and Discourses*. Translated by G. D. H. Cole. Revised by J. M. Brumfitt, and John Hall. London: Dent, 1983.

Rummel, R. J. "Libertarianism and International Violence." *Journal of Conflict Resolution* 27 (1983), 457–479.

Rummel, R. J. "Democracies Are less Warlike than Other Regimes." *European Journal of International Relations* 1 (1995), 457–479.

Russett, Bruce. *Grasping the Democratic Peace: Principles for a Post-Cold War World*. Princeton: Princeton University Press, 1993.

Russett, Bruce, and John R. O'neal. *Triangulating Peace: Democracy, Interdependence, and International Organizations*. New York: W. W. Norton, 2001.

Said, Edward W. *Orientalism*. New York: Random House, 1978.

Shani, Giorgio. "Toward a Post-Western IR: The *Umma, Khalsa Panth,* and Critical International Relations Theory." *International Studies Review* 10, 4 (December 2008), 722–734.

Shapiro, Michael J. "Textualizing Global Politics." In *International/Intertextual Relations: Postmodern Readings of World Politics*. James Der Derian, and Michael J. Shapiro, eds. Lexington: Massachusetts: Lexington Books, 1989.

Shirk, Susan. *China: Fragile Superpower*. New York: Oxford University Press, 2007.

Sinclair, Timothy J. "Beyond International Relations Theory: Robert W. Cox and Approaches to World Order." In *Approaches to World Order*. Robert W. Cox with Timothy J. Sinclair, eds. Cambridge: Cambridge University Press, 1996.

Singer, David J. "The Level-of-Analysis Problem in International Relations." In *The International System*. Klaus Knorr, and Sydney Verba, eds. Princeton: Princeton University Press, 1961.

Singer, David J. "The Global System and Its Subsystems: A Developmental View." In *Linkage Politics: Essays on the Convergence of National and International Systems*. James Rosenau, ed. New York: Free Press, 1969.

Skocpol, Theda. *States and Social Revolutions*. Cambridge: Cambridge University Press, 1979.

Small, Melvin, and David Singer. "The War-Proneness of Democratic Regimes." *Jerusalem Journal of International Relations* 1 (1976), 49–69.

Smith, Adam. "The Theory of Moral Sentiments." In *The Work of Adam Smith*, vol. 1. Otto Zieler, ed., New York: Lowman, 1963.

Smith, Adam. *An Inquiry into the Nature and Causes of the Wealth of Nations*. Edwin Cannan, ed. Chicago: University of Chicago Press, 1976.

Smith, Steve, Ken Booth, and Marysia Zalewski, eds. *International Theory: Positivism and Beyond*. Cambridge: Cambridge University Press, 1996.

Smith, Steven B. "Defending Hegel from Kant." In *Essays on Kant's Political Philosophy.* Howard Lloyd Williamsed, ed. Chicago: University of Chicago Press, 1992.

Snyder, Glenn H., and Paul Diesing. *Conflict Among Nations. Bargaining, Decision Making, and System Structure in International Crises.* Princeton: Princeton University Press, 1977.

Sopiee, Noordin. "Malaysia's Doctrine of Comprehensive Security." *Journal of Asiatic Studies* XXVII 2, 259–265.

Spivak, Gayatri Chakravorty. *Toward a History of the Vanishing Present.* Cambridge, Massachusetts: Harvard University Press, 1999.

Strauss, Leo. *Thoughts on Machiavelli.* Chicago: University of Chicago Press, 1958.

Thiparat, Pranee, ed. *The Quest for Human Security: The Next Phase of ASEAN?* Bangkok: Institute of Security and International Studies, 2001.

Tickner, Arlene B., and Ole Waever, eds. *International Relations Scholarship around the World. (Worlding Beyond the West).* London: Routledge, 2009.

Tilly, Charles. *Coercion, Capital, and European States,* A.D. *990–1990.* Oxford: Basil Blackwell, 1990.

United Nations Development Program (UNDP) "Redefining Security: The Human Dimension." *Current History* 94 (May 1995), 229–236.

Van Der Pijl, Kees. *Nomads, Empires, States: Modes of Foreign Relations and Political Economy,* vol. 1. London: Pluto Press, 2007.

Wa Thiong'o, Ngugi. *Decolonizing the Mind: The Politics of Language in African Literature.* Portsmouth: Heinemann, 1986.

Waever, Ole. "The Sociology of a Not So International Discipline: American and European Developments in International Relations." *International Organization* 52 (Autumn 1998), 687–723.

Walker, R. B. J. *Inside/outside: International Relations as Political Theory.* Cambridge: Cambridge University Press, 1993.

Wallerstein, Immanuel. *The Modern World-System,* vol. 1: *Capitalist Agriculture and the Origins of the European World-Economy in the Sixteenth Century.* San Diego: Academic Press, 1974.

Wallerstein, Immanuel. *The Capitalist World-Economy.* Cambridge: Cambridge University Press, 1979.

Wallerstein, Immanuel. *The Modern World-System,* vol. 2: *Mercantilism and the Consolidation of the European World-Economy, 1600–1750.* San Diego: Academic Press, 1980.

Wallerstein, Immanuel. *The Second Era of Great Expansion of the Capitalist World-Economy.* San Diego: Academic Press, 1989.

Walt, Stephen M. "International Relations: One World, Many Theories." *Foreign Policy* 110 (Spring 1998), 29–46.

Waltz, Kenneth N. *Man, the State and War.* New York: Columbia University Press, 1954.

Waltz, Kenneth N. *Theory of International Politics.* Reading, Massachusetts: Addison-Wesley, 1979.

Watkins, J. W. N. *Hobbes's System of Ideas.* Second edition. London: Hutchinson and Company, 1973.

Wendt, Alexander. "Anarchy Is What States Make of It: The Social Construction of Power Politics." *International Organization* 46 (1992), 391–425.

Wendt, Alexander. *Social Theory of International Politics.* Cambridge: Cambridge University Press, 1999.

Wight, Martin. *International Theory: The Three Traditions.* Gabriele Wight, and Brian Porter, eds. London and Leicester: University of Leicester Press, 1991.

Williams, Michael C. "Rousseau, Realism and *Realpolitic.*" *Millennium* 18, 2 (1989), 185–204.

Wohlforth, W. C. "Reality Check: Revising Theories of International Politics in Response to the End of the Cold War." *World Politics* 50, 4 (July 1998), 650–680.

Wolin, Sheldon. *Politics and Vision.* Boston: Little, Brown, 1960.

Wolin, Sheldon. "Violence and the Western Political Tradition." *American Journal of Orthopsychiatry* 33 (1963), 15–28.

Yoffie, David. *Power and Protectionism: Strategies of the Newly Industrializing Countries.* New York: Columbia University Press, 1983.

Yeung, Henry Wai-chung. "The Limits of Globalization Theory: A Geographic Perspective on Global Economic Change." *Economic Geography* 78, 3 (July 2002), 285–305.

Young, I. M. *Justice and the Politics of Difference.* Princeton: Princeton University Press, 1991.

Zakaria, Fareed. "The Future of American Power." *Foreign Affairs* 87, 3 (May/June 2008), 18–43.

Zakaria, Fareed. *The Post-American World.* New York: W. W. Norton & Company, 2008.

Zakaria, Fareed. "The Rise of the Rest." *Newsweek* (May 12, 2008).

Zehfuss, Maja. *Constructivism in International Relations.* Cambridge: Cambridge University Press, 2002.

Index

CPSIA information can be obtained
at www.ICGtesting.com
Printed in the USA
LVHW021418230619
622080LV00007B/55/P